Bingham and Berrymans'
Personal Injury and Motor Claims Cases

Whilst every care has been taken to ensure the accuracy of this work, no responsibility for loss or damage occasioned to any person acting or refraining from action as a result of any statement in it can be accepted by the authors or publishers.

Bingham and Berrymans' Personal Injury and Motor Claims Cases

Fourteenth Edition Supplement

Ruth Graham
Partner, Berrymans Lace Mawer

Sarah Cartlidge
Berrymans Lace Mawer

Kerris Dale
Berrymans Lace Mawer

Christopher Drayton
Berrymans Lace Mawer

Stuart Furniss
Berrymans Lace Mawer

Andrew Guirguis
Berrymans Lace Mawer

Simon Hammond
Berrymans Lace Mawer

Stuart Hardy
Berrymans Lace Mawer

Ben Howson
Berrymans Lace Mawer

Alistair Kinley
Berrymans Lace Mawer

Adam Lidster

Berrymans Lace Mawer

Louisa Martindale
Berrymans Lace Mawer

Cathie Mortimer
Berrymans Lace Mawer

Joanna Peters
Berrymans Lace Mawer

Ian Walker
Berrymans Lace Mawer

LexisNexis®

Members of the LexisNexis Group worldwide

United Kingdom	RELX (UK) Limited, trading as LexisNexis, 1–3 Strand, London, WC2N 5JR
Argentina	LexisNexis Argentina, Buenos Aires
Australia	LexisNexis Butterworths, Chatswood, New South Wales
Austria	LexisNexis Verlag ARD Orac GmbH & Co KG, Vienna
Benelux	LexisNexis Benelux, Amsterdam
Canada	LexisNexis Canada, Markham, Ontario
Chile	LexisNexis Chile Ltda, Santiago
China	LexisNexis China, Beijing and Shanghai
France	LexisNexis SA, Paris
Germany	LexisNexis GmbH, Dusseldorf
Hong Kong	LexisNexis Hong Kong, Hong Kong
India	LexisNexis India, New Delhi
Italy	Giuffrè Editore, Milan
Japan	LexisNexis Japan, Tokyo
Malaysia	Malayan Law Journal Sdn Bhd, Kuala Lumpur
New Zealand	LexisNexis NZ Ltd, Wellington
Singapore	LexisNexis Singapore, Singapore
South Africa	LexisNexis Butterworths, Durban
USA	LexisNexis, Dayton, Ohio

First published 1946 as Bingham and Berrymans' Motor Claims Cases

© Reed Elsevier (UK) Ltd 2016

Published by LexisNexis Butterworths

All rights reserved. No part of this publication may be reproduced in any material form (including photocopying or storing it in any medium by electronic means and whether or not transiently or incidentally to some other use of this publication) without the written permission of the copyright owner except in accordance with the provisions of the Copyright, Designs and Patents Act 1988 or under the terms of a licence issued by the Copyright Licensing Agency Ltd, 90 Tottenham Court Road, London, England W1T 4LP. Applications for the copyright owner's written permission to reproduce any part of this publication should be addressed to the publisher.
Warning: The doing of an unauthorised act in relation to a copyright work may result in both a civil claim for damages and criminal prosecution.

Crown copyright material is reproduced with the permission of the Controller of HMSO and the Queen's Printer for Scotland. Parliamentary copyright material is reproduced with the permission of the Controller of Her Majesty's Stationery Office on behalf of Parliament. Any European material in this work which has been reproduced from EUR-lex, the official European Communities legislation website, is European Communities copyright.
A CIP Catalogue record for this book is available from the British Library.

ISBN for this volume: 9781474303088

Printed and bound in Great Britain by CPI Group (UK) Ltd, Croydon, CR0 4YY

Visit LexisNexis at http://www.lexisnexis.co.uk

Preface

This Supplement to the 14th edition brings the law up to date to 31 July 2016 (or 3 August, to allow the inclusion of the Supreme Court judgment in *Moreno v MIB*). It seems hard to believe it has been two years since the 14th edition was completed. In this supplement we include various cases in our chapters on procedure which illustrate how the courts have applied the principles in *Denton* to applications for relief from sanctions. We also comment on the amendments to the general Pre-Action Protocol for Personal Injury Claims that were made in April 2015.

We have been able to include several decisions of the Supreme Court. In *Knauer v Ministry of Justice* the Supreme Court finally reformed the common law calculation of multipliers in fatal accident claims. The change brings the law in England and Wales into line with that in Scotland and we comment on how the method of quantification has changed in practice.

The Supreme Court also recently ruled on two important fraud matters which are covered in the supplement to the fraud chapter. The first decision was in *Versloot Dredging v HDI Gerling* and examined the effect a policyholder's collateral lies - previously analysed under the 'fraudulent devices' doctrine - have on the recoverability of their claim.

This was closely followed by the decision in *Zurich Insurance v Hayward*. This is a significant case detailing the circumstances in which a compromise agreement to settle a personal injury claim (here, a *Tomlin* order) may be set aside on the basis of fraudulent misrepresentation. Lord Toulson pointed out that 'Hayward's deceitful conduct was intended to influence the mind of the insurers, not necessarily by causing them to believe him, but by causing them to value his litigation claim more highly than it was worth if the true facts had been disclosed.' Lord Clarke added the important qualification that the insurer had 'done as much as it reasonably could to investigate the accuracy and ramifications of Hayward's representations'.

We also have new cases to refer to the in the world of credit hire, with commentary on the case of *Stevens v Equity* and how the courts should approach assessment of the basic hire rate (BHR) and also we feature the case of *Willis v Phillips* in the Court of Appeal, dealing with credit hire in the MoJ Portal.

Finally, there is commentary on the European case *Vnuk v Zararovalnica Triglav* and its potential impact on the insurance measures set out in Part VI of the Road Traffic Act 1998. These may need to be rewritten some time in the short to medium term (and while the UK remains a member of the EU, albeit having decided in the referendum of 23 July to leave).

As always I would like to thank my co-editors for their contributions to this supplement, in particular Stuart Hardy, Stuart Furniss, Simon Hammond, Ian

Preface

Walker, Andrew Guirguis, Cathie Mortimer, Louisa Martindale, Chris Drayton, Ben Howson, Alistair Kinley, Kerris Dale, Sarah Cartledge and Adam Lidster – for some of them this is the first time they have contributed to *Bingham and Berrymans*. Also we could not manage without the invaluable assistance of Helen Cafferata and the rest of the information services team and Charlotte Reay, our hardworking secretary.

I hope you find the Supplement useful and interesting. Please, as always, if you have any comments do not hesitate to get in touch.

Ruth Graham
August 2016

Table of Contents

Preface	vii
Table of Statutes	xi
Table of Statutory Instruments	xiii
Table of European Legislation	xv
Table of Cases	xvii
CHAPTER 1 Insurance Principles	1
CHAPTER 2 Coverage	3
CHAPTER 3 Motor Insurers' Bureau	7
CHAPTER 4 General Principles of Negligence	11
CHAPTER 5 Vicarious Liability	15
CHAPTER 6 Res Ipsa Loquitur	19
CHAPTER 7 Defences	21
CHAPTER 8 Fraud	25
CHAPTER 9 Liability of Road Users	33
CHAPTER 10 Driving, Manoeuvring and Parking	35
CHAPTER 11 Pedestrians	37
CHAPTER 12 Liability of Children	39
CHAPTER 13 Passengers	41
CHAPTER 15 Highways	43
CHAPTER 17 Animals on Highway	45
CHAPTER 18 Limitation	49
CHAPTER 19 Introduction to Civil Procedure	53
CHAPTER 20 The MOJ Process	67
CHAPTER 21 Parties	73
CHAPTER 22 Issuing Proceedings	77
CHAPTER 23 Service	79
CHAPTER 24 Defence	83
CHAPTER 25 Summary Judgment	89

Table of Contents

CHAPTER 26	Additional Claims	91
CHAPTER 27	Allocation	93
CHAPTER 28	Disclosure	95
CHAPTER 29	Witnesses	99
CHAPTER 30	Evidence and Admissibility	101
CHAPTER 31	Expert Evidence	103
CHAPTER 32	Applications	107
CHAPTER 33	Part 36 Offers	111
CHAPTER 34	Trial	131
CHAPTER 35	Appeals	133
CHAPTER 36	Accidents Abroad	137
CHAPTER 37	General Principles of Quantum	143
CHAPTER 38	Quantification of Damages	147
CHAPTER 39	Damages in Fatal Cases	159
CHAPTER 40	Credit Hire	175
CHAPTER 41	Costs	161

Table of Statutes

Paragraph references printed in **bold** type indicate where the Statute is set out in part or in full.

A

Access to Justice Act 1999
.... 41.33B
Administration of justice Act 1982
s 12(2)(a) 38.218A
Animals Act 1971
s 10, 11 .... **17.2A**

C

Consumer Insurance Act 2012
.... 2.271
County Court Act 1984
s 51(2)(a) 38.218A
Courts and Legal Services Act 1990
s 58(4B) 41.35A, 41.35C

D

Dangerous Dogs Act 1991
s 3 .... 17.3
s 6 .... 17.3
10 .... 17.3
Deregulation Act 2015
.... 3.65A

E

Equality Act 2010 .... 38.94A

F

Fatal Accidents Act 1976
.... 36.25

H

Health and social care (Community Health and Standards) Act 2003
s 158 .... 38.218A
Highways Act 1980
s 41 .... 15.12A
(3) 18.35FA

I

Insurance Act 2015
.... 2.268, 2.270, 2.271

Insurance Act 2015 – *cont.*
s 9 .... 2.272

J

Judgements Act 1838
.... 38.246A

L

Law Reform (Miscellaneous Provision) Act 1934 .... 36.25
Legal Services Act 2007
s 194(3) 19.68AA
Limitation Act 1980
.... 19.8
s 10(1) 18.82A
(4) 18.82A
11 .... 18.62F
14(1) 18.35H
33 . 18.35H, 18.60D, 18.62D, 18.62F, 18.62G

R

Road Traffic Act 1988
s 143 .... 1.7A
(3) 3.30D
144, 145 .... 1.7A
151(4) 3.30D

S

Senior Court Act 1981
s 32A(2)(a) 38.218A
Social Security (Recovery of Benefits) Act 1997 .... 38.185A
Supreme Court Act 1981
s 51 .... 41.260A

W

Welfare Reform Act 2012
.... 38.203A, 38.218A

Table of Statutory Instruments

Paragraph references printed in **bold** type indicate where the Statutory Instrument is set out in part or in full.

C

Cancellation of Contracts made in
 a Consumer's Home or Place of Work
 etc Regulations 2008, SI 2008/1816
 .... 40.14A, 40.14B, 41.43A
Civil Procedure Rules 1998, SI 1998/3132
 .... 8.4E, 41.216A
Pt 1
 r 1.2 .... **19.33A**
   (b) 8.49A
  1.3 .... 23.59BA
Pt 3
 r 3.1(2) 26.16A
   m 19.33A
   (4)–(6) 19.19A
   (7) 8.16C, 32.26HA
  3.4(2)(a) 23.1A3
    (b) 8.16F
  3.7 .... 19.61A
  3.8 .... 23.59BA
  3.9 .... 32.26HA, 32.26R, 35.20B
   (1)(a) 19.94B, 19.94D
    b) 19.94B
  3.17 .... 8.27
Pt 4
 r 4.3A **22.16A**
Pt 6 .... 24.21A
 r 6.9(2) 23.1A3
  6.15 .... 23.22C, 23.36B
   (1) 23.36C
  6.16 .... 23.1A3
  6.20(1) 32.26Q
  6.27 .... 23.22C
PD 6A
para 4.1 .... 23.36C
Pt 7 .... 20.8A, 20.8B, 20.12A, 20.18A,
       20.34A, 20.57A, 24.21A
 r 7 .... 41.94D
  7.4 .... **23.61**
Pt 8
 r 8.1(3) 20.57A
PD 8B
para 7.2 .... 20.57A, 41.94D
Pt 10
 r 10.3 .... 24.7A
Pt 12
 r 12.6 .... 38.246A
  12.7 .... 24.17A
  12.10 .... 24.13

Civil Procedure Rules 1998, SI 1998/3132 – *cont.*
Pt 13
 r 13.3 .... 24.21A
  (1)(b) 32.26R
Pt 14
 r 14.1 .... **24.32**
  14.1A 19.8
  14.1B 20.18A
Pt 19
 r 19.2 .... 26.16A
Pt 20 .... 26.25A
 r 20.96 .... 26.16A
Pt 21
 r 21.1 .... **21.1**
Pt 24
 r 24 .... 25.12C
  24.4 .... 25.12B
Pt 25
 r 25.7(4) 32.31A
Pt 26
 r 26.2A 27.3A
  26.3 .... 19.68AA
  26.8 .... 27.11B
  26.10 .... 27.17A
Pt 28
 r 28.5 .... 19.68AA
Pt 29
 r 29.6 .... 19.68AA
Pt 31 .... 19.8, 28.1A
 r 31.6 .... 28.14B
  31.16 .... 28.6E
Pt 32 .... 28.1A
 r 32.5 .... 29.7A
  32.10 .... 29.9A
Pt 33 .... 33.2A
Pt 35 .... 19.8, 20.34C, 31.3
 r 35.4 .... **31.12**
   (1) 19.19A
PD 35 .... 31.2
Pt 36 ... 18.82A, 19.8, 19.19A, 33.13B,
       33.23B, 33.41G, 33.41H, 33.41I,
       33.41J, 33.50A, 33.60A, 41.148B
 r 36.2 .... **33.2A**
  36.3 .... **33.8**
  36.5 .... **33.7**
  36.7 .... **33.10**
  36.8 .... **33.18**
  36.9 .... **33.23A**
  36.10 .... **33.23C**

xiii

Table of Statutory Instruments

Civil Procedure Rules 1998, SI 1998/3132 – *cont.*
r 36.11 .... 33.24
36.12 .... 33.25C
36.13 .... 33.26
36.14 .... 33.27, 33.50A
36.15 .... 33.29, 33.49
36.16 .... 33.30
36.17 .... 33.34, 33.50A
36.18 .... 33.46A
36.19 .... 33.46B
36.22 .... 33.49
    (1)(d) 36.30
36.23 .... 33.29A
36.24 .... 33.55
36.26 .... 33.57
36.27 .... 33.56, 33.58
36.28 .... 33.59
36.29 .... 33.60
36.30 .... 33.61
Pt 39
r 39.3(5)(a) 34.4A
Pt 44
r 44 .... 41.127A
44.2 .... 33.2A
44.3 .... 41.216B
    (5) 19.19A
    (a) 19.19A
44.3B 41.221A
    (1) 41.38A
44.9 .... 19.68AA
44.13 .... 41.217D
    (1) 41.217C
44.16 .... 8.20B

Civil Procedure Rules 1998, SI 1998/3132 – *cont.*
r 44.16(1) 41.217B
Pt 45
r 45 .... 41.94A, 41.94B
45.24(2)(b), (c) 20.12A
45.29 .... 41.94A
45.29A 8.49A, 41.94A, 41.94B
45.29C 41.94C
Section IIIA (rr 45.29A–45.29L)
.... 8.49A, 33.60A
r 45.29C 33.60A
Pt 52
r 52.3 .... 35.10
52.6 .... 35.20B
52.12 .... 33.31
Pt 54
r 54.12 .... 19.68AA

I

Income Support (General) Regulations 1987, SI 1987/1967
Sch 10
para 44(1)(b) 38.112B

M

Motor Vehicles (Compulsory Insurance) (Information Centre and Compensation Body) Regulations 2003, SI 2003/37 .... 6.27
reg 13(2) 36.28
    (b) 36.29

Table of European Legislation

Paragraph references printed in **bold** type indicate where the Legislation is set out in part or in full.

Primary Legislation

Conventions

Convention for the Protection of Human Rights and Fundamental Freedoms (Rome 1950)
- art 1 .... 41.33B
- 6 .... 41.33B

Treaties and Agreements

Uninsured Drivers Agreement 2015 (13 August 1999) 3.30B
Uninsured Drivers Agreement 2015 (August 2015) 3.30B, 3.30H, 3.65A

Secondary Legislation

Directives

Council Directive No 72/166/EEC
- art 1(1) 1.7A

Council Directive No 72/166/EEC – *cont.*
- art 3(1) **1.7A**

Council Directive No 84/5/EEC
- art 1 .... 36.28

European Parliament and of the Council Directive No 2009/103/EC (VIth MID) 1.7A

Regulations

Council Regulation (EC) No 44/2001
- art 9 .... 36.6B
- 11 .... 36.6B

European Parliament and the Council Regulations No 883/2004/EC
- art 85 .... 36.25

European Parliament and the Council Regulation (EC) No 864/2007 (Rome II regulation)
- art 4(1) .. 36.22A, 36.24, 36.26, 36.27, 36.28
- (2), (3) 36.24, 36.28
- 15 .... 36.26, 36.27
- 16 .... 36.26

Table of Cases

Decisions of the European Court of Justice are listed below numerically. These decisions are also included in the preceding alphabetical list.

A

A v Hoare and other appeals [2008] UKHL 6, [2008] 1 AC 844, [2008] 2 All ER 1, [2008] 2 WLR 311, [2008] 1 FLR 771, [2008] Fam Law 402, 100 BMLR 1, [2008] NLJR 218, (2008) Times, 31 January, [2008] All ER (D) 251 (Jan) 18.62F
A v Trustees of the Watchtower Bible & Tract Society, Trustees of the Loughborough Blackbrook Congregation of Jehovah's Witnesses and Trustees of the Loughborough Southwood Congregation of Jehovah's Witnesses [2015] EWHC 1722 (QB), 165 NLJ 7692 .... 5.23J, 18.35H
AB (By his mother and next friend CD) v Lisa Main [2015] EWHC 3183 (QB) 12.15B
Abid Anwar v Severn Trent Water Ltd (2015) unreported 8.16C
Agapitos v Agnew [2002] EWCA Civ 247, [2003] QB 556, [2002] 1 All ER (Comm) 714, [2002] 3 WLR 616, [2002] 2 Lloyd's Rep 42, [2002] Lloyd's Rep IR 191, [2002] 16 LS Gaz R 38, [2002] All ER (D) 54 (Mar) 8.10D
Aggouche v TNT UK Ltd (2011), unreported 40.14B
Aileen Webb v Bromley London Borough Council (18 February 2016, unreported) 41.35C
Akinrodoye v Esure Services Ltd (16 February 2015, unreported) 20.34A
Alcock v Chief Constable of South Yorkshire Police [1992] 1 AC 310, [1991] 4 All ER 907, [1991] 3 WLR 1057, 8 BMLR 37, [1992] 3 LS Gaz R 34, 136 Sol Jo LB 9, HL 38.43A
Ali v Spirit Motor Transport Ltd (12 May 2014, unreported) 40.14B, 40.19A
American Leisure Group Ltd v Sir David Eardley Garrard [2014] EWHC 2101 (Ch), [2014] 1 WLR 4102, 164 NLJ 7613, [2014] All ER (D) 218 (Jun) 23.22A
Andrew and Claire Foulds v Devon County Council [2015] EWHC 40 (QB), [2015] All ER (D) 74 (Jan) 15.12A
Atkins (Desmond) v Co-Operative Group Ltd [2016] EWHC 80 (QB), [2016] All ER (D) 205 (Jan) 30.7C

B

Barton v Wright Hassall LLP [2016] EWCA Civ 177, [2016] All ER (D) 202 (Mar) 23.36C
Beaumont & O'Neill v Ferrer [2016] EWCA Civ 768 .... 37.66E
Bent v Highways and Utilities Construction and Allianz [2011] EWCA Civ 1539 ... 40.39C
Berwick Copley v Ibeh (5 June 2014, unreported) 20.33A, 20.33B
Bhatti v Ashgar [2016] EWHC 1049 (QB) 25.13A
Bianco (Widow and Administratrix of the estate of the late Vladimiro Capano on behalf of herself and dependant children) v Bennett [2015] EWHC 626 (QB), [2015] All ER (D) 178 (Mar) 36.25
Billett v Ministry of Defence [2015] EWCA Civ 773, [2016] PIQR Q1, [2015] All ER (D) 256 (Jul) 38.94A, 38.95B
Blankley (Diann) (by her litigation friend Andrew MG Cusworth) v Central Manchester and Manchester Children's University Hospitals NHS Trust [2015] EWCA Civ 18, [2015] 1 WLR 4307, 165 NLJ 7639, [2015] 1 Costs LR 119, [2015] All ER (D) 207 (Jan) 41.41A
Bloy v Motor Insurers' Bureau [2013] EWCA Civ 1543, [2014] Lloyd's Rep IR 75, [2014] PIQR P171, [2013] All ER (D) 344 (Nov) 36.27, 36.29

xvii

Table of Cases

Bristow v The Princess Alexander Hospital NHS Trust (4 November 2015, unreported) 41.418C
British Gas Trading Ltd v Oak Cash & Carry Ltd [2016] EWCA Civ 153, 166 NLJ 7692, [2016] All ER (D) 128 (Mar) 19.94F
Broadhurst v Tan [2016] EWCA Civ 94, [2016] 1 WLR 1928, 166 NLJ 7689, [2016] All ER (D) 219 (Feb) 33.60A
Budana v Leeds Teaching Hospitals NHS Trust (14 September 2015, unreported) ... 41.35B
Budd v Abayle (2015), unreported 20.38A
Burgess v Lejonvarn [2016] EWHC 40 (TCC), 164 ConLR 165, [2016] All ER (D) 132 (Jan) 37.38A
Burrett v Mencap Ltd (14 May 2014, unreported) .... [33.23B]
Bushell v Parry (27 March 2015, unreported) 20.33A, 20.33B
Buswell v Symes and MIB [2015] EWHC 1379 (QB), [2015] All ER (D) 154 (May) 9.10A

C

Caliendo and another company v Mishcon de Reya (a firm) [2015] EWCA Civ 1029, [2015] All ER (D) 99 (Oct) 19.94D, 41.221B
Cammack v Naqvi (2015), unreported 27.11B
Cassley v GMP Securities Europe LLP [2015] EWHC 722 (QB), [2015] All ER (D) 05 (Apr) 4.44C
Catholic Child Welfare Society v Various Claimants (FC) [2012] UKSC 56, [2013] 2 AC 1, [2013] 1 All ER 670, [2012] 3 WLR 1319, [2013] IRLR 219, [2012] NLJR 1504, (2012) Times, 18 December, 156 Sol Jo (no 45) 31, [2013] 4 LRC 242, [2012] All ER (D) 238 (Nov) 5.23J
Cavell (Philip) v Transport for London [2015] EWHC 2283 (QB), [2015] All ER (D) 36 (Aug) 24.41E
Chadwick (Matthew) (trustee in bankruptcy of Anthony Burling) v Linda Burling [2015] EWHC 1610 (Ch), [2015] 3 Costs LR 589, [2015] BPIR 1019, [2015] All ER (D) 98 (Jun) 19.94B
Chief Constable of Hampshire Constabulary v Southampton City Council [2014] EWCA Civ 1541, [2015] PIQR P61, [2014] All ER (D) 01 (Dec) 18.82A
Chopra (Renu) and Vivek Rattan v Bank of Singapore Ltd and Oversea-Chinese Banking Corpn Ltd [2015] EWHC 1549 (Ch), [2015] All ER (D) 42 (Jun) 23.1A3
Christian v South East London and Kent Bus Co [2014] EWCA Civ 944 .... 13.43A
Collins (George) v Secretary of State for Business Innovation and Skills and Stena Lane Irish Sea Ferries Ltd [2013] EWHC 1117 (QB), [2013] All ER (D) 116 (May); affd [2014] EWCA Civ 717, [2014] PIQR P324, 164 NLJ 7610, [2014] All ER (D) 44 (Jun) 18.35FA
Coventry v Lawrence [2015] UKSC 50, [2016] 2 All ER 97, 165 NLJ 7663, [2015] 4 Costs LO 507, [2015] All ER (D) 234 (Jul), sub nom Lawrence v Fen Tigers Ltd (Secretary of State for Justice intervening) [2015] 1 WLR 3485, (2015) Times, 17 August 41.33B
Cox v Ministry of Justice [2016] UKSC 10, [2016] 2 WLR 806, [2016] ICR 470, [2016] PIQR P8, (2016) Times, 10 March 5.7BA
Cox v Woodlands Manor Care Home [2015] EWCA Civ 415, [2015] 3 Costs LO 327, [2015] All ER (D) 268 (Jan) 41.43A
Crofton v National Health Service Litigation Authority [2007] EWCA Civ 71, [2007] 1 WLR 923, [2007] LGR 507, [2015] CP Rep 25, [2007] PIQR Q37, (2007) Times, 15 February, [2007] All ER (D) 106 (Feb) 38.118C
Crooks v Hendricks Lovell Ltd [2016] EWCA Civ 8, 166 NLJ 7684, [2016] All ER (D) 100 (Jan) 33.50A

D

DB UK Bank Ltd (t/a DB Mortgages) v Jacobs Solicitors [2016] EWCA Civ 8 ...... 33.13B
Delaney v Secretary of State for Transport [2015] EWCA Civ 172, [2015] 3 All ER 329, [2015] 2 CMLR 914, [2015] RTR 169, [2015] Lloyd's Rep IR 441, [2015] PIQR P 266, [2015] All ER (D) 97 (Mar) 3.30D, 7.46AA

Table of Cases

Denton v TH White Ltd [2014] EWCA Civ 906, [2015] 1 All ER 880, [2014] 1 WLR 3926, 154 Con LR 1, [2014] BLR 547, 164 NLJ 7614, [2014] 4 Costs LR 752, [2014] All ER (D) 53 (Jul) ... 19.68AA, 19.94B, 19.94C, 19.94D, 19.94E, 19.94F, 19.94G, 32.26Q, 32.26R, 34.4A, 35.20B, 41.221A, 41.221B, 41.221C
Deutsche Bank AG v Sebastian Holdings Incorporated [2016] EWCA Civ 23, [2016] 4 WLR 17, (2016) Times, 25 February, [2016] All ER (D) 185 (Jan) 41.260A
Diamanttek Ltd v Mr Jonathon James, (8 February 2016, unreported) 8.20B
Dingley v Chief Constable, Strathclyde Police 1998 SC 548, Ct of Sess; affd (2000) 55 BMLR 1, 2000 SC (HL) 77, [2000] All ER (D) 304, HL 31.6A
Dunbar Assets plc v BCP Premier Ltd [2015] EWHC 10 (Ch), [2015] All ER (D) 64 (Jan) 23.36B
Dursan v J Sainsbury plc [2015] EWHC 233 (QB), [2015] RTR 113, [2015] All ER (D) 131 (Feb) 4.34D, 11.10E
Dusek v Stormharbour Securities LLP [2015] EWHC 37 (QB), [2015] All ER (D) 138 (Jan) 4.44C

E

Easton v B & Q plc [2015] EWHC 880 (QB), [2015] All ER (D) 40 (Apr) 38.41A
Edward Power v Meloy Whittle Robinson Solicitors [2014] EWCA Civ 898 .... 23.22B
Edward Williams v Santander UK plc (2015), unreported 27.17A
Eeles v Cobham Hire Services Ltd [2009] EWCA Civ 204, [2010] 1 WLR 409, [2009] PIQR P273, 153 Sol Jo (no 11) 30, [2009] All ER (D) 144 (Mar) 32.31A
8 Representative Claimants v MGN Ltd [2016] EWHC 855 (Ch), [2016] All ER (D) 127 (Apr) 41.33A
Euro-Asian Oil SA v Abilo (UK), Credit Suisse AG and Dan Igniska [2015] EWHC 1741 (Comm), [2015] All ER (D) 239 (Jun) 28.14B
Excalibur Ventures LLC v Texas Keystone Inc [2015] EWHC 566 (Comm), 165 NLJ 7645, [2015] All ER (D) 109 (Mar) 41.127A
EXP v Barker [2015] EWHC 1289 (QB), 165 NLJ 7656, [2015] All ER (D) 12 (Jun) 31.8B

F

Fathollahipour v Aliabadienis [2014] EWCA Civ 1633, [2015] 1 WLR 2472, (2015) Times, 22 January, [2015] 2 Costs LR 191, [2014] All ER (D) 165 (Dec) 35.20B
Finglands Coachways Ltd v O'Hare (a protected party by his sister and litigation friend Ms Portia Crees) [2014] EWHC 1513 (QB), [2014] 4 Costs LO 668, [2014] All ER (D) 131 (May) 41.216A
Framlington Court, The. See H (minors) (sexual abuse: standard of proof), Re

G

Gee 7 Group Ltd v Personal Management Solutions [2016] EWHC 891 (Ch) 23.22C
Gentry (Stuart John) v Miller and UK Insurance [2016] EWCA Civ 141, (2016) Times, 21 April, [2016] All ER (D) 107 (Mar) 8.4E, 34.4A, 41.221C
Ghising (Roshan) v Secretary of State for the Home Department [2015] EWHC 3706 (QB), [2015] All ER (D) 213 (Dec) 41.38B
Gohil v Gohil [2015] UKSC 61, [2016] 1 All ER 685, [2015] 3 WLR 1085, [2015] 3 FCR 497, [2015] 2 FLR 1289, [2015] Fam Law 1459, 165 NLJ 7673, (2015) Times, 03 November, [2015] All ER (D) 100 (Oct) 8.16D
Graham v Commercial Bodyworks Ltd [2015] EWCA Civ 47, [2015] ICR 665, [2015] PIQR P240, (2015) Times, 27 March, [2015] All ER (D) 72 (Feb) 5.23H
Greenway v Johnson Matthey plc [2016] EWCA Civ 408, [2016] All ER (D) 207 (Apr) 37.38B
Greig (Kenneth) v Anthony Francis Stirling and Anthony Tomas Etridge [2014] EWHC 4017 (QB), [2014] All ER (D) 20 (Dec) 25.12B
Grieves v FT Everard & Sons Ltd [2007] UKHL 39, [2008] PIQR P95 .... 18.60D

Table of Cases

Grovit v Doctor [1997] 2 All ER 417, [1997] 1 WLR 640, [1997] NLJR 633, 141 Sol Jo LB 107, HL 32.66C

H

H (minors) (sexual abuse: standard of proof), Re [1996] AC 563, [1996] 1 All ER 1, [1996] 2 WLR 8, [1996] 1 FCR 509, [1996] 1 FLR 80, [1996] Fam Law 74, 140 Sol Jo LB 24, HL 8.9A
HS v Lancashire Teaching Hospitals NHS Trust [2015] EWHC 1376 (QB), [2015] All ER (D) 167 (May) 38.131B
Hallam Estates Ltd and Michael Stainer v Baker [2014] EWCA Civ 661, 164 NLJ 7608, [2014] 4 Costs LR 660, [2014] All ER (D) 163 (May) 23.59BA
Harman v East Kent Hospitals NHS Foundation Trust [2015] EWHC 1662 (QB), [2015] PIQR Q92, [2015] All ER (D) 182 (Jun) 38.118C
Hassan v Cooper and Accident Claims Consultants Ltd [2015] EWHC 540 (QB), [2015] RTR 288 .... 41.217B
Hatton v Sutherland [2002] EWCA Civ 76, [2002] 2 All ER 1, [2002] ICR 613, [2002] IRLR 263, 68 BMLR 115, (2002) Times, 11 February, [2002] All ER (D) 53 (Feb 38.41A
Hayden v Maidstone and Tunbridge Wells NHS Trust [2016] EWHC 1121 (QB), [2016] All ER (D) 108 (May) 30.12F
Hayward v Zurich Insurance Company plc [2015] EWCA Civ 327, [2015] Lloyd's Rep IR 585, [2015] All ER (D) 04 (Apr) 8.16D, 8.20ia, 30.7D
Hedley Byrne & Co Ltd v Heller & Partners Ltd [1964] AC 465, [1963] 2 All ER 575, [1963] 3 WLR 101, [1963] 1 Lloyd's Rep 485, 8 LDAB 155, 107 Sol Jo 454, HL ... 4.29E, 37.38A
Henderson v Merrett Syndicates Ltd (No 1) [1995] 2 AC 145, [1994] 3 All ER 506, [1994] 3 WLR 761, [1994] NLJR 1204, [1994] 4 LRC 355, HL 37.38A
Hobbs v Guy's and St Thomas' NHS Foundation Trust [2015] EWHC B20 (Costs) 41.216C
Hockley (Sharon) v North Lincolnshire & Goole NHS Foundation Trust (19 September 2014, unreported), QC 24.7A, 24.25A, 32.26R
Home Office v Dorset Yacht Co Ltd [1970] AC 1004, [1970] 2 All ER 294, [1970] 2 WLR 1140, [1970] 1 Lloyd's Rep 453, 114 Sol Jo 375, HL 4.29E
Horner v Norman [2015] EWCA Civ 1055, [2015] All ER (D) 216 (Oct) 11.10D
Hoteles Pinero & Keefe (by his litigation friend Eyton) v Mapfre Mutualidad Compania De Seguros Y Reaseguros SA [2015] EWCA Civ 598, [2016] 1 WLR 905, [2016] Lloyd's Rep IR 94, [2015] All ER (D) 213 (Jun) 36.5A
Howe v Motor Insurers' Bureau [2016] EWHC 640 (QB), 166 NLJ 7694, [2016] All ER (D) 210 (Mar) 36.29
Hussain (Khalid) v Robert Parry (2013), unreported 24.21A

I

Ifede v Ministry of Defence [2015] EWHC 3835 (QB) 18.62G
Iqbal v Whipps Cross University NHS Trust [2007] EWCA Civ 1190, [2008] PIQR P161, [2007] All ER (D) 300 (Nov) 38.118B

J

Jacobs v Motor Insurers' Bureau [2010] EWCA Civ 1208, [2011] 1 All ER 844, [2011] 1 All ER (Comm) 445, [2011] 1 WLR 2609, [2011] RTR 16, [2011] Lloyd's Rep IR 355, [2010] All ER (D) 256 (Oct) 36.24, 36.27, 36.29
Jet Airways (India) Ltd v Barloworld Handling Ltd [2014] EWCA Civ 1311, [2014] All ER (D) 133 (Oct) 28.6E
Jones v Spire Healthcare Ltd (2016), unreported 41.35A

K

Kennedy v Cordia (Services) LLP [2016] UKSC 6, [2016] 1 WLR 597, [2016] ICR 325, 2016 SLT 209, [2016] All ER (D) 99 (Feb) 31.6A

L

LBI HF (formerly Landsbani Island HF) v Kevin Gerald Stanford & Landsbanki Luxembourg SA [2014] EWHC 3273 (Comm) 24.62
Ladd v Marshall [1954] 3 All ER 745, [1954] 1 WLR 1489, 98 Sol Jo 870, CA 8.16D
Landau v Big Bus Co Ltd and Pawel Zeital [2013] EWHC 3281 (QB), [2013] All ER (D) 64 (Oct) 41.217A
Lawrence v Fen Tigers Ltd (Secretary of State for Justice intervening). See Coventry v Lawrence
Lawson v Mullen (22 June, 2015, unreported) 40.39B
Legg v Sterte Garage Ltd and Aviva UK Ltd [2016] EWCA Civ 97, [2016] All ER (D) 215 (Feb) 41.250A
Lewis v Ward Hadaway (A Firm) [2015] EWHC 3503 (Ch), [2016] 4 WLR 6, [2016] All ER (D) 46 (Jan) 25.12C, 32.66B
Linda Engeham v London & Quandrant Housing Trust Ltd and Academy of Plumbing Ltd '(In voluntary liq)', sub nom Linda Engeham v London & Quandrant Housing Trust Ltd and Academy of Plumbing Ltd (In Voluntary Liq) [2015] EWCA Civ 1530 .... 41.44A
Liverpool Women's Hospital NHS Foundation Trust v Ronayne [2015] EWCA Civ 588, 145 BMLR 110, [2015] PIQR P337, 165 NLJ 7659, (2015) Times, 08 July, [2015] All ER (D) 195 (Jun) 38.43B
Lloyd v Humphreys & Glasgow Ltd [2015] EWHC 525 (QB), [2015] All ER (D) 243 (Mar) 18.60D
Long v Value Properties Ltd and Ocean Trade Ltd [2014] EWHC 2981 (Ch), [2015] 3 All ER 419, [2014] 5 Costs LR 915, [2014] All ER (D) 103 (Oct) 41.221A
Luftu Ali v CIS General Insurance (2015), unreported 28.29D

M

McCracken (a protected party suing by his mother and litigation friend Deborah Norris) v Smith, MIB and Bell [2015] EWCA Civ 380, [2016] Lloyd's Rep IR 171, [2015] PIQR P305, [2015] All ER (D) 188 (Apr) 7.46CA, 37.66C
MacLeod (Donald) (a protected party suing by his litigation friend Barbara MacLeod) v Metropolitan Police Comrs [2015] EWCA Civ 688, [2015] All ER (D) 98 (Jul) 6.25A, 10.46D, 29.7A
Maddocks v Lyne (22 January 2016, unreported) 20.33B
Malak v Nasim [2015] LTLPI 20.18A
Malone v Reylon Heating Engineering Ltd [2014] EWCA Civ 904, [2014] All ER (D) 34 (Jul) 18.62D
Manna (Lamarieo) (a child and protected party by his father and litigation friend, Samuel Manna) v Central Manchester University Hospitals NHS Foundation Trust [2015] EWHC 2279 (QB), [2015] All ER (D) 39 (Aug) 38.118B, 38.131A, 38.185A
Marshall v Motor Insurers' Bureau, Pickard & Generali [2015] EWHC 3421 (QB), [2016] PIQR Q65, [2015] All ER (D) 78 (Dec) 36.28, 36.29
Massey v Tameside and Glossop Acute Services NHS Trust [2007] EWHC 317 (QB), [2007] All ER (D) 301 (Feb) 38.112A, 38.118B
May v Robinson [2014] EWCA Civ 1633, [2015] 1 WLR 2472, (2015) Times, 22 January, [2015] 2 Costs LR 191, [2014] All ER (D) 165 (Dec) 35.20B
Mendes v Hochtief (UK) Construction Ltd [2016] EWHC 976 (QB), [2016] All ER (D) 18 (May) 41.94C
Michael v The Chief Constable of South Wales Police [2015] UKSC 2, [2015] AC 1732, [2015] 2 All ER 635, [2015] 2 WLR 343, 165 NLJ 7639, (2015) Times, 16 January, [2015] All ER (D) 215 (Jan) 4.29E
Mills (Jonathan) v Farmfoods Distribution Ltd (27 November 2015, unreported) ... 41.94B

Table of Cases

Milton Keynes NHS Foundation Trust v Hyde [2016] EWHC 72 (QB), 166 NLJ 7688, [2016] All ER (D) 158 (Feb) 41.34A
Mishcon De Reya (a firm) and Mishcon De Reya LLP v Antonio Caliendo and Barnaby Holdings Ltd [2015] EWCA Civ 1029, [2015] All ER (D) 99 (Oct) 19.94D
Mitchell v News Group Newspapers Ltd [2013] EWCA Civ 1537, [2014] 2 All ER 430, [2014] 1 WLR 795, [2014] BLR 89, [2013] 6 Costs LR 1008, [2013] All ER (D) 314 (Nov) 19.68AA, 19.94C, 23.59BA, 32.26HA, 34.4A, 35.20B, 41.221A
Modhwadia v Modhwadia (20 January 2015, unreported) 20.8B
Mohamed Rizan & Mohammed Rilshad v Barry Hayes & Allianz Insurance plc [2016] EWCA Civ 481 .... 8.9A
Mohamud v WM Morrison Supermarkets plc [2016] UKSC 11, [2016] 2 WLR 821, [2016] ICR 485, [2016] IRLR 362, 166 NLJ 7690, (2016) Times, 14 March, [2016] All ER (D) 19 (Mar) 5.23GA
Moreno v Motor Insurers' Bureau [2015] EWHC 1142 (QB), [2015] All ER (D) 213 (Apr) 36.27
Morris (Annie) v Sandra Sanda Htay (2 February 2015, unreported) 41.148A
Mosson v Spousal (London) Ltd [2015] EWHC 53 (QB), [2016] 4 WLR 28, [2016] All ER (D) 214 (Jan) 38.132B
Murphy v Ministry of Defence [2016] EWHC 3 (QB) 38.94B
Murray v BAE Systems plc (2016) unreported 19.94G

N

NA v Nottinghamshire County Council [2015] EWCA Civ 1139, [2016] 1 FCR 419, [2016] Fam Law 171, 165 NLJ 7678, [2015] All ER (D) 126 (Nov) 5.23I
Nesham v Sunrich Clothing Ltd (2016), unreported 8.20C

O

O'Brien (John Joseph) (a protected party suing by his father and litigation friend Authur O'Brien) v Michael Shorrock and Motor Insurers Bureau [2015] EWHC 1630 (QB), [2015] 4 Costs LO 439, [2015] All ER (D) 209 (Jun) 41.38A
OOO Abbott and Godfrey Victor Chasmer v Econowall UK Ltd, Project Consultancy and Construction Ltd, Smith Brewer Ltd and Retail Display Connections Ltd [2016] EWHC 660 (IPEC), [2016] All ER (D) 41 (Apr) 23.59F
Oyesanya v Mid-Yorkshire Hospital NHS Trust [2015] EWCA Civ 1049, [2015] 5 Costs LR 911, [2015] All ER (D) 170 (Oct) 38.246A

P

PGF II SA v OMFS Co 1 Ltd [2013] EWCA Civ 1288, [2014] 1 All ER 970, [2014] 1 WLR 1386, 152 ConLR 72, [2013] 3 EGLR 16, [2014] BLR 1, [2013] 6 Costs LR 973, [2013] All ER (D) 264 (Oct) 33.41J
PM Law Ltd v Motorplus Ltd and Members of Equity 218 at Lloyds (t/a Equity Red Star) [2016] EWHC 193 (QB), [2016] All ER (D) 89 (Feb) 25.6D
Parker v Butler [2016] EWHC 1251 (QB) 41.217D
Pattni v First Leicester Buses Ltd [2010] All ER (D) 201 (Nov) 40.35A
Payne v Scott (19 August 2015, unreported), LTL 20.8C
Peters v East Midlands Strategic Health Authority [2009] EWCA Civ 145, [2010] QB 48, [2009] 3 WLR 737, [2009] PIQR Q1, (2009) Times, 16 March, 153 Sol Jo (no 9) 30, [2009] All ER (D) 24 (Mar) 38.118C
Phillips v Willis [2016] EWCA Civ 401, [2016] All ER (D) 149 (Apr) 20.57A, 40.46, 41.94D
Picard v Motor Insurers' Bureau [2015] EWHC 3421 (QB), [2016] PIQR Q65, [2015] All ER (D) 78 (Dec) 36.28, 36.29
Pipe (Barbara) v Spicer Haart Estate Agents Ltd (t/a Haart) [2016] EWHC 61 (QB), [2016] All ER (D) 152 (Jan) 19.94E
Platt (Howard) v BRB (Residuary) Ltd [2014] EWCA Civ 1401, [2014] PIQR P80, [2014] All ER (D) 07 (Nov) 18.62E

Table of Cases

Popi M, The. See Rhesa Shipping Co SA v Edmunds, The Popi M
Purefuture Ltd v Simmons & Simmons [2001] CP Rep 30 .... 32.66C

Q

Qader (Shahow) v Esure Services Ltd [2015] All ER (D) 295 (Oct) 41.94A

R

R (on the application of Hysaj) v Secretary of State for the Home Department [2014] EWCA Civ 1633, [2015] 1 WLR 2472, (2015) Times, 22 January, [2015] 2 Costs LR 191, [2014] All ER (D) 165 (Dec) 35.20B
R (on the application of ZYN) v Walsall Metropolitan Borough Council [2014] EWHC 1918 (Admin), [2015] 1 All ER 165, [2014] PTSR 1356, [2014] WTLR 1649, [2014] All ER (D) 108 (Jun) 38.112B
RE v GE [2015] EWCA Civ 287, [2015] All ER (D) 88 (Apr) 18.62F
Rafiania v All Type Scaffolding Ltd (14 October 2015, unreported) 20.12A
Rahman v Arearose Ltd [2001] QB 351, [2000] 3 WLR 1184, 62 BMLR 84, [2000] All ER (D) 813 .... 37.17A
Raja v Day and MIB (2 March 2015, unreported) 20.12A
Reaney (Christine) v University Hospital of North Staffordshire and Mid Staffordshire NHS Foundation Trust [2015] EWCA Civ 1119, [2015] All ER (D) 16 (Nov) 37.17A, 38.118A
Reid v Buckinghamshire Healthcare NHS Trust [2015] EWHC B21 (Costs) 41.148B
Rhesa Shipping Co SA v Edmunds, The Popi M [1985] 2 All ER 712, [1985] 1 WLR 948, [1985] 2 Lloyd's Rep 1, 129 Sol Jo 503, [1985] LS Gaz R 2995, HL 8.9A
Riff Trading Ltd (in liq), Timothy James Bramston v John Saunders (dec'd), Paul Oliver Saunders, John Gerrard Saunders, Waterleaf Ltd (a company registered in the British Virgin Islands) and Prestwood Property Ltd (a company registered in the British Virgin Islands) [2014] EWHC 2116 (Ch) 19.68AA, 29.9A
Roberts v Johnstone (1986) Times, 26 July; on appeal [1989] QB 878, [1988] 3 WLR 1247, [1989] 5 LS Gaz R 44, CA 38.131A
Robshaw (A Child) v United Lincolnshire Hospitals NHS Trust [2015] EWHC 923 (QB), [2015] All ER (D) 21 (Apr) 38.131B
Royal Bank of Scotland plc v Highland Financial Partners LP [2013] EWCA Civ 328, [2013] All ER (D) 65 (Apr) 34.4A

S

Salter (Matthew) v Muller UK & Ireland Group LLP (27 November 2015, unreported) 41.94B
Savoye v Spicers Ltd [2015] EWHC 33 (TCC), [2015] 1 Costs LR 99 .... 41.216B
Seers (Mr Jason) v Creighton & Sons Ltd [2015] EWHC 959 (QB) 38.132A
Selcuk Fertek and Canan Peker v Aviva Insurance UK Ltd (2016) unreported 8.34B
Shahow Qadar v Esure Services Ltd (15 October 2015, unreported), QBD 8.49A
Sharland v Sharland [2015] UKSC 60, [2016] 1 All ER 671, [2015] 3 WLR 1070, [2015] 3 FCR 481, [2015] 2 FLR 1367, [2015] Fam Law 1461, (2015) Times, 02 November, [2015] All ER (D) 108 (Oct) 8.16E
Sheikh v Beaumont [2015] EWHC 1923 (QB), [2015] All ER (D) 68 (Jul) 21.17AA
Shorter v Surrey and Sussex Healthcare NHS Trust [2015] EWHC 614 (QB), 144 BMLR 136, [2015] All ER (D) 312 (Mar) 38.43C
Sienkiewicz v Greif (UK) Ltd [2011] UKSC 10, [2011] 2 AC 229, [2011] 2 All ER 857, [2011] 2 WLR 523, [2011] ICR 391, 119 BMLR 54, (2011) Times, 10 March, 155 Sol Jo (no 10) 30, [2011] All ER (D) 107 (Mar), CSRC vol 35 iss 1/2 .... 8.9A
Simone Vasile v Pop Ioan and Axa Insurance (17 November 2015, unreported) 8.16F
Sinclair v Joyner [2015] EWHC 1800 (QB), [2015] RTR 349, [2015] All ER (D) 235 (Jun) 10.150D
Smith v Kay (1859) VII HLC 749 .... 8.16E

Table of Cases

Smith v Manchester City Council (or Manchester Corpn) (1974) 17 KIR 1, 118 Sol Jo 597 .... 38.94A, 38.95B
Smith (by his mother and litigation friend Mrs. Banner) v Stratton [2015] EWCA Civ 1413, [2015] All ER (D) 259 (Dec) 37.66D
Sobrany v UAB Transtira [2016] EWCA Civ 28, [2016] Lloyd's Rep IR 266, [2016] All ER (D) 03 (Feb) 40.14A
Solland International Ltd v Clifford Harris & Co [2015] EWHC 3295 (Ch), [2015] All ER (D) 33 (Dec) 32.66C
Sowden v Lodge [2004] EWCA Civ 1370, [2005] 1 All ER 581, [2005] 1 WLR 2129, 148 Sol Jo LB 1282, [2004] All ER (D) 304 (Oct) 38.118C
Sparrow v Andre [2016] EWHC 739 (QB), [2016] All ER (D) 61 (Apr) 10.119B
Stevens v Equity Syndicate Management Ltd [2015] EWCA Civ 93, [2015] 4 All ER 458, [2015] RTR 257, [2015] Lloyd's Rep IR 503, 165 NLJ 7644, [2015] GCCR 13001, [2015] All ER (D) 301 (Feb) 40.35A, 40.39A
Stobart Group Ltd, William Andrew Tinkler, William Stobart, Eddie Stobart Ltd, WA Developments International Ltd v Peter Elliott [2015] EWCA Civ 449, [2015] All ER (D) 121 (May) 30.7B
Stubbings v Webb [1993] AC 498, [1993] 1 All ER 322, [1993] 2 WLR 120, [1993] 2 FCR 699, [1993] 1 FLR 714, [1993] Fam Law 342, 11 BMLR 1, [1993] 6 LS Gaz R 41, 137 Sol Jo LB 32, HL 18.62F
Sugar Hut Group Ltd v AJ Insurance Service (a partnership) [2016] EWCA Civ 46, [2016] All ER (D) 51 (Feb) 33.41J
Symes (Timothy) v St Georges Healthcare NHS Trust [2014] EWHC 2505 (QB), 140 BMLR 171, [2014] All ER (D) 292 (Jul) 24.17A
Syred v Powszecnny Zaklad Ubezpieczen (PZU) SA, Bednorz & HDI Gerling [2016] EWHC 254 (QB), [2016] All ER (D) 157 (Feb) 36.26

T

Taj v Isran (22 October 2015, unreported) 40.39C
Taylor v Smith [2016] EWCA Civ 94, [2016] 1 WLR 1928, 166 NLJ 7689, [2016] All ER (D) 219 (Feb) 33.60A
Tennant v W Cottrell Ltd (11 December 2014, unreported) 20.8A
Thai Airways International Public Company Ltd v KI Holdings Co Ltd (formerly known as Koito Industries Ltd) and Asia Fleet Services (Singapore) PTE Ltd [2015] EWHC 1476 (Comm), [2015] 3 Costs LR 545, [2015] All ER (D) 41 (Jun) 33.41H
Thevarajah v Riordan [2015] UKSC 78, [2016] 1 WLR 76, (2015) Times, 23 December, [2015] All ER (D) 146 (Dec) 32.26HA

U

UK Insurance Ltd v Farrow and Farrow (t/a R Farrow & Sons) (19 January 2016, unreported) Waksman QC 17.37B

V

Vann v Ocidental-Companhia de Seguros SA [2015] EWCA Civ 572, [2015] All ER (D) 36 (Jun) 36.22A
Vaughan v Ministry of Defence [2015] EWHC 1404 (QB), [2015] All ER (D) 207 (May) 4.29F
Versloot Dredging BV and SO DC Merwestone BV v HDI Gerling Industrie Versicherung AG, The DC Merwestone [2014] EWCA Civ 1349, [2015] QB 608, [2015] 2 WLR 1063, [2015] 1 Lloyd's Rep 32, [2015] Lloyd's Rep IR 115, [2014] All ER (D) 202 (Oct) 8.10D
Viridor Waste Management Ltd v Veolia Es Ltd [2015] EWHC 2321 (Comm) 19.94C, 32.26Q
Vnuk v Zavarovalnica Triglav d.d: C-162/13 (2014) ECLI:EU:C:2014:2146, [2016] RTR 188, [2015] Lloyd's Rep IR 142, [2014] All ER (D) 121 (Sep), ECJ 1.7A

W

Wagenaar v Weekend Travel Ltd t/a Ski Weekend [2014] EWCA Civ 1105, [2016]
  1 All ER 643, [2015] 1 WLR 1968, [2014] PIQR P392, 164 NLJ 7619, [2014] 5 Costs
  LO 803, [2014] All ER (D) 24 (Aug) 26.25A, 41.217A
Walsham Chalet Park Ltd (t/a Dream Lodge Group) v Tallington Lakes Ltd [2014]
  EWCA Civ 1607, [2015] 1 Costs LO 157, [2014] All ER (D) 155 (Dec) 19.68AA
Watson v Ministry of Defence (8 April 2016, unreported), QBD 30.12E
West Sussex County Council v Fuller [2015] EWCA Civ 189, [2015] All ER (D) 140
  (Mar) 4.44B
White v White [2001] UKHL 9, [2001] 2 All ER 43, [2001] 1 All ER (Comm) 1105,
  [2001] 1 WLR 481, [2001] 2 CMLR 1, [2001] RTR 379, [2001] 1 Lloyd's Rep 679,
  151 NLJ 350, (2001) Times, 6 March, 145 Sol Jo LB 67, [2001] All ER (D) 07
  (Mar) 3.30D
Wild (Lisa Diane) and Ian Daniel Wild v Southend University Hospital NHS Foundation
  Trust [2014] EWHC 4053 (QB), [2014] All ER (D) 46 (Dec) 38.43A
Winrow v Hemphill [2014] EWHC 3164 (QB), 164 NLJ 7629, [2014] All ER (D) 65
  (Oct) 36.24
Wood (S E) v Days Health UK Ltd [2016] EWHC 1079 (QB), [2016] All ER (D) 85
  (May) 24.41F
Worthington v 03918424 Ltd (16 June 2015, unreported) 33.41I

X

XP v Compensa Towarzystwo SA [2016] EWHC 1728 (QB) 37.17A
XYZ v Various (Including Transform Medical Group (CS) Ltd and Spire Healthcare Ltd)
  [2014] EWHC 4056 (QB), [2014] All ER (D) 85 (Dec) 26.16A

Y

Yason (Aso) v Peshraw Karim and Sabre Insurance (17 April 2015, unreported) 8.4D

CHAPTER 1

Insurance Principles

2. STATUTORY PROVISIONS

SUB-SECTION (1)(A): 'ROAD OR ANY OTHER PUBLIC PLACE'

[1.7A]   Vnuk v Zavarovalnica Triglav dd

C-162/13 (2014) ECLI:EU:C:2014:2146, [2016] RTR 188, [2015] Lloyd's Rep IR 142

The ECJ judgement from September 2014 in the case of *Damijan Vnuk v Zavarovalnica Triglav d.d (Vnuk)* has significant ramifications for the scope of compulsory RTA insurance, and general insurance in the UK.

The ECJ concluded that the insurance obligation in respect of motor vehicles set out in the EU Motor Insurance Directives (MID) is now to be interpreted as extending to 'any use of a vehicle consistent with the normal function of that vehicle'. The use of a vehicle is to be widely construed to include 'any use' and no longer restricted in geographic scope such as by reference to 'public' or 'private' land.

Mr Vnuk brought an action for compensation for injury in his native Slovenia following an accident on 13 August 2007. Mr Vnuk, whilst working as a farmhand, suffered injury when he was knocked from a ladder he had climbed, whilst storing bales of hay in a barn. He was knocked from the ladder by a trailer attached to a tractor. The tractor was reversing on private property, the courtyard of a farm, in order to position the trailer in the barn.

Mr Vnuk sought payment of the sum of EUR 15 944.10 as compensation for his non-pecuniary damage, together with default interest, against Zavarovalnica Triglav, the insurance company with whom the owner of the tractor had taken out compulsory motor insurance.

At first and second instance the claim failed. The Slovenian court dismissed the appeal stating that compulsory insurance in respect of the use of a motor vehicle covered damage caused by the use of a tractor as means of transport, but not damage caused when a tractor is used as a propulsion device.

HELD: The Slovenian appeal court, though, went on to refer the case to the Court of Justice of the European Union (CJEU) to determine whether the duty to insure 'the use of vehicles' within the meaning of Article 3(1) of Council Directive 72/166/EEC, the 1st Motor Directive (MID), covered such circumstances as manoeuvring of a tractor in the courtyard of a farm in order to bring the trailer attached to that tractor into a barn. Article 3(1) of the First Directive states:

> 'Each Member State shall, subject to Article 4, take all appropriate measures to ensure that civil liability in respect of the use of vehicles normally based in its territory is covered by insurance. The extent of the liability covered and the terms and conditions of the cover shall be determined on the basis of these measures.'

The Slovenian court noted that the 1st to the 5th MIDs did not specify what may be regarded as the use of a motor vehicle. It was thus possible to take the view that compulsory insurance covers any damage howsoever connected to the use or operation of a vehicle, irrespective of whether the situation may be defined as a situation involving road use.

[1.7A] *Insurance Principles*

Prior to the CJEU ruling the case was the subject of an Opinion from Advocate General Mengozzi ('the AG'). The AG found that a broad interpretation of movement and 'use' implies no requirement for the vehicle to be on a road. Reversing a tractor in a farmyard must be regarded as use of a vehicle.

The CJEU, in delivering its judgment, followed the AG's approach. At its outset the judgment sought to put in context EU law underpinning compulsory motor insurance, and highlighted the relevant parts of the 1st to 5th MIDs now codified in Directive 2009/103/EC, the 6th MID. Running through of the development of compulsory motor insurance, and it's broadening scope over time, the judgment highlighted that the definition of 'vehicle' is unconnected with the use which is made or may be made of the vehicle in question. Consequently, the fact that a tractor, possibly with a trailer attached, may, in certain circumstances, by used as an agricultural machine has no effect on the finding that such a vehicle corresponds to the concept of 'vehicle' in Article 1(1) of the 1st MID.

So, what are the implications for UK law? In short the judgment in *Vnuk* implies compulsory insurance extends to any use, consistent with normal function of the vehicle and anywhere. *Vnuk* will not have immediate impact on the application of the Road Traffic Act 1988 (RTA 1988) or on insurers in the UK but has led to a review of the RTA 1988 and ss 143 and 145 in terms of the definition of 'vehicle' and 'use' and extending it beyond the road and removing any restriction or exclusion on use of a vehicle. It is likely that the RTA 1988 will be amended but at the time of preparing this update the review into the *Vnuk* decision remains ongoing.

CHAPTER 2

Coverage

12. NON-CONSUMER INSURANCE CONTRACTS

(A) INSURANCE ACT 2015

(i) Introduction

[2.268] From 12 August 2016, non-consumer contracts and will be governed by the Insurance Act 2015.

(ii) Duty of fair presentation

[2.269] From that date, a positive duty of disclosure remains, although this is defined as a 'duty of fair presentation'. This means that before entering into a contract of insurance, the parties will be required to disclose 'every matter which they know, or ought to know, that would influence the judgement of an insurer in deciding whether to insure the risk and on what terms' or 'sufficient information to put an insurer on notice that it needs to make further enquiries about potentially material circumstances'.

The first part of the duty is very similar to that which is already required and will include matters which could have been revealed by a reasonable search of documentation or which is known personally to an individual, but not necessarily the individual making the proposal. The duty may include information held by a broker, although not to the extent that the proposer will be imputed to know confidential information acquired through a business relationship which is unconnected to the contract of insurance in question. The depth of the search will depend on the size and complexity of the business, therefore a reasonable search by a multinational retail organisation will be greater than that expected from a proprietor of a corner shop.

The policyholder will be deemed to have access to documentation or information which may be known to a broker, their own senior management, or to those who are responsible for making the insurance arrangements. This means that even if the person making the proposal is not personally aware of a piece of information which is known to their manager, and which may affect the insurance proposal, the knowledge is still imputed to him/her. Furthermore, if there was a suspicion about an issue, but a deliberate decision was taken to refrain from making further enquiries about that suspicion, knowledge of that issue is deemed to be imputed.

In return, insurers are no longer able to rely upon a passive approach to disclosure, when it comes to seeking to exercise remedies for non-disclosure. They will be considered to have known or ought to have known matters known to the underwriting team and readily available or known by an employee or agent of the insurer and which could reasonably have been passed

[2.269] Coverage

on to the underwriter prior to accepting the risk. In effect an insurer will be presumed to know things which are common knowledge or which they should have been expected to know in the ordinary course of their business.

The duty of fair presentation will continue from the time of the proposal until renewal, unless there is a change in circumstances which affect the policy cover, for example an increase in sums insured, changes to size of vehicle fleet etc which will need to be notified.

(iii) BREACH OF THE DUTY OF FAIR PRESENTATION

[2.270] Under the Insurance Act 2015, insurers retain the right to review the entitlement to indemnity where the policyholder has not given 'a fair presentation', but only if the insurer can prove it would not have entered the contract at all, or would have done so only on different terms. If this can be shown, the remedy will be determined by the action the underwriters would have taken had 'a fair presentation' been made in the first place.

(iv) REMEDIES

[2.271] Before an insurer can consider its remedy, the nature of the breach needs to be considered. A 'qualifying breach' is defined as:

> 'Deliberate or reckless — the policyholder knew or did not care they were in breach of their duty of fair presentation. The burden is on the insurer to show that the breach was deliberate or reckless, as opposed to other qualifying breaches—which are neither deliberate or reckless and are likely to be innocent or careless breaches (although these terms are not mentioned in the Act).'

The distinction between these two definitions is important since the remedies which are available for each will differ. Where there is a deliberate or reckless breach, the insurer may avoid the contract of insurance and refuse to pay all claims, as covered by current legislation. However the Insurance Act 2015 goes a step further, in that an insurer is not required to return any of the premiums paid to them. Where the qualifying breach has been neither deliberate nor reckless, the Insurance Act 2015 introduces a concept of proportionate remedies, similar to those adopted by the Consumer Insurance Act 2012:

(1) If the insurer would not have entered into the policy on any terms, the insurer may avoid the policy and refuse to pay all claims, but must return the premium paid.
(2) If the insurer would have entered into the contract on different terms (other than premium), the policy is to be treated as if it had been entered into on those different terms.
(3) If the insurer would have entered into the policy but with a higher premium, the insurer is entitled to reduced proportionately, the amount to be paid on a claim.

Thus, if the policy would have been taken but with a theft exclusion, a claim for theft made under the policy could be rejected by the insurers. Similarly, if the underwriters would have accepted the risk but with an increased premium of 25%, then any theft claim would be reduced by the same percentage (25%).

(v) WARRANTIES, 'SUSPENSIVE CONDITIONS' AND POLICY TERMS

[2.272] Historically insurers sought to include a 'basis of the contract' clause into their policies. The effect of such a clause is to turn all of the representations made in the proposal into a warranty, to ensure the policyholder kept the promises made in the proposal. A breach of one of these promises would bring the contract to an end from the time of the breach and generally discharge the insurer from liability for a claim. Section 9 of the Insurance Act 2015 will mean such clauses will also be ineffective in relation to non-consumer contracts. Instead such warranties become 'suspensive conditions' meaning that, where possible and notwithstanding the breach of warranty, an insurer will be liable for losses provided the breach has been remedied. Where the warranty relates to a loss of a particular kind, location or time, the insurer cannot rely on that breach to discharge its liability, if the policyholder can show the breach did not increase the risk of the loss that actually occurred. However, where the non-compliance could potentially have had some bearing on the risk of the loss which actually occurred, the insurers may have a defence.

CHAPTER 3

Motor Insurers' Bureau

2.   THE UNTRACED DRIVERS' AGREEMENT

(D) THE UNINSURED DRIVERS' AGREEMENTS

(i)   INTRODUCTION

[3.30B] The Motor Insurers' Bureau (MIB) has updated the Uninsured Drivers' Agreement (UNIDA), its agreement with the Secretary of State which provides a 'safety net' for innocent victims of identified, uninsured drivers.

There have also been revisions made to the MIB's Articles of Association, in particular Article 75 which sets out the basis for an insurer to be liable to pay the innocent victim's damages, while acting 'in the shoes' of the MIB.

The aim of the revisions is to incorporate into the UNIDA changes in the law and legislation, as well as making the Agreement as a whole easier to read and more user friendly.

The new Uninsured Drivers' Agreement (dated 3 July 2015) applies to accidents which occur on or after 1 August 2015. The Uninsured Drivers' Agreement dated 13 August 1999 continues to apply in respect of accidents occurring between 1 October 1999 and 31 July 2015. The main changes are set out below.

(ii) NOTICE PROVISIONS

[3.30C] The notice provisions within the Agreement are significantly simplified by the new clause 13(1) which requires the MIB to be joined to the proceedings as a named party from the outset. Therefore, the MIB should no longer have to apply to be added to proceedings.

The new clause 13(2) provides that the MIB does not need to be added from the outset where a claimant reasonably believes that there is an RTA insurer and has given RTA notice accordingly.

An insurer is to explain to a claimant pre-issue where they have Article 75 status. In these circumstances, the claimant should join in the insurer from the outset and the insurer should be sued as 'The Motor Insurers' Bureau (acting through its agent [insurance company name])'.

(iii) PASSENGER CLAIMS

[3.30D] The wording of clause 8 of the 2015 Agreement, which deals with passenger claims, has been amended from 'ought to have known' to 'had reason to believe' so the Agreement is in line with the definition of 'knowledge' in ss 143(3) and 151(4) of the Road Traffic Act 1988 and reflects the legal position following *White v White* [2001] UKHL 9, [2001] 2 All ER 43, [2001] 1 WLR 481.

[3.30D] *Motor Insurers' Bureau*

The 1999 Agreement excludes from compensation, claimants who have knowingly allowed themselves to be carried in vehicles used in furtherance of a crime. This is now removed in line with the outcome of *Delaney v Secretary of State* [2015] EWCA Civ 172, [2015] 3 All ER 329, [2015] CP Rep 25.

The 1999 Agreement also excludes from compensation, claimants who have knowingly allowed themselves to be carried in vehicles to escape or avoid lawful apprehension. This is also removed.

Clause 6(3)(d) of the 1999 Agreement (knowledge of no clear link to user of vehicle) has also been removed.

The new clause 8(4) provides that the exclusions applying to passengers with knowledge also apply to those cases involving fatalities. This is not the case under the 1999 Agreement. It should be noted that it is the deceased's knowledge that counts, rather than the dependants.

(iv)   TERRORISM EXCLUSION

[3.30E] The new Agreement makes it clear that the MIB has no liability for terrorist acts.

(v)   SUBROGATED CLAIMS

[3.30F] The new clause 6(1)(c) extends the scope of what is deemed a subrogated claim. True subrogated claims remain excluded. Claims where the claimant has other sources of redress available to him are now also excluded. For example, the MIB will not be liable to pay the cost of repair of a claimant's vehicle where they have a comprehensive insurance policy available to cover this cost.

(vi)   LIMITATION ON MIB'S OBLIGATIONS

[3.30G] The new clause 11 formally incorporates the £1 million property damage limit from the supplementary agreement together with wording as to how to apply the limit.

(vii)   RECOVERY RIGHTS

[3.30H] The Agreement is extended to recognise the common practice of settlement of a claimant's claim using a form of assignment. The new clause 15(b) now makes it a mandatory requirement for a victim to agree to assign their cause of action to the MIB ahead of settlement of their claim.

It should be noted that an Article 75 insurer will also be able to compel a claimant to complete a form of assignment ahead of settlement.

Note: The full 2015 Uninsured Drivers' Agreement, new Notes for Guidance and a Correlation Table highlighting the differences between the current and new Agreement can be found on the MIB's website at: www.mib.org.uk

(5) UNINSURED DRIVERS' AGREEMENT 2015

(A) INTRODUCTION

[3.65A] The Deregulation Act 2015 came into force on 30 June 2015. This Act simplifies the process of cancelling motor insurance and reduces the chances of a motor insurer continuing to have an RTA or Article 75 liability.

The Articles of Association (and Article 75) have been updated to reflect the changes brought about by the Deregulation Act. The key differences include: Clause (2)(2)(iii) removed; NB All subsequent numbering affected. Clause (2)(2)(iv) - revised. Becomes Clause (2)(2)(iii) 1 & 2.

A Member ceases to be Article 75 Insurer where the policy is cancelled before the date the liability incurred and:

(1) on policies cancelled on or after 30 June 2015, any record on MID to show the policy has been cancelled, (2) on policies prior to 30 June 2015, the certificate of insurance has been surrendered, Statutory Declaration has been made or proceedings for failure to surrender certificate commenced.

Clauses (2)(2)(v)-(viii) become Clauses (2)(2)(iv)-(vii) respectively.

Clause (2)(3) revised - Where there is more than one Article 75 Insurer, costs are now shared in proportion to the number of policies issued, rather than equally.

CHAPTER 4

General Principles of Negligence

2   THE DUTY OF CARE

(D) FAIR, JUST AND REASONABLE

[4.29E]   Michael v The Chief Constable of South Wales Police
[2015] UKSC 2, [2015] AC 1732, [2015] 2 All ER 635

The claimants were the parents and children of a woman who had been murdered by her former partner. She had made a 999 call in which she explained that her ex-boyfriend had come to her house and found her with another man. The former partner told her that he was going to kill her. The call was subsequently graded as only requiring a response within 60 minutes. The woman called 999 again; she screamed and the line went dead. The defendant force was informed and arrived eight minutes later. They found the claimant stabbed to death by her ex-partner. The Court of Appeal held that the police did not owe the woman a duty of care. The claimants appealed.

HELD, ON APPEAL: English law does not, as a general rule, impose liability on a defendant for injury caused to the claimant by a third party. There are two exceptions: where the defendant was in a position of control over the third party and should have foreseen the likelihood of the third party causing damage to somebody in close proximity and the defendant failed to take reasonable care in exercising that control (ie *Home Office v Dorset Yacht Co Ltd*) at para [**4.45**]; or where the defendant assumes a positive responsibility to safeguard the claimant as per *Hedley Byrne & Co Ltd v Heller & Partner Ltd* [1964] AC 465, [1963] 2 All ER 575, [1963] 3 WLR 101. It does not follow that, if the police fails to achieve its purpose through individual fault, the public should bear the burden of compensating the victim for harm caused by the actions of a third party, and for whose behaviour the state is not responsible.

[4.29F]   Vaughan v Ministry of Defence
[2015] EWHC 1404 (QB), [2015] All ER (D) 207 (May)

The claimant, a Royal Marine, was taking part in an adventure training exercise abroad. While off duty and visiting a tourist beach, the claimant performed a shallow dive into the sea and fractured his spine. The claimant alleged that he was exercising, which was part of his training and duty as a marine, and therefore should have been warned about the risks of diving in the sea by the defendant. In addition, he claimed that he considered himself to be on duty from the moment he left home for the training until his return home. The claimant sued the defendant for negligence.

HELD: An employer's liability does not extend to free time. The claimant had not been on duty at the time, his superior officer had not known where he was going, diving was not part of the training and it was determined the claim-ant had gone to the beach for recreational purposes only. Whilst marines are expected to maintain a general level of

[4.29F] *General Principles of Negligence*

fitness, even if it was found that the activities he had undertaken formed part of training, that does not place a limitless duty on employers to carry out risk assessments for all exercises, even those during a holiday. The claimant was not acting in the course of his employment therefore any warning by his superior would have made no difference to the outcome. The claimant had a genuine and informed choice as to how he entered the sea. He was not acting under orders therefore the defendant owed no duty of care.

3. BREACH

[4.34D] Dursan v J Sainsbury plc

[2015] EWHC 233 (QB), [2015] All ER (D) 131 (Feb) , [2015] RTR 13

The claimant had been hit and and killed by the defendant's lorry. He had been crossing a two-lane road, between lines of queuing traffic. He had begun crossing the inside lane of traffic behind a bus and continued across in front of the defendant's lorry. As he did so, the lorry moved forward and hit him. It was dark at the time of the accident but the road was lit by vehicle, street and building lighting. The claimant was wearing dark clothing; it was raining; the traffic was stopping and starting and pedestrians were crossing the road in various places. The defendant driver was found to have carried out checks of all his mirrors before pulling off.

HELD, ON APPEAL: While the circumstances demanded extra vigilance from the driver, there could be no justifiable criticism of his not re-checking mirrors again and again before moving forward. The claimant therefore failed to establish any lack of reasonable care on the defendant's part and as such there had been no breach. The defendant driver had done all that he reasonably could in the discharge of his duty of care and therefore could not be considered to be negligent. In the absence of authoritative guidance as to the sequence in which visual checks to mirrors should be made, it was for the driver to determine the appropriate sequence.

4. CAUSATION

CAUSATION OF INJURY

[4.44B] West Sussex County Council v Fuller

[2015] EWCA Civ 189, [2015] All ER (D) 140 (Mar)

The claimant tripped up the stairs whilst carrying post at work, spraining her wrist She said that at the time she was carrying a large amount of post of both considerable bulk and weight. She had to use both hands in order to carry the post so that she could not use either of the handrails and could not see where she was walking. As she was going up the stairs, one foot did not lift off as she was anticipating because of the presence of a sticky patch. She fell forward, putting out her right hand to break her fall. She alleged the local authority was responsible for having not carried out a risk assessment in respect of carrying post. At first instance it was held that the defendant had breached their duty. The defendant appealed.

HELD, ON APPEAL: The claimant's accident was entirely unconnected with the circumstance that she was at the time carrying post. The circumstance may be described as the occasion for her injury but it was not the cause of it. The claimant had simply misjudged her footing when climbing a staircase while she happened to be carrying one or more items of post. The defendant was arguably in breach of duty in failing to carry out a risk assessment in relation to the task which it asked the claimant to perform but the accident the claimant had did not fall within the ambit of the risk which the defendant was required to assess.

[4.44C]   Cassley v GMP Securities Europe LLP and Sundance Resources Ltd
[2015] EWHC 722 (QB), [2015] All ER (D) 05 (Apr)

The claimant was an employee of the first defendant and was invited by the second defendant's board of directors on a private flight to a mine project in the Congo. Just before the flight the aircraft carrier was changed from the one the first defendant had been advised would be used. The aircraft struck the side of a mountain and all aboard were killed. The claim against the first defendant was brought both for breach of statutory duty and in negligence at common law, based on the non-delegable duties owed by an employer to its employee. It was alleged that the first defendant made no risk assessment and no enquiries into the air carrier chartered for the flight. Had they done so, the results of those enquiries would have led them to conclude that it was not safe for the claimant to have boarded the flight.

HELD: The claim against the first defendant failed on causation. There was no evidence that the original air carrier, which the employer had expected would be used, was anything but safe. Even if the employer had found out about the change in carrier, enquiries that it could reasonably have made would have led it to reach the conclusion that the substitute air carrier was a safe carrier also. Although the first defendant did breach their duty of care, the claimant would still have been on the flight that crashed. The accident and the causes of the accident were not reasonably foreseeable and too remote. The claimant sought to make the first defendant liable for the selection of the carrier for the flight but the first defendant was actually two steps removed from that decision. There is no general liability on a defendant for the action of a third party unless what happened was a 'highly likely' consequence of the actions of that third party. The actions of the pilots that caused the accident were not 'highly likely'. In those circumstances, the duty owed by the first defendant did not extend to the performance of the carrier once the flight had started. No risk assessment performed by the first defendant would have identified the risk of pilot error, which was the primary cause of the accident.

See also *Dusek v Stormharbour Securities LLP* [2015] EWHC 37 (QB), [2015] All ER (D) 138 (Jan), in which causation was successfully made out in the death of an employee in a helicopter crash. The employee was visiting a remote, inaccessible, inhospitable and mountainous area of the Andes. There were reasonably foreseeable potential dangers involved in such a trip and the trip was held to be essentially an accident waiting to happen. A reasonable employer would have realised that, if their employee was to fly on a helicopter from high altitude across such an environment, there was a real risk of danger and the safety of their employee would be entirely dependent on the safe operation and performance of that flight. The extreme nature of the trip was such that there was sufficient to put the employer on notice that some enquiry was required.

CHAPTER 5

Vicarious Liability

1. LIABILITY FOR EMPLOYERS

(A) WHO IS AN EMPLOYEE?

[5.7BA] Cox v Ministry of Justice
[2016] UKSC 10, [2016] 2 WLR 806, [2016] ICR 470

The claimant was employed as a catering manager at a prison. Whilst unloading sacks of food a prisoner working in the kitchen dropped a sack, causing a spillage. The claimant instructed the prisoners to stop working until the spillage was cleared. Negligently, and contrary to the claimant's instructions, another prisoner worker continued and dropped a sack on the claimant's back whilst she was clearing the spillage. The negligence of the prisoner was not in question. At first instance the claimant's claim was dismissed. The Court of Appeal allowed her appeal and found the defendant vicariously liable. The defendant then appealed to the Supreme Court.

HELD, ON APPEAL: Appeal dismissed. Lord Reed clarified that the individual for whose conduct a defendant may be vicariously liable must carry on activities assigned to him by the defendant as an integral part of its operation and for its benefit. The defendant must, by assigning activities, have created a risk of a tort being committed. A wide range of circumstances can satisfy those requirements and defendants cannot avoid vicarious liability on the basis of arguments about the employment status of the person to whom activities are assigned. Prisoners working in kitchens are integrated into the operation of the prison. The activities assigned to them form an integral part of the activities the prison carries on in the furtherance of its aims. The defendant's arguments that requiring prisoners to work serves the purpose of rehabilitation and that the prisoners have no interest in furthering the defendant's objectives were rejected. Rehabilitation is not the sole objective. On the contrary, the fact that a prisoner is required to undertake work for nominal wages actually binds him into a closer relationship with the prison service than would be the case for an employee, and strengthens the case for imposing vicarious liability.

2. LIABILITY OF EMPLOYER

(A) SCOPE OF EMPLOYMENT

[5.23GA] Mohamud v WM Morrison Supermarkets plc
[2016] UKSC 11, [2016] 2 WLR 821, [2016] ICR 485

The claimant had visited a petrol station run by the defendant and asked an employee, K, if he could print some documents. K responded in an abusive fashion including racist language. As the claimant got back in his car, K approached and kicked and punched the claimant a number of times in an unprovoked attack. It was found that before the attack K's supervisor had told him not to follow the claimant

[5.23GA] *Vicarious Liability*

and that during the attack the supervisor was encouraging K to go back inside the petrol station. The claim was dismissed at first instance and the Court of Appeal upheld the decision. The claimant appealed to the Supreme Court on the grounds that the defendant supermarket was vicariously liable for the attack carried out by its employee.

HELD, ON APPEAL: Appeal allowed. The court had to consider two matters. First, the court must ask what function or field of activities has been entrusted to the employee by the employer. This is to be viewed broadly. Second, the court must decide whether there was a sufficient connection between the position in which the employee was employed and his wrongful conduct to make it just for the employer to be held liable. It was the employee's job to attend to customers and respond to their inquiries. Whilst the employee's actions in responding were extreme and inexcusable, interacting with customers was within the field of activities assigned to him. What happened in the following moments was an unbroken chain of events. It was not correct to regard the employee as having left the scope of his employment the moment he stepped out from behind the counter – he was following up on what he said to the claimant. Secondly, when the employee followed the claimant to his car and told him not to come back to the petrol station that was not something personal between them but an order to keep away from his employer's premises. In giving the order he was purporting to act pursuant to his employer's business. The employee's motive in the attack was irrelevant.

[5.23H] **Graham v Commercial Bodyworks Ltd**

[2015] EWCA Civ 47, [2015] ICR 665, [2015] PIQR P240

The claimant worked at a bodywork repair shop. He worked with flammable thinning agents and a co-worker had sprayed some of it onto the claimant's overalls. The same co-worker lit a cigarette near the claimant and this caused the claimant's overalls to set on fire. The claimant sustained serious injuries. It was never alleged that the co-worker intended to cause any harm. The judge at first instance labelled the co-worker's action as deliberate and '*clearly reckless*' and dismissed the claim against the employer. The claimant appealed.

HELD, ON APPEAL: Appeal dismissed. The fact that the defendant can be said to have vested discretion in the employee to use the thinners and that he was obliged to do so carefully by reason of his contractual obligations was not a strong argument. Those circumstances are the same for every employer/employee relationship. Also, the fact that the defendant could be said to have created the risk is insufficient to impose liability. The real cause of the claimant's injuries was the reckless frolic of the co-worker which cannot be said to have occurred in the course of his employment.

[5.23I] **NA v Nottinghamshire County Council**

[2015] EWCA Civ 1139, [2016] 1 FCR 419, [2016] Fam Law 171

The claimant had been placed in the care of the defendant local authority until her majority, initially with Mr and Mrs A and then with Mr and Mrs B. She was physically abused with couple A and sexually abused with couple B. She sued the local authority. At first instance the claim was dismissed. The claimant appealed. The issue to be determined was whether the local authority was liable for the foster parents' abuse.

HELD, ON APPEAL: Appeal dismissed. The relationship between a local authority and a foster parent is not 'akin to employment'. Consequently a local authority cannot be vicariously liable for the deliberate wrongful acts of foster parents. In order to be non-delegable, a duty must relate to a function which the purported delegator has assumed for itself. Fostering is a function which the local authority must entrust to others. By arranging the foster placement the local authority discharged rather than delegated its duty. To impose a non-delegable duty on a local authority would be unreasonably burdensome and contrary to the interests of the children for whom they have to care.

[5.23J] A v The Trustees of the Watchtower Bible and Tract Society
[2015] EWHC 1722 (QB), 165 NLJ 7692

The claimant sought damages for personal injury from sexual assaults carried out by S, a Jehovah's Witness ministerial servant. The first defendant was the over-arching body of the Jehovah's Witnesses, whilst the second and third were descendants of the congregation. A argued that the defendants were vicariously liable for the sexual assaults committed by S.

HELD, ON APPEAL: The claimant was successful and all three defendants were held vicariously liable for the actions of the ministerial servant. The judge confirmed that the two stage test in *Catholic Child Welfare Society v Various Claimants (FC)* [2012] UKSC 56, [2013] 2 AC 1, [2013] 1 All ER 670 (at para **[5.23A]**) was satisfied. The relationship between the Jehovah's Witness elders and the ministerial servants was capable of giving rise to vicarious liability. As to stage two, the sexual abuse was not as a result of the mere opportunity of the servant's presence in the claimant's company for reasons outside any role he was playing as a Jehovah's Witness. Whether the abuse took place at or after book study at whoever's home, on field service or other premises, he was ostensibly performing his duties as a Jehovah's Witness ministerial servant. It was only possible because he had the status of a ministerial servant that meant no one who saw him questioned his being alone with the claimant. It is that which provides the close connection between the abuse and what he was authorised to do. In respect of the second and third defendants, it was held that the elders had additional responsibilities to those held by ministerial servants. The elders had owed a duty of care to warn the congregation and individual parents about the risks and they had breached that duty. They were even closer and more integrated with congregational issues than were ministerial servants. They had a spiritual role and partly exercised that role via the judicial committee. The decisions that emanated from the judicial committee and thereafter from the body of elders were a fundamental part of the role of the defendants within the organisation. The defendants were unincorporated associations who had taken over the responsibility of the congregations.

CHAPTER 6

Res Ipsa Loquitor

3. EVENTS IMPLYING NEGLIGENCE

(C) OTHER CIRCUMSTANCES IMPLYING NEGLIGENCE

[6.25A]　Donald Macleod (a protected party suing by his litigation friend Barbara MacLeod) v Metropolitan Police Commissioner
[2015] EWCA Civ 688, [2015] All ER (D) 98 (Jul)

The claimant had been cycling home when he was hit by a police car responding to an emergency call. The dispute centred on the direction from which the claimant had approached the junction. The claimant was so severely injured he could not give evidence. The judge found the evidence of two of the independent witnesses to be reliable and concluded that the police car had been driving too fast and without the degree of care and skill which would have been reasonable in the circumstances. The defendant appealed submitting that the judge had erred in making findings of fact against the weight of the evidence and rejecting the possibility of an alternative scenario based on expert evidence.

HELD, ON APPEAL: Appeal dismissed. The judge had been entitled to rely on the evidence of the two independent witnesses. The inference he drew that the claimant had approached the junction from the south was a powerful one. The judge was not obliged to accept the expert evidence; he was entitled to apply his common sense and experience when evaluating everything in the round.

CHAPTER 7

Defences

5. EX TURPI CAUSA NON ORITUR ACTIO

[7.46AA] Delaney v Secretary of State for Transport
[2015] EWCA Civ 172, [2015] 3 All ER 329, [2015] CP Rep 25

A car passenger could claim under the Motor Insurers' Bureau Agreement after he had been injured while in possession of cannabis with intent to supply. The Court of Appeal found that as a matter of causation the damage suffered by the claimant was not caused by his criminal activity but was caused by the tortious act of the defendant driving in a negligent way. The illegal acts were incidental to those of the criminal acts. Clause 6(1)(e)(iii) of the MIB agreement was not one of the permitted exceptions under the Directive and the exclusion of liability under that clause was in breach of the UK's obligations under EU law (see para **[3.52B]**).

[7.46CA] McCracken (a protected party suing by his mother and litigation friend Deborah Norris) v Smith, MIB and Bell
[2015] EWCA Civ 380, [2016] Lloyd's Rep IR 171, [2015] PIQR P305

The claimant was a pillion passenger on a trial bike being ridden by the first defendant which was invoked in an accident with the third defendant. The first defendant did not have insurance nor a driving licence and neither boy was wearing a helmet when their bike collided with a mini-bus being driven by the third defendant. The motorbike they had been riding was stolen, was not designed to carry passengers and was not suitable for riding on roads. The first defendant's negligence was not in question. The MIB pleaded, inter alia, that *ex turpi causa* applied and the claimant's claim should fail on the basis that he was participating in the first defendant's wrongdoing.

At first instance it was accepted that the bike was being ridden in an unsafe manner but the judge held that there was nothing to suggest that the claimant was encouraging the first defendant to ride in that way. The claimant's criminal conduct consisted of him allowing himself to be a pillion passenger on the bike when he knew that it had not been designed for pillion passengers and that it would be ridden without insurance or a valid driving licence. These factors were not the cause of the claimant's injuries; the cause of his injuries was the way the bike was ridden by the defendant and the negligent driving of the third defendant. The claimant was merely 'along for the ride' and not partaking in a joint criminal enterprise with the first defendant. The defence of *ex turpi causa* accordingly failed and the effect of the claimant's conduct reflected in a reduction of damages for his own contributory negligence. Mr Bell appealed.

HELD, ON APPEAL: Appeal allowed. The judge had been generous to the claimant in distancing him as he had done from the first defendant's dangerous riding. The correct inference was that the two boys were parties to a joint enterprise, the essence of which was joy riding. As to *ex turpi causa*, the conduct had to be taken to have been the claimant's participation with the first defendant in a joint enterprise to ride the bike dangerously. Such conduct had to amount to turpitude. The question was therefore what relationship did the turpitude have to the claim. Applied to the claim against the first defendant (and by virtue the MIB), the judge had been wrong to reject

[7.46CA] *Defences*

the defence of *ex turpi causa*. Those issues were not appealed however. As to the third defendant, the right approach was to give effect to both causes by allowing the claimant to claim in negligence against the third defendant but, if negligence was established, by reducing any recoverable damages in accordance with the principles of contributory negligence. The *ex turpi causa* defence was rooted in the public interest and the public interest was served by this approach. A fair reflection of the claimant's degree of blameworthiness would be a deduction of 50%.

See also *John Clarke v Phoebe Clarke and Motor Insurers* (at para **[1.5A]**) where the defence of ex turpi causa failed because the cause of the claimant's injury was the defendant's tortious driving and not the claimant's involvement in the fight that preceded.

[7.46DA]   Beaumont & O'Neill v Ferrer
[2016] EWCA civ 768

The claimants, who were both minors, had planned with others to take a taxi then make off without paying the fare. When they reached their destination, three of the gang got out of the taxi and ran off. The defendant, seeing what was happening, drove on. The claimants attempted to get out of the taxi as it was moving and sustained significant injuries.

The claimants argued, inter alia, that the doctrine of *ex turpi causa* did not apply, as no crime had been committed by them; the defendant left the scene before he gave the claimants time or opportunity to pay. They also argued that, even if they were found to have committed a crime, their offending was not so serious so as to engage the defence of *ex turpi causa*. Their claims were dismissed at first instance and the claimants appealed.

HELD, ON APPEAL: Appeal dismissed. The claimants were involved in a criminal joint enterprise, with three of the gang already having run away, and this caused the defendant to drive on because he wanted to stop the claimants from also exiting and making off without payment. Even though it was correct that the defendant had been in breach of his duty of care to the claimants, any fault on the part of the defendant followed from the criminal actions of the claimants.

The defendant had not caused the claimants' injuries. The action of each of them in jumping out of the taxi broke the casual link between any fault on the part of the defendant and the claimants' damage. This was a case where public policy and justice dictated that the claimants brought about the injuries themselves. The correct approach to deciding whether *ex turpi causa* applied was to ask whether the criminal act was no more than the circumstances in which the damage occurred or whether the damage was caused by the criminal act itself; if the latter was the case, the doctrine would apply.

6.   CONTRIBUTORY NEGLIGENCE

(C) EXAMPLES OF CONTRIBUTORY NEGLIGENCE

[7.52B]   Jackson v Murray
[2015] UKSC 5, [2015] 2 All ER 805, 2015 SC (UKSC) 105

The claimant got off a mini bus and tried to cross the road. She stepped out suddenly from behind into the path of the defendant's oncoming car. The defendant was driving too fast: he had seen the bus, but had made no allowance for the possibility that a child might attempt to cross in front of him. He was not keeping a proper look-out, and did not see her. He was going too fast to have stopped in time even if he had seen her. It was found that if he had been driving at a reasonable speed, and had been keeping a proper look-out, he would not have hit her. At first instance the claimant was held to be 90% contributorily negligent. The claimant appealed.

HELD, ON APPEAL: Appeal allowed. It is necessary to consider the relative importance of the claimant's actions compared to the defendant's as well as blameworthiness. It was therefore often the case that a motorist is found to be much more to blame than a pedestrian due to the fact that a pedestrian is generally not posing a danger to anyone else whereas a driver travelling at speed without properly observing is. A pedestrian also has to look in all directions when crossing whereas a driver does not. Therefore this disparity between a pedestrian and the driver of a vehicle meant that the courts placed a higher burden on drivers. An assessment of contributory negligence at 50% was held to be appropriate.

It is to be noted that the Supreme Court was at pains to emphasise the limited role of a court of appeal when asked to review a judgment from a lower court. In the absence of an identifiable error, such as an error of law, or the taking into account of an irrelevant matter, or the failure to take account of a relevant matter, it is only a difference of opinion as to the apportionment of responsibility which exceeds what is reasonable disagreement and as such warrants the conclusion that the court below has gone wrong. In the absence of an identifiable error, the appellate court must be satisfied that the apportionment made by the court below was not one which was reasonably open to it. An appeal court must focus not on the precise apportionment figure but on the question of whether the lower court has correctly identified the party who should bear the greater share of responsibility.

8. ESTOPPEL

[7.70A]   Deighton v Collett and Roberts Express Deliveries Ltd
(19 April 2016, unreported), QBD

The first defendant, an employee of the second defendant, had collided with a lorry. The lorry in turn hit the claimant's car, and the claimant was injured. The lorry operator brought a claim against both defendants. At trial, it was held that the first defendant had been driving in a state of automatism and as such it was held that he was not negligent. Subsequently, the claimant brought a claim for personal injury, citing new evidence. The defendants applied to strike out the claim on the basis that the matter had already been litigated and that it was unfair to bring further proceedings based on the same incident. The judge found that the claimant had not been party to the proceedings brought by the lorry operator, and that allowing the claim to continue would not be an abuse of process. The defendants appealed. The issues were whether:
(a)   the claimant had been privy to the first action; and
(b)   allowing the claim to continue would be an abuse of process.

The defendants submitted that the claimant was to be regarded as privy to the first action as the cause of action was the same and he had been aware of the lorry operator's claim against the defendant but had not done anything.

HELD, ON APPEAL: Appeal dismissed. A mere interest or concern in the outcome of prior litigation was not sufficient to establish privity of action. In the absence of an identifiable involvement, a claimant was not estopped merely because they stood by. Privity of interest required a precursory relationship between the parties; the accident itself was not sufficient. There had been no previous relationship between the claimant and the lorry operator capable of creating privity. The claimant had indeed done nothing during the proceedings brought by the lorry operator. He went to the hearing, but that was insufficient in law to create estoppel. The determination of privity could not depend on loose behavioural factors.

[7.70A] *Defences*

It was only an abuse of process to challenge the factual findings of the judge in a previous action if it would be manifestly unfair to a party to the later proceedings that the same issues should be re-litigated, or permitting re-litigation would bring the administration of justice into disrepute, and only if a party to proceedings was not a party to or privy of those who were parties to the earlier proceedings. In the instant case, the judge had not been satisfied of these requirements. The claimant argued that the outcome could be different based on different neurological evidence in respect of the first defendant. His case was that the first defendant's seizure was not completely beyond his control and that he should have reported his condition. Had there been no new evidence, the defendants' case would be much stronger. The judge had been entitled to conclude that it was not unfair to subject the first defendant to a further trial. The claimant had sustained very serious injuries. It was correct to say that he should have been involved in the first trial, but that was not a significant factor in the balance that his claim should be struck out. The claimant was not precluded by law from bringing the claim, and it would not be manifestly unfair on the first defendant. The claimant might have a difficult task at any new trial, but the claim was not 'very weak'.

CHAPTER 8

Fraud

1. PROFESSIONAL OBLIGATIONS

(B) OBLIGATIONS WHEN PLEADING

[8.4D] Aso Yason v Peshraw Karim and Sabre Insurance
(17 April unreported, 2015) CC (Kingston upon Hull) Judge Jeremy Richardson QC

The claim arose following a road traffic accident. D2 had doubts that the claim was genuine but did not have enough evidence to plead fraud in its defence. As such, the defence stated that D2 was not pleading fraud but made a number of assertions which implied concerns, for example, inconsistent information given and the fact that D1 had since vanished and that D1 had previously acted dishonestly in other claims. The judge ordered that part of D2's defence should be struck out on the basis that fraud was not pleaded.
    D2 appealed against the decision.

HELD: The judge found that if there was evidence of fraud, then this must be 'clearly and unequivocally pleaded', however stated that 'it is necessary for the parties to place on the table, by way of express pleading, ammunition and artillery that is in their possession. These sorts of cases are not a form of intellectual game. It is important that the parties place their case on the table for all to see. Ambush and springing points upon opponents at the last minute would not be right. In this case D2 placed their cards on the table.' He found that each case should be considered on its own facts and as to whether it falls into the 'fraud category' or 'inference category' and found that in this case the pleadings fall within the second of these categories.
    Appeal allowed.

[8.4E] Stuart John Gentry v Lee Miller and UK Insurance Ltd
[2016] EWCA Civ 141, (2016) Times, 21 April

The first defendant's insurer (D2) admitted liability for a road traffic accident which took place in March 2013. D2 made no offers of settlement and failed to engage with the claimant's solicitors. As a result, proceedings were issued. Despite the admission of liability, D2, who had been made aware of the claimant's intention to issue proceedings failed to instruct solicitors to accept service or took any steps to protect its position. No acknowledgment of service was served and default judgement was entered. Damages were later assessed at a disposal hearing to which the defendant failed to attend. An application was made for judgment to be set aside and that D2 be joined as second defendant. It was their assertion that the claimant and D1 were known to each other and that this was a fraudulent claim.
    The judge set aside judgment on the basis that claims of alleged fraud are the one type of claim which should now be exempt from the structures of the current CPR rules and views of the Court of Appeal in *Mitchell* and other recent cases.
    The claimant appealed the decision on the basis that more emphasis should have been put on the compliance with the CPR and orders and that the full rigours of *Mitchell* and *Denton* should be applied.

[8.4E] *Fraud*

HELD: The allegation of fraud was not an exemption and the test in *Mitchell* and *Denton* needed to be observed. Whilst the insurer had shown that there was a real prospect of successfully defending the claim, it had not acted promptly to deal with the matter and it had failed to protect its own interest.

Appeal allowed.

2. STANDARD/BURDEN OF PROOF

(B) BURDEN OF PROOF REMAINS WITH THE CLAIMANT

[8.9A] Mohamed Rizan & Mohammed Rilshad v Barry Hayes & Allianz Insurance plc

[2016] EWCA Civ 481

The claimants alleged that the first defendant had driven into the side of their car. The second defendant insurer alleged that either the accident was staged and the insured had been complicit, or the claimants had deliberately halted their vehicle intending to cause an accident. The claimants changed their evidence to fit expert engineering evidence and witness statements served. The judge dismissed the claims on the basis he found the claimants to be unreliable and inconsistent. Following the judgment, the judge stated that, although it was unnecessary to make a finding, it was more likely than not that the claim had been fraudulent.

The claimants appealed stating that the judge had been wrong to make a finding of fraud, and without a finding of fraud he could not have dismissed the claim, because the evidence before him demonstrated either a conspiracy or an accident.

HELD ON APPEAL: The appeal was dismissed. The judge was unwise to express a view on the question whether the claim was fraudulent, and doubly unwise to do so without giving reasons for his conclusion over and above those which he had already given for his dismissal of the claim. The judge would have been better advised to leave to his initial correct, view that, as the claimants had failed to satisfy the burden of proof on them concerning the occurrence of the alleged accident, it was unnecessary to address the question of fraud. The judge did not spell out whether he regarded all three actors, the claimants and Mr Hayes, as implicated in the fraud. The second defendant put forward two alternatives, one that the accident was staged and that Mr Hayes was complicit, the other that the first claimant deliberately brought the vehicle to a halt without reason intending to cause an accident. Judge Harris plainly had in mind the guidance given in cases such as *In Re H (minors) (sexual abuse: standard of proof)* [1996] AC 563, [1996] 1 All ER 1, [1996] 2 WLR 8 by Lord Nicholls of Birkenhead. What the judge did not do however was to enunciate his reasons for his conclusion that a fraudulent scheme such as one or other of those proposed by the second defendant had occurred. He did not, at any rate overtly, ask himself whether there were any inherent improbabilities in that conclusion which needed to be overcome or explained, such as the good character of the actors involved, their different ethnic, cultural and linguistic backgrounds, the recent acquisition of the vehicle and its use for chauffeuring or taxi services, the potentially modest size of any award for whiplash injury, all of which might at first blush tell against a fraudulent conspiracy, or against one including all three actors.

However, the judge was not faced with a binary choice between conspiracy or an accident as alleged. It had not been for the insurer or the judge to explain how the damage had occurred, This learning was succinctly summarised by Lord Mance in *Sienkiewicz v Greif UK Ltd* [2011] 2 AC 229 at 296:

> 'In other cases, there will be continuing good sense in the House of Lords' reminder to fact-finders in *Rhesa Shipping Co SA v Edmunds (The 'Popi M')* [1985] 1 WLR 948 that it is not

their duty to reach conclusions of fact, one way or the other, in every case. There are cases where, as a matter of justice and policy, a court should say that the evidence adduced (whatever its type) is too weak to prove anything to an appropriate standard, so that the claim should fail.'

The judge gave his reasons for regarding the evidence before him as unreliable and we would not be justified in interfering with that conclusion unless we regarded it as a conclusion to which no reasonable judge could have come. His reasons were cogent and compelling.

3.   COLLATERAL FRAUD – FIRST PARTY CLAIMS

[8.10D]   Versloot Dredging BV and SO DC Merwestone BV v HDI Gerling Industrie Versicherung AG, The DC Merwestone

[2014] EWCA Civ 1349, [2015] QB 608, [2015] 2 WLR 1063

An insured claimed for an indemnity under a marine insurance policy following damage to the ship's engine occasioned by an ingress of sea water. The insurer sought to repudiate the claim on the basis that the claim was supported by a fraudulent device in the form of a letter from a crew member. The contents of the letter, if believed, would not have had the effect of validating the claim which otherwise would not have been covered, nor would it have increased the sum claimed or due under the indemnity. It was simply provided to promote the prospects of the claim being settled promptly.

At first instance it was found the letter contained a reckless statement. The insurer did not have to prove that they had been deceived or relied upon the untruth. Simply the fact the insured attempted to deceive was sufficient to render the claim forfeit, irrespective that this seemed a disproportionate sanction.

The insured appealed.

HELD: Whilst the comments made in the decision in *Agapitos v Agnew* [2002] EWCA Civ 247, [2003] QB 556, [2002] 1 All ER (Comm) 714 were obiter, the Court of Appeal considered that this should apply as matter of ratio as it was authoritative. The fraudulent device must be directly related to the claim; the device must have been intended by the assured to promote his prospect of success; it must not be irrelevant, but such that, if believed, it would have tended to yield a not insignificant improvement in the assureds prospect of success. The test was satisfied and the appeal dismissed.

Note - The case proceeded to the Supreme Court in March 2016 and the judgement is awaited.

4.   COLLATERAL FRAUD – THIRD PARTY CLAIMS

(A) INTRODUCTION

[8.16C]   Abid Anwar v Severn Trent Water

(13 July 2015, unreported) Birmingham CC, District Judge Truman

The claim arose from a road traffic accident in which the claimants claimed they had suffered personal injury as a result of the negligence of the defendant's employee. Ten days before the trial, the district judge heard an application made by the defendant to strike out the claims on the basis that an unless order had not been fully complied with. The district judge declined to strike out the claims.

[8.16C] *Fraud*

At trial the judge found that the first two claimants were passengers in the car, but that the third claimant was making a fraudulent claim. Despite the first two claimants having supported the fraudulent claim of the third claimant, damages were awarded for their injuries.

Following the trial, the defendant made an application asking the court to revisit the previous order to strike out the claims using its powers under CPR r 3.1(7).

HELD: The court found that it was appropriate to revisit the order. The unless order provided that the claimants provide full and complete CPR-compliant responses to requests for further information. Having found that the third claimant was not present in the vehicle; the responses given to the requests for further information were untrue and therefore could not be described as full and complete. Had the judge been aware of the truth when considering the application, the matter would not have proceeded to trial. Accordingly, the earlier order was set aside and the claims were struck out.

[8.16D] Gohil v Gohil

[2015] UKSC 61, [2016] 1 All ER 685, [2015] 3 WLR 1085

Mrs G's claim for financial relief in divorce proceedings was settled by consent in 2004 on the basis of a recital to the order recording that she believed that Mr G had not provided full and frank disclosure of his financial circumstances. In 2007, Mrs G applied to set aside the financial order on the ground that Mr G had fraudulently failed to disclose his assets. The proceedings were delayed when he was convicted of serious money-laundering offences and committed to prison in 2011 with confiscation proceedings against him ongoing.

The judge allowed the wife's application and set aside the order, having found that she had adduced evidence, some from the husband's criminal trial, which satisfied *Ladd v Marshall* [1954] 3 All ER 745, [1954] 1 WLR 1489, 98 Sol Jo 870, CA principles and established that there had been material non-disclosure by the husband.

Mr G appealed and the Court of Appeal allowed the appeal, having found that the judge had incorrectly applied the *Ladd v Marshall* criteria. It held that there was insufficient admissible evidence for the judge to have made a finding of material non-disclosure, and therefore no reason to set aside the order, which was reinstated. Mrs G appealed: [2015] UKSC 6.

HELD, ON APPEAL:
(1) The *Ladd v Marshall* principles had no relevance to the determination of an application to set aside a financial order on the ground of fraudulent non-disclosure and the Court of Appeal's errors in its considerations as to the admissibility of all the evidence adduced by Mrs G could not stand.
(2) A party to financial relief proceedings had a duty to the court to make full and frank disclosure of his resources. In the context of a financial order in divorce proceedings, wording such as that in the recital to the order had no legal effect, *Hayward v Zurich Insurance Company plc* [2015] EWCA Civ 327, [2015] Lloyd's Rep IR 585 considered.
(3) The judge would still have found Mr G to have been guilty of material non-disclosure even with only the admissible evidence before him.

[8.16E] Sharland v Sharland

[2015] UKSC 60, [2016] 1 All ER 671, [1985] 3 WLR 1070

The parties had agreed a comprise agreement in relation to financial provision proceedings during a matrimonial separation. Mr S gave evidence concerning the status and value of his company. Following the hearing and before the order was sealed it became apparent the company was subject to an initial public offering that placed the value of the company at a substantially higher amount. Mrs S sought an order setting aside the agreement in view of Mr S's misleading statements and for the hearing to be resumed. The judge found that Mr S had knowingly misled experts and had given false evidence at the hearing, however, his order would not have differed if proper disclosure had taken place.

The Court of Appeal decided that misrepresentation that would normally allow a wife to rescind a contract and have a consent order set aside, did not necessarily entitle her to renounce the agreement and resume proceedings. Mrs S appealed to the Supreme Court.

HELD, ON APPEAL: At common law, the general effect of any misrepresentation, whether fraudulent, negligent or innocent, or of non-disclosure where there was a duty to disclose, was to render a contract voidable at the instance of a party who had been induced to enter into it. There is no need to decide here whether the greater flexibility which the court now has in cases of innocent or negligent misrepresentation in contract should apply to consent orders in civil or family cases. It was clear from case law that the misrepresentation or non-disclosure had to be material to the decision made. It would be extraordinary if the victim of a fraudulent misrepresentation which had led her to compromise her claim to financial remedies in a matrimonial case, were in a worse position than the victim of a fraudulent misrepresentation in an ordinary contract case, including a contract to settle a civil claim. As was held in *Smith v Kay* (1859) VII HLC 749, a party who had practised deception with a view to a particular end, which had been attained, could not be allowed to deny its materiality. The only exception was where the court was satisfied that, when it made the consent order, the fraud would not have influenced a reasonable person to agree to it, or, if the court had known the true position when making the order, it would not have made a significantly different order regardless of whether the parties had agreed to it. The burden of satisfying the court had to lie with the fraudster. The order should have been set aside. The wife was entitled to re-open the case, when she might seek to negotiate a new settlement or a rehearing when all the relevant facts were known.

[8.16F] Simone Vasile v Pop Ioan and Axa Insurance

(17 November 2015 unreported), Wilesden CC

The claimant claimed that her parked and unattended vehicle was struck on the nearside by the first defendant. The claimant sought to recover damages for the alleged damage to her vehicle, miscellaneous expenses and hire, storage and recovery charges. The second defendant insurer, was joined to satisfy any judgment obtained against the first defendant insofar as it is was proved that there was a valid contract of insurance in place at the material time with indemnity not confirmed. Evidence was adduced that the claimant had intimated fraudulent claims for personal injury alleged to have been sustained in the accident through two separate firms of solicitors. Handwritten documents verified by a statement of truth from the claimant confirmed that she was not in the vehicle despite two separate CNF's and medical evidence having been submitted for personal injury claims. A defence pleading fraud was produced in these proceedings based both on this dishonesty and the result of other investigations of concern with a counterclaim in the tort of deceit.

HELD: The court decided that it was quite clear in this case that the claimant had been dishonest, that this was a fraudulent claim made by her. It was quite clear that while she made a claim that she had not been in the car in relation to this particular case she had made other claims in relation to the same incident through different solicitors where she had said that she suffered personal injury and was in the car. The claim was struck out pursuant to r 3.4(2)(b) as an abuse of process and the judge gave judgment on the counterclaim in the tort of deceit awarding damages for wasted administrative expenses and resources in the sum of £1500 associated with investigating and processing the alleged claim and injuries and exemplary damages of

[8.16F] *Fraud*

£15000 and costs. The judge would still have found Mr G to have been guilty of material non-disclosure even with only the admissible evidence before him.

5. EXAGGERATION

(B) FIRST PARTY CLAIMS AND EXAGGERATION

[8.20ia] Hayward v Zurich Insurance Company plc

[2015] EWCA Civ 327, [2015] Lloyd's Rep IR 585

In June 1998 the claimant suffered an accident at work in which he injured his back. He brought a claim against his employer. He alleged that his injury continued to cause him serious lumbar pain which restricted his mobility; that he had also developed a depressive illness and that his ability to work was seriously impaired. Liability was admitted, subject to a 20% reduction for contributory negligence and settlement was reached by consent.

Two years later the claimant's neighbours approached the insurer to say that they believed that the claim was dishonest and that they considered he was recovered from his injuries at least a year before settlement. On receipt of this information, Z commenced proceedings for deceit and fraudulent misrepresentation. The agreed settlement was subsequently set aside.

The claimant appealed the decision.

HELD: Whilst the judge commented that the decision is unattractive because C retains a settlement in excess of excess of his loss; the contract which Z sought to rescind was a contract to compromise a disputed claim and Z was aware of the probable untruth of C's statement. By settling the claim, Z took the risk that those statements would not be proved at trial and paid a sum commensurate with their assessment of that risk. Z could not now have that opportunity for a Court to consider the C's claim.

Appeal allowed.

Note - This matter is proceeding to the Supreme Court in 2016 and the judgement is awaited.

(D) FUNDAMENTAL DISHONESTY

[8.20B] Diamanttek Ltd v Mr Jonathon James

(8 February 2016, unreported) His Honour Judge Gregory, Coventry County Court

The claimant alleged noise induced hearing loss as a result of his employment between 2002 and 2014 with the defendant employer. The evidence as to availability of hearing protection and over what period was in dispute and the claimant's evidence changed. The judge found that the claimant had not been telling the truth at the hearing and rejected his claim with costs. The defendant applied for permission to enforce the costs order under r 44.16 of the CPR 1998, on the basis that the claim had been found to be fundamentally dishonest. The judge declined the application on the basis that finding that he did not tell the truth on the day does not mean that he was dishonest. The defendant appealed.

HELD: The judge did not appear to have addressed the specific wording of r 44.16. What she should have considered was whether the claim was, on the balance of probabilities, fundamentally dishonest. Having found that the claimant was not at any time during his employment deprived of hearing protection as he had alleged, the court failed to see how she could justifiably have concluded that the claim was not fundamentally dishonest. An appellate court should be slow to interfere as the first instance judge is in the best position to form a view about fundamental dishonesty. But in a case in which findings of fact have been made which have included that the claimant has not told the truth, she then failed to reach a conclusion in any way consistent with that finding. The judge seemed to have thought that she had to categorise the claimant as a dishonest person in order to justify a finding, whereas, in fact, she should have been asking was this on the balance of probabilities a fundamentally dishonest claim? There was fundamental dishonesty in bringing the claim. One of the fundamentals of the claim was the alleged deprivation of the use of ear defenders; in regard to that matter, the claimant had lied. That finding should have led the judge to conclude that it was a fundamentally dishonest claim. Her decision to the contrary was perverse. The defendant should have been permitted to enforce the costs order made in its favour.

[8.20C] Nesham v Sunrich Clothing Ltd (unreported)

(22 April 2016, unreported), Newcastle County Court, HHJ Freedman

The trial concerned a road traffic accident where a collision occurred between the front of the defendant's vehicle and the rear of the claimant's truck. The claimant alleged he was stationary and that the defendant had simply drove into the rear of his vehicle. The defendant said that the claimant had driven from a slip road into his path, making a collision unavoidable. The engineering evidence strongly suggested that the collision had occurred between the two vehicles at a time when the vehicles were at an angle to each other rather than it being a rear end shunt. The judge preferred the defendant's evidence and dismissed the claim as not proven with costs. The defendant applied to disapply QOCS protection and enforce the costs order which was refused. The defendant applied for permission to appeal this refusal.

HELD ON APPEAL: Declined. The district judge listened to submissions about whether the claimant was fundamentally dishonest and did not find that he was. She preferred not to accept his version of the accident but it does not necessarily follow that he was fundamentally dishonest. This was a finding for the district judge who heard the case to make. There was no proper basis here to invite an appellate court to reverse that finding. Merely because an account of an accident has been rejected does not equate to fundamental dishonesty. This appeal, in such circumstances where an appellate court is being asked to overturn the finding as to assessment of a witness had no prospect of success.

9. DELIBERATE ACT

[8.34B] Selcuk Fertek and Canan Peker v Aviva Insurance UK Ltd

CA (Civ Div) (Floyd LJ, Vos LJ) 11/02/2016

The first claimant was driving a vehicle; the second claimant was his wife and was one of three passenger in the vehicle. Behind the first claimant was a vehicle being driven by the defendant's insured. A vehicle swerved in front of the claimant's vehicle and the claimant performed an emergency stop. The defendant driver attempted to stop his vehicle but collided with the claimant's vehicle. This claim was one of eight conjoined cases arising out of similar alleged 'slam-on' collisions. The eight cases were heard by HHJ Mitchell in June 2013. In this particular case, the Judge found that it could not be proven that the collision was staged or that a decoy vehicle was involved. The judge found that the collision was caused by the first claimant executing an emergency stop with the intention of inducing a collision.

The claimants appealed the decision on the basis that it was not open to the judge to reach that conclusion on the basis of the pleaded case.

[8.34B] *Fraud*

HELD: The Court of Appeal found that dishonesty had been pleaded and addressed in cross-examination. Having found that there was no reason for the first claimant to have stopped the vehicle, the judge was entitled to arrive at an explanation as to why the claimant had stopped the vehicle.

Appeal dismissed.

11. COSTS

[8.49A] Shahow Qadar v Esure Services Ltd
(15 October 2015, unreported) QBD (TCC) (Judge David Grant)

The claimants made a personal injury claim after allegedly being involved in a road traffic accident in October 2013. The claim was valued at between £5,000 and £15,000 and therefore started under the RTA Protocol. The claim was allocated to the multi-track on the basis of the pleaded case by the defendant, being the claimant deliberately caused the accident. At first instance, the judge ordered that fixed costs would apply on the basis of the value of the claim rather than the track to which it was allocated and that the CPR allowed for costs on the multi-track to be awarded as fixed costs.

The appellant appealed against an order holding that fixed costs were applicable pursuant to CPR r 45.29A. The decision was challenged as to whether CPR r 45.29A had been interpreted correctly in light of the Jackson reforms and in accordance with the overriding objective.

HELD: HHJ Grant rejected the appellants' arguments. He found that r 45.29A is clear and does not require interpretation from the Court and that therefore the provisions of CPR r 1(2)(b), concerning the interpretation of rules in accordance with the overriding objective, were not engaged.

The judge stated the effect of inserting Section IIIA into Part 45 was to implement a fixed recoverable costs scheme in low-value personal injury claims arising out of a road traffic accident, which start under the RTA protocol but no longer continue under that protocol or the stage 3 procedure, but instead now proceed on the multi-track. It would appear that by amendment to the CPR, such a scheme of fixed recoverable costs has indeed been introduced into 'the lower reaches of the multi-track', certainly as regards cases which began via either the RTA protocol or the EL/PL protocol.

CHAPTER 9

Liability of Road Users

2.   OBSTRUCTING THE HIGHWAY

[9.10A]   Buswell v Symes and MIB
[2015] EWHC 1379 (QB), [2015] All ER (D) 154 (May)

The claimant motorcyclist travelling on the main road was involved in a collision with a tractor as it exited a field into the main road. A speed limit of 60 mph applied, and the claimant was travelling with a pillion passenger towards where the tractor was exiting when the collision occurred. As the collision was just over the brow of a hill, the claimant had limited visibility, until reaching the top of the hill.

It was accepted by the 1st defendant that in conducting the manoeuvre this would result in the whole road being blocked however he admitted that he did not consider the possibility of it presenting a hazard to other road users approaching from the same direction as the claimant. It was argued that the 1st defendant could not have done anything different, and that the accident was caused by the speed of the motorcyclist.

The court held that the 1st defendant (who was unrepresented) gave an inconsistent account, and had incorrectly stated that there was no alternative access to the field. In any event, the fact that the 1st defendant either failed to appreciate the risk, or foresaw it and took a chance meant that he was negligent.

However, as the claimant's speed which was assessed as being close to 70 mph, with knowledge of the road meant that he was aware of the not only the exit but also the possibility of slow moving tractors driving out of fields. As such contributory negligence was assessed at 66.6%.

CHAPTER 10

Driving Manoeuvring and Parking

3. SPEED

(C) POLICE VEHICLES AND FIRE ENGINES

[10.46D] Donald Macleod (a protected party by his litigation friend Barbara Macleod) v Metropolitan Police Commissioner
[2015] EWCA Civ 688, [2015] All ER (D) 98 (Jul)

The claim involves an incident which occurred at a crossroads junction in London, when the claimant was cycling home. The incident arose when the claimant was struck by the defendant's vehicle proceeding on an emergency call out on a dark road at about 55 mph. A speed limit of 30 mph applied.

The claimant cyclist was wearing a high-visibility jacket and the bike was brightly coloured with its lights on.

There was a dispute about which direction the claimant had been travelling prior to impact, and the claimant who sustained serious head injuries was unable to give any evidence about the accident circumstances.

The defendant asserted that the claimant had been travelling across the junction from west to east, although there were two independent witnesses, one of whom said he saw the claimant travelling south to north (the same as the defendant), with the other saying that although she did not see the incident was able to confirm that she had not seen the claimant travelling west to east, which is where she was positioned.

At first instance, the judge found in favour of the claimant on the basis that the independent witness evidence was supportive of the suggestion that he was travelling in the same direction of the defendant. In addition, he found that the defendant driver had been travelling too quickly without reasonable care and skill.

The defendant appealed on the basis that the judge erred in:
(1) Making findings of fact contrary to the weight of evidence.
(2) Reject the possibility of an alternative scenario.
(3) Finding that the respondent (claimant) turned right immediately before the collision when there was no evidence to support this theory.

It was held on appeal, that the trial judge was entitled to reach the conclusions he did, and rely on the evidence of the independent witnesses. The Court of Appeal accepted that the inference that the claimant had approached the junction from the South was a powerful one. The Court of Appeal further stated that judge was entitled to reject the hypothesis put forward by the accident reconstruction expert and was entitled to apply his common sense and experience when assessing the totality of the evidence. As there was nothing to suggest that the conclusions reached were not one that a reasonable judge could reach the appeal was dismissed.

[10.119B] *Driving Manoeuvring and Parking*

8. NEGLIGENT PARKING/OPENING DOOR OF VEHICLE

(A) CAR PARKS

[10.119B] Sparrow v Andre
[2016] EWHC 739 (QB), [2016] All ER (D) 61 (Apr)

The rear of the claimant and defendant's vehicle collided as both drivers attempted to manoeuvre in a crowded car park.

Following the collision the claimant exited his vehicle to inspect the damage. The defendant moved his car, which resulted in the claimant's vehicle rolling backwards down a slope towards the service area. As the claimant's children were in the car, obviously concerned for their safety he attempted to hold the car back as it rolled down the slope sustaining a serious leg injury.

The defendant conceded that he breached his duty of care in failing to keep a proper lookout. However, causation was in issue. The court held that the claimant was able to satisfy the 'but for' test in that if not for the initial collision caused by the defendant's breach of duty the claimant would not have needed to exit his vehicle. The judge was satisfied that there had been no intervening event, although he found the claimant 60% contributory negligent for failing to apply the foot brake and place the car in '*park*' mode before exiting.

10. TRAFFIC SIGNS

(D) WHITE LINES AND DOTTED LINES

[10.150D] Sinclair v Joyner
[2015] EWHC 1800 (QB), [2015] RTR 349

The claimant a cyclist was riding along a rural road in the opposite direction to the defendant. As both parties came around a bend they collided resulting in the claimant falling off her bicycle and sustaining significant injuries.

The claimant alleged that the defendant failed to keep a proper lookout and failed to properly assess the presentation of the hazard by the claimant who was cycling in the middle of the road while standing on the pedals. The claimant asserted that the defendant ought to have stopped to allow her to pass, and it was that failure that amounted to negligence.

The defendant denied liability on the basis that she was driving slowly and cautiously with her family and took the view that there was sufficient space for her to pass safely without incident. The defendant sought to rely on the fact that her carriageway was 2.5 metres wide with her vehicle being 2.1 metres wide. Therefore this left 0.4 metres of width without encroaching into the opposite carriageway.

As the claimant was barely on her side of the road (close to the middle of the road), and was riding while standing on the pedals, the court was satisfied that the defendant failed to assess that the claimant was not a '*serious cyclist*' which a prudent road user would have and as such should have allowed her to pass. This is because it is for motorists to anticipate hazards, particularly from vulnerable road users.

The court assessed contributory negligence at 25% on the basis that the claimant should not have been cycling in the centre of the road.

CHAPTER 11

Pedestrians

1. DRIVERS

(A) DRIVER NOT LIABLE

[11.10D]   Horner v Norman

[2015] EWCA Civ 1055, [2015] All ER (D) 216 (Oct)

The claimant, a pedestrian, ran across a dual carriageway into the path of the defendant driver.

The claimant alleged that if the defendant had braked as quickly and as forcefully as could be reasonably expected the accident would not have occurred. The claimant relied on evidence from an accident reconstruction expert who put forward evidence to support the claim.

As there was evidence of icy patches on the road, the defendant expert asserted that the braking forces would have been sufficient in damp conditions to confirm the evidence of the claimant's instructed expert. However, given the evidence of icy conditions the braking forces would have been lower making a collision unavoidable.

At first instance the judge found in favour of the defendant on the basis that the road was icy at the time of this incident (this was confirmed by the police report). As the judge accepted that the defendant braked as hard as she could and that her actions accorded with that of a careful and competent driver faced with an emergency she was not negligent.

The claimant appealed on the basis that the evidence from the collision investigator about braking and stopping distance supported his allegations against the claimant.

HELD: Held on appeal that the judge was right to reach the decision he did, as the assessment of the claimant's expert evidence relied on a number of assumptions none of which were sufficiently clear to compel acceptance.

Given the icy road conditions the Court of Appeal concluded that the trial judge was unable to say with any confidence that the state of the road allowed for maximum braking efficiency as suggested by the claimant's instructed expert.

As the trial judge was satisfied that the defendant had done everything possible in the circumstances, the appeal was dismissed.

[11.10E]   Dursan v J Sainsbury plc

[2015] EWHC 233 (QB), [2015] RTR 113

The claim involved a fatal road traffic accident which occurred on 22 December 2011 at 5.40 pm, when the deceased (a pedestrian) was struck by the defendant's LGV as he attempted to cross a street.

The deceased who was wearing dark clothing was in the process of attempting to cross a two-lane carriageway by stepping off the kerb, walking behind a bus in the bus lane, and into the path of the LGV, which was slowly proceeding in stop start traffic in the second carriageway. It was dark and although there was light provided by cars and

[11.10E] Pedestrians

street and shop lighting the deceased would not have been obviously conspicuous to the defendant driver.

The defendant's vehicle was fitted with EU compliant mirrors which included class V and class VI mirrors.

It was alleged that the defendant driver was negligent in failing to see the deceased as he attempted to cross the road, and in failing to properly check the class VI mirrors.

It was held after hearing evidence from the police collision investigator, the defendant driver, and the accident reconstruction experts instructed by the claimant and defendant respectively that the drivers mirror checks prior to moving forward were reasonable. In addition, the judge was satisfied that the defendant driver was careful and conscientious, and that the deceased was not visible to the driver in either his class V or class VI mirrors when he moved forward. Therefore the judge was satisfied that the collision did not arise because of any lack of observations on the part of the defendant driver, as the deceased was not in the drivers field of vision at the time when he carried out his mirror checks.

In addition the judge was satisfied that given the limited lighting and the deceased dark clothing, and reduced visibility that there was no guarantee that the driver would have seen the deceased in any event.

As the claimant was unable to prove negligence on the part of the defendant driver the claim was dismissed, with the judge commenting that the deceased by taking the steps he did was the 'author of this tragic incident'.

[11.10F]   Scott v Gavigan

[2016] EWCA Civ 544

The defendant was riding a motorcycle along Valley Road in Streatham, the defendant saw the claimant on the pavement on the opposite side of the road. The claimant suddenly and without warning ran diagonally towards the defendant's motorcycle resulting in a collision despite the defendant's best efforts to avoid impact.

The claimant sustained serious injuries and pursued a claim for compensation. The claim was dismissed at first instance on the basis that the claimant's actions were highly careless due to his drunken state and were not foreseeable to the defendant. The judge did however criticise the defendant by suggesting that his speed was excessive in the circumstances.

However, there was no finding of liability as the claimant's actions were sufficient to absolve the defendant of any liability as it constituted an intervening event.

The claimant appealed asserting that his actions should not be sufficient to eclipse any wrong doing on the part of the defendant, and that they did not amount to an intervening act which broke the chain of causation.

It was held on appeal that it was not unreasonable for the judge to find that the claimant's actions were not foreseeable, in that he ran out into the road at an angle towards the defendant.

The Court of Appeal did not accept that the defendant's speed was excessive, and given the finding on foreseeability could not support the notion that the defendant rider had been negligent.

The Court of Appeal did not specifically deal with the issue of novus actus, but did state that it should be exceptional for a claimant to be denied a remedy if he was able to establish foreseeability, negligence, and causation.

CHAPTER 12

Liability of Children

2. **NEGLIGENCE OF CHILDREN**

(A) CONTRIBUTORY NEGLIGENCE

[12.15BA]   AB (By his mother and next friend CD) v Lisa Main
[2015] EWHC 3183 (QB)

The claimant an eight year old boy was seriously injured when he ran out into the road and collided with the wheel arch of the defendant's vehicle. The speed limit for the road was 40 mph, and the defendant stated that she was travelling at around 25 mph and 30 mph at the time of impact.

Prior to the collision the defendant had seen the claimant with another boy standing at the side of the road, when one of them (the claimant) suddenly ran out.

In deciding the issue of fault the court considered the relevant standard of care of a careful and competent driver, and what they would have done armed with common sense, in the face of real and possible danger.

In considering this issue the judge took account of the actions of the claimant prior to the collision, namely standing by the side of the road, observing traffic, and an object on the other side of the road, which should have put the defendant driver on notice that there was a risk that he may run out. In anticipating that risk the defendant ought to have taken her foot off the accelerator and covered the brakes, or sounded her horn, as she failed to take any of these steps the accumulation of these failings amounted to negligence despite her modest speed.

Contributory negligence was assessed at 20% to reflect the claimant's young age.

CHAPTER 13

Passengers

4. PASSENGERS ON PUBLIC TRANSPORT

(B) PASSENGERS INJURED EN ROUTE

[13.43A]   Christian v South East London and Kent Bus Co
[2014] EWCA Civ 944

The claimant a passenger on the defendant's bus was thrown forward after the driver performed emergency braking. Another passenger then fell onto her which caused her to suffer personal injuries.

The claimant alleged that the driver was travelling too quickly towards a queue of traffic and that his negligent speed on approach was the reason for her injury. It was the defendant's case that its driver was forced to perform emergency braking because of the actions of a red vehicle which tried to cut in front of him.

At first instance the trial judge heard evidence from the claimant and defendant driver and viewed CCTV footage and stills from the bus on board camera.

The judge accepted the evidence of the defendant driver as the CCTV footage showed the movement of the red vehicle into the path of the defendant's bus which meant that the driver had to react to avoid a collision. The judge rejected the claimant's allegation that the driver ought to have braked earlier and found that the driver of the red vehicle was to blame.

The claimant appealed. The appeal was dismissed as the Court of Appeal was satisfied that the trial judge had properly considered the facts and was entitled to reach the conclusions he did. Further the Court of Appeal accepted that the driver acted on the spur of the moment to a hazard by taking evasive action, and as such it was wrong to interfere with the first instance decision. Appeal dismissed.

CHAPTER 15

Highways

2. THE HIGHWAYS ACT 1980

(A) APPLICATION OF SECTION 41

(ii) Nature of duty

[15.12A] Andrew and Claire Foulds v Devon County Council
[2015] EWHC 40 (QB), [2015] All ER (D) 74 (Jan)

The claimants brought an action on behalf of their son who sustained serious injuries, when his bicycle collided with some railings which broke on impact causing him to fall a significant distance into the road below.

It was alleged that the local authority were negligent in failing to ensure that the railings were sufficiently strong to prevent the claimants son from falling into the road below.

The claimant's son lost control of his bicycle before crashing into the railings which broke on impact.

It was held that the actions of the local authority were reasonable as the railings were included in the inspection and repair regime. Further it was held that although the local authority were responsible for maintaining and inspecting the railings this did not amount to the creation of a crash barrier.

Therefore as the force applied on impact with the railings by the claimant's son was significantly more than its anticipated use of steadying, a stumbling pedestrian or cyclist the duty of care owed by the local authority had not been breached. The claim was therefore dismissed.

CHAPTER 17

Animals on Highway

2. STATUTORY PROVISIONS

(A) ANIMALS ACT 1971

[17.2A]

'10. Application of certain enactments to liability under sections 2 to 4A

For the purposes of the Fatal Accidents Acts 1846 to 1959, the Law Reform (Contributory Negligence) Act 1945 and the Limitation Act 1980 any damage for which a person is liable under sections 2 to 4A of this Act shall be treated as due to his fault.

'11. General interpretation

In this Act—

"damage" includes the death of, or injury to, any person (including any disease and any impairment of physical or mental condition);

"fault" has the same meaning as in the Law Reform (Contributory Negligence) Act 1945;

"fencing" includes the construction of any obstacle designed to prevent animals from straying;

"horse" includes an ass, mule or hinny;

"livestock" means cattle, horses, sheep, pigs, goats and poultry, and also deer not in the wild state and, in sections 3 and 9, also, while in captivity, pheasants, partridges and grouse;

"poultry" means the domestic varieties of the following, that is to say, fowls, turkeys, geese, ducks, guinea-fowls, pigeons, peacocks and quails;

"public place" includes—

(a) any common land or town or village green;
(b) any highway (and the verges of any highway); and

"species" includes sub-species and variety.

In England—

"common land" means–

(a) land registered as common land in a register of common land kept under Part 1 of the Commons Act 2006;
(b) and to which Part 1 of that Act does not apply and which is subject to rights of common within the meaning of that Act;

"town or village green" means land registered as a town or village green in a register of town or village greens kept under Part 1 of the Commons Act 2006;

[17.2A] *Animals on Highway*

In Wales—

"common land", and "town or village green" have the same meanings as in the Commons Registration Act 1965;'

(B) DANGEROUS DOGS ACT 1991

[17.3] The relevant sections of this Act were brought into force on 13 May 2014 by the Anti-social Behaviour, Crime and Policing Act 2014, SI 2014/949:

'**3. Keeping dogs under proper control**
- (1) If a dog is dangerously out of control in any place in England or Wales (whether or not a public place)—
  - (a) the owner; and
  - (b) if different, the person for the time being in charge of the dog,

is guilty of an offence, or, if the dog while so out of control injures any person or assistance dog, an aggravated offence, under this subsection.

- (1A) A person ("D") is not guilty of an offence under subsection (1) in a case which is a householder case.
- (1B) For the purposes of subsection (1A) "a householder case" is a case where—
  - (a) the dog is dangerously out of control while in or partly in a building, or part of a building, that is a dwelling or is forces accommodation (or is both), and
  - (b) at that time—
    - (i) the person in relation to whom the dog is dangerously out of control ("V") is in, or is entering, the building or part as a trespasser, or
    - (ii) D (if present at that time) believed V to be in, or entering, the building or part as a trespasser.

Section 76(8B) to (8F) of the Criminal Justice and Immigration Act 2008 (use of force at place of residence) apply for the purposes of this subsection as they apply for the purposes of subsection

- (8A) of that section (and for those purposes the reference in section 76(8D) to subsection (8A)(d) is to be read as if it were a reference to paragraph (b)(ii) of this subsection).
- (2) In proceedings for an offence under subsection (1) above against a person who is the owner of a dog but was not at the material time in charge of it, it shall be a defence for the accused to prove that the dog was at the material time in the charge of a person whom he reasonably believed to be a fit and proper person to be in charge of it.
- (3) . . .
- (4) A person guilty of an offence under subsection (1) above other than an aggravated offence is liable on summary conviction to imprisonment for a term not exceeding six months or a fine not exceeding level 5 on the standard scale or both; and a person guilty of an aggravated offence under that subsection is liable—
  - (a) on summary conviction, to imprisonment for a term not exceeding six months or a fine not exceeding the statutory maximum or both;
  - (b) on conviction on indictment, to imprisonment for a term not exceeding the relevant maximum specified in subsection (4A) or a fine or both.
- (4A) For the purposes of subsection (4)(b), the relevant maximum is—
  - (a) 14 years if a person dies as a result of being injured;

- (b) 5 years in any other case where a person is injured;
- (c) 3 years in any case where an assistance dog is injured (whether or not it dies).

(5) It is hereby declared for the avoidance of doubt that an order under section 2 of the Dogs Act 1871 (order on complaint that dog is dangerous and not kept under proper control)—

- (a) may be made whether or not the dog is shown to have injured any person; and
- (b) may specify the measures to be taken for keeping the dog under proper control, whether by muzzling, keeping on a lead, excluding it from specified places or otherwise.

(6) If it appears to a court on a complaint under section 2 of the said Act of 1871 that the dog to which the complaint relates is a male and would be less dangerous if neutered the court may under that section make an order requiring it to be neutered.

(7) The reference in section 1(3) of the Dangerous Dogs Act 1989 (penalties) to failing to comply with an order under section 2 of the said Act of 1871 to keep a dog under proper control shall include a reference to failing to comply with any other order made under that section; but no order shall be made under that section by virtue of subsection (6) above where the matters complained of arose before the coming into force of that subsection.

6. Dogs owned by young persons.

Where a dog is owned by a person who is less than sixteen years old any reference to its owner in section 1(2)(d) or (e) or 3 above shall include a reference to the head of the household, if any, of which that person is a member or, in Scotland, to the person who has his actual care and control.

10. Short title, interpretation, commencement and extent.

(1) This Act may be cited as the Dangerous Dogs Act 1991.

(2) In this Act—

"advertisement" includes any means of bringing a matter to the attention of the public and

"advertise" shall be construed accordingly;

"assistance dog" has the meaning given by section 173(1) of the Equality Act 2010;

"public place" means any street, road or other place (whether or not enclosed) to which the

public have or are permitted to have access whether for payment or otherwise and includes

the common parts of a building containing two or more separate dwellings.

(3) For the purposes of this Act a dog shall be regarded as dangerously out of control on any occasion on which there are grounds for reasonable apprehension that it will injure any person or assistance dog, whether or not it actually does so, but references to a dog injuring a person or assistance dog or there being grounds for reasonable apprehension that it will do so do not include references to any case in which the dog is being used for a lawful purpose by a constable or a person in the service of the Crown.'

[17.37B] *Animals on Highway*

3. CASE LAW

(A) NEGLIGENCE

(i) SECTION 2(1)

[17.37B]   UK Insurance Ltd v Farrow and Farrow (t/a R Farrow & Sons)
(19 January 2016, unreported), Waksman QC

The applicant insurer issued proceedings for a declaration that the indemnity sought by their insureds was outside of the scope of their public liability policy. The insureds owned a large dog that was used to guard their scrap metal business, which was a business specifically excluded from cover. The policy also specifically excluded any liability arising from animals, except when being used 'in connection with the [insured] business' (a largely historical beef farm) or when being used for private purposes only.

The guard dog was kept shackled by a chain but broke free, ran into the road, and caused an accident in which a motorcycle passenger was badly injured. The motorcycle passenger subsequently bought a personal injury claim against the insureds.

The insureds submitted that the dog had either caused the accident when guarding the premises, which included the insured business, or alternatively that the animal was being put to private use.

HELD: The dog's essential role to guard the scrap business; it was not a family pet. Its protection of other parts of the premises was incidental to its essential role.

Accordingly, the exclusion(s) applied and the insurer's declaration was granted. The insurer would not be required to indemnify the policyholder(s) in respect of the liability arising from the road traffic accident.

CHAPTER 18

Limitation

3. CALCULATING THE PERIOD

(A) WHEN TIME BEGINS TO RUN: S 14 'DATE OF KNOWLEDGE'

[18.35FA] George Collins v Secretary of State for Business Innovation and Skills and Stena Lane Irish Sea Ferries Ltd
[2014] EWCA Civ 717, [2014] PIQR P324, 164 NLJ 7610

The claimant worked at the London docks between 1947 and 1967. In May 2002 he was diagnosed with lung cancer. In May 2012 he issued proceedings alleging that his condition had been caused by exposure to asbestos whilst unloading bags of asbestos from ships. Limitation was tried as a preliminary issue. The judge at first instance dismissed the claim: [2013] EWHC 1117 (QB).
Court of Appeal's findings
Knowledge
The claimant's doctor examined him on numerous occasions between 2002 and 2008. The judge was correct to find that a reasonable person in the claimant's position would have asked about the possible causes of his lung cancer by mid-2003. The medical records in 2002 contained several references to the claimant's employment history and his exposure to asbestos. If asked about the matter in 2002/3 it was inevitable that the doctor would have mentioned exposure to asbestos as a possible cause of the claimant's lung cancer, however the claimant had formulated his question. The claimant did not ask about these matters until 2008. The claimant had constructive knowledge by the middle of 2003.
Section 33 discretion
The court, when deciding whether or not to disapply the limitation period, can take into account the passage of time between the date of the alleged breach and the claimant's date of knowledge:
(1) The period of time between the alleged breach of duty and the start of the limitation period is part of the circumstances of the case. within s 33(3).
(2) The primary factors to consider are those listed in s 33(3) (such as the length of and reasons for the claimant's delay).
(3) The court will have regard to time elapsed before the claimant's date of knowledge – but will accord less weight to this factor.
(4) Both parties may rely upon pre-limitation passage of time for different purposes. It is for the court to assess these considerations.
Appeal dismissed.

[18.35H] A v Trustees of the Watchtower Bible & Tract Society, Trustees of the Loughborough Blackbrook Congregation of Jehovah's Witnesses and Trustees of the Loughborough Southwood Congregation of Jehovah's Witnesses
[2015] EWHC 1722 (QB), 165 NLJ 7692

The claimant sought damages in respect of sexual abuse she suffered from 1989 to 1994. She claimed the defendants were vicariously liable for the sexual assaults of the deceased ministerial servant and that they had failed to take reasonable steps to

[18.35H] *Limitation*

protect her because they had been aware since 1990 that he had abused another child in the congregation, from his own admission. The primary limitation period expired on 4 September 2006. Proceedings were commenced in March 2013. The claimant also sought the court's discretion to set aside the primary limitation period under the Limitation Act 1980, s 33.

The defendants were found vicariously liable for the actions of their ministerial servant between 1989 and 1994, as the relationship between the elders and ministerial servants was akin to that of an employer and employee. Further, his admission provided foreseeability of risk. The elders therefore had assumed a duty of care to protect the claimant from this risk and the defendants were vicariously liable for their breach of duty in failing to do so.

In relation to limitation and the negligence claim it was held the claimant did not have sufficient knowledge within the meaning of s 14(1) until March 2014 therefore, proceedings issued in March 2013 were within the statutory limitation period. In any event, the court would have allowed the s 33 application were she deemed to have had sufficient knowledge prior to this date, as there could still be a fair trial. The claim succeeded.

4. EXTENDING THE STATUTORY PERIOD

(B) DISCRETION EXERCISED IN THE CLAIMANT'S FAVOUR

[18.60D]   Lloyd v Humphreys and Glasgow Ltd
[2015] EWHC 525 (QB), [2015] All ER (D) 243 (Mar)

In 2008 L was diagnosed with asbestosis. The claim handlers for H, one of L's former employers, were contacted in 2008 but refused to consider the claim until the House of Lords had delivered its judgment in *Grieves v FT Everard and Sons Ltd* [2007] UKHL 39, [2008] PIQR P95. L claimed against two other former employers in 2011; both were settled. L was diagnosed with mesothelioma in 2012 and died shortly thereafter. L's estate sought to bring a claim against H, but H contested the claim was an abuse of process and that the limitation date had passed. Exercising its discretion under s 33 of the Limitation Act 1980, the court held that the claim was not statute barred. The court confirmed that L was not required to sue all former employers at once and, in any event, H's insurers had been aware of the possible claim since 2008. The evidence showed L had developed mesothelioma shortly before a scan in 2008, so the limitation period technically expired in October 2011. The court considered L had acted promptly once he was aware of his possible claim against H and had sought out suitable legal and medical advice.

(C) DISCRETION EXERCISED IN THE DEFENDANT'S FAVOUR

[18.62D]   Malone v Relyon Heating Engineering Ltd
[2014] EWCA Civ 904, [2014] All ER (D) 34 (Jul)

The claimant brought a claim against his previous employers for noise-induced hearing loss and tinnitus due to noise exposure during his employment between 1977 and 2004. The letter of claim was sent in March 2009 and proceedings issued in January 2011.

The claimant had constructive knowledge by the end of January 2001, when his GP referred him to an ENT consultant who issued a hearing aid. However, exposure allegedly continued until his employment terminated in 2004, so the claimant said the primary limitation period expired in 2007 and should be disapplied under s 33 of the Limitation Act 1980.

The judge at first instance accepted the limitation period expired in 2007 for the entire claim, as the damage continued until 2004. Whilst the delay between 2004 and 2009 prejudiced the defendant, the delay between 2007 and 2009 did not materially compromise the defendant's ability to investigate and defend the claim, so the judge disapplied the limitation period.

The Court of Appeal allowed the defendant's appeal. The court held this was a divisible injury (pre- and post-2001). There were two periods of delay. With regards to the pre-2001 injury, the claimant's delay between 2004 and 2009 caused considerable prejudice to the defendant which outweighed that to the claimant. As to the post-2001 injury, the prejudice caused by the previous delay had to be taken into account along with proportionality: the value of the claim attributable to that period was minimal as most of the injury had occurred beforehand. The court refused to exercise its discretion for either period.

[18.62E]   Howard Platt v BRB (Residuary) Ltd

[2014] EWCA Civ 1401, [2014] PIQR P80

The claimant alleged he had been exposed to excessive noise during the course of his employment with the defendant between 1953 and 1988. He first attended upon his GP complaining of hearing problems in 1982. Following a further attendance in May 1997 complaining of right tinnitus and reduction in hearing, the claimant was referred to an ENT specialist. Upon examination the latter asked the claimant whether he had worked in a noisy environment to which he replied that he had. It was the claimant's case that he did not go on to ask the relevance of this, nor was he told that he was suffering from noise induced hearing loss.

In August 2010 the claimant read an article about occupational hearing loss, he contacted solicitors and subsequently brought a claim. The claimant succeeded at first instance. However, the court gave the defendant permission to appeal on the ground there was a lack of clear authority as to the extent to which a claimant who seeks medical advice is expected to question his doctors when no cause for the condition was given. The defendant's appeal was successful, the Court of Appeal finding that having been asked about his occupational exposure it was for the claimant to make enquiries as to whether this could have caused his present problems. Accordingly the claimant had constructive knowledge of the cause of his hearing loss for more than three years prior to issue of proceedings and the claim was statute-barred.

[18.62F]   RE v GE

[2015] EWCA Civ 287, [2015] All ER (D) 88 (Apr)

The case of *Stubbings v Webb* [1993] AC 498, [1998] 1 All ER 322, [1993] 2 WLR 120 held that personal injury claims for deliberate assault were subject to a strict six year limitation period. In *A v Hoare* the House of Lords held that ss 11 and 33 of the Limitation Act 1980 allowed the limitation period for such claims to be extended in certain cases. R was born in 1968 and alleged that between the ages of 6 and 14 she had been abused by G. R visited solicitors in 2001 and 2006 but had not pursued her claim in light of *Stubbings*. Following *A v Hoare* [2008] UKHL 6, [2008] 1 AC 844, [2008] 2 All ER 1 R's solicitors advised her to pursue a claim and a letter of claim was sent to G in 2009. The claim was issued in September 2012 but the judge at first instance held that limitation had passed and the claim was statute barred. On appeal the Court of Appeal held the judge had correctly identified that s 33 was only to be used in exceptional cases. The court had to consider whether it would be equitable to let the action proceed taking into account all the circumstances of the case. The judge

[18.62F] *Limitation*

was entitled to conclude that R's explanation for the delay was not adequate. In particular the court considered that, limitation having expired well before the decision in *A v Hoare*, R should have issued her claim urgently rather than wait a further four years after that decision. Appeal dismissed.

[18.62G] Ifede v Ministry of Defence
[2015] EWHC 3835 (QB)

The court was required to determine whether it should exercise its discretion pursuant to s 33 of the Limitation Act 1980 and disapply the three year limitation period to a personal injury claim that was issued out of time.

The claimant was an infantry training centre recruit. On 22 February 2010, he sustained injury during a tactical exercise. It was alleged that the Ministry of Defence was negligent and/or in breach of statutory duty on the basis that the route was not safe because of the snow and ice.

The three year limitation period expired on 22 February 2013. Proceedings were not issued until 17 September 2014, some 19 months following the expiry date. The claimant accepted that at the time of the fall, he knew an accident had occurred, that he had been injured and it was the MOD's fault.

The court held that this was a weak claim with a number of reasons to doubt the claimant's credibility. It was not accepted that the claimant was misled into believing he could not bring a civil claim against the MOD or that he was unable to do so until he was discharged in August 2013. It was not accepted that the claimant was unaware he could bring a civil negligence claim also.

It was held that this was a stale claim that was significantly delayed without justification with prejudice to the defendant. The judge was not persuaded that the three years should be dis-applied.

7.   THIRD PARTY CASES

(A) LIMITATION ACT 1980, S 10

[18.82A] Chief Constable of Hampshire v Southampton City Council
[2014] EWCA Civ 1541, [2015] PIQR P61

The issue before the court of appeal was when, in a claim for contribution, time starts to run where the original claim has been settled by way of acceptance of a Part 36 offer, but a consent order embodying the settlement is subsequently agreed.

HELD, ON APPEAL: The limitation period specified in s 10(1) of the Limitation Act 1980 was two years from the date on which the right to recover contribution occurred. By operation of s 10(4) of that Act, the start date was the date of acceptance of the Part 36 offer and not the date of the consent order.

CHAPTER 19

Introduction to Civil Procedure

2. THE PERSONAL INJURY PRE-ACTION PROTOCOL

(A) TEXT OF THE PROTOCOL

[19.18]
1.1 Introduction
1.1.1 This Protocol is primarily designed for personal injury claims which are likely to be allocated to the fast track and to the entirety of those claims: not only to the personal injury element of a claim which also includes, for instance, property damage. It is not intended to apply to claims which proceed under—
(a) the Pre-Action Protocol for Low Value Personal Injury Claims in Road Traffic Accidents from 31 July 2013;
(b) the Pre-Action Protocol for Low Value Personal Injury (Employers' Liability and Public Liability) Claims;
(c) the Pre-Action Protocol for the Resolution of Clinical Disputes; and
(d) the Pre-Action Protocol for Disease and Illness Claims.
1.1.2 If at any stage the claimant values the claim at more than the upper limit of the fast track, the claimant should notify the defendant as soon as possible. However, the "cards on the table" approach advocated by this Protocol is equally appropriate to higher value claims. The spirit, if not the letter of the Protocol, should still be followed for claims which could potentially be allocated multi-track.
1.2 Claims which exit either of the low value pre-action protocols listed at paragraph 1.1.1(a) and (b) ("the low value protocols") prior to Stage 2 will proceed under this Protocol from the point specified in those protocols, and as set out in paragraph 1.3.
1.3 1.3.1. Where a claim exits a low value protocol because the defendant considers that there is inadequate mandatory information in the Claim Notification Form ("CNF"), the claim will proceed under this Protocol from paragraph 5.1.
1.3.2 Where a defendant—
(a) alleges contributory negligence;
(b) does not complete and send the CNF Response; or
(c) does not admit liability,
the claim will proceed under this Protocol from paragraph 5.5.
1.4 1.4.1 This Protocol sets out conduct that the court would normally expect prospective parties to follow prior to the commencement of proceedings. It establishes a reasonable process and timetable for the exchange of

information relevant to a dispute, sets standards for the content and quality of letters of claim, and in particular, the conduct of pre-action negotiations. In particular, the parts of this Protocol that are concerned with rehabilitation are likely to be of application in all claims.

1.4.2 The timetable and the arrangements for disclosing documents and obtaining expert evidence may need to be varied to suit the circumstances of the case. Where one or both parties consider the detail of the Protocol is not appropriate to the case, and proceedings are subsequently issued, the court will expect an explanation as to why the Protocol has not been followed, or has been varied.

1.5 Where either party fails to comply with this Protocol, the court may impose sanctions. When deciding whether to do so, the court will look at whether the parties have complied in substance with the relevant principles and requirements. It will also consider the effect any non-compliance has had on another party. It is not likely to be concerned with minor or technical shortcomings (see paragraphs 13 to 15 of the Practice Direction on Pre-Action Conduct and Protocols).

Early Issue

1.6 The Protocol recommends that a defendant be given three months to investigate and respond to a claim before proceedings are issued. This may not always be possible, particularly where a claimant only consults a legal representative close to the end of any relevant limitation period. In these circumstances, the claimant's solicitor should give as much notice of the intention to issue proceedings as is practicable and the parties should consider whether the court might be invited to extend time for service of the claimant's supporting documents and for service of any defence, or alternatively, to stay the proceedings while the recommended steps in the Protocol are followed.

Litigants in Person

1.7 If a party to the claim does not have a legal representative they should still, in so far as reasonably possible, fully comply with this Protocol. Any reference to a claimant in this Protocol will also mean the claimant's legal representative.

2. OVERVIEW OF PROTOCOL – GENERAL AIM
  2.1 The Protocol's objectives are to—
(a) encourage the exchange of early and full information about the dispute;
(b) encourage better and earlier pre-action investigation by all parties;
(c) enable the parties to avoid litigation by agreeing a settlement of the dispute before proceedings are commenced;
(d) support the just, proportionate and efficient management of proceedings where litigation cannot be avoided; and
(e) promote the provision of medical or rehabilitation treatment (not just in high value cases) to address the needs of the Claimant at the earliest possible opportunity.

3. THE PROTOCOL

An illustrative flow chart is attached at Annexe A which shows each of the steps that the parties are expected to take before the commencement of proceedings.

Letter of Notification

3.1 The claimant or his legal representative may wish to notify a defendant and/or the insurer as soon as they know a claim is likely to be made, but before they are able to send a detailed Letter of Claim, particularly, for instance, when the defendant has no or limited knowledge of the incident giving rise to the claim, or where the claimant is incurring significant expenditure as a result of the accident which he hopes the defendant might pay for, in whole or in part.

3.2 The Letter of Notification should advise the defendant and/or the insurer of any relevant information that is available to assist with determining issues of liability/suitability of the claim for an interim payment and/or early rehabilitation.

3.3 If the claimant or his legal representative gives notification before sending a Letter of Claim, it will not start the timetable for the Letter of Response. However the Letter of Notification should be acknowledged within 14 days of receipt.

4. REHABILITATION

4.1 The parties should consider as early as possible whether the claimant has reasonable needs that could be met by medical treatment or other rehabilitative measures. They should discuss how these needs might be addressed.

4.2 The Rehabilitation Code (which can be found at: http://www.iua.co.uk/IUA_member/publications) is likely to be helpful in considering how to identify the claimant's needs and how to address the cost of providing for those needs.

4.3 The time limit set out in paragraph 6.3 of this Protocol shall not be shortened, except by consent to allow these issues to be addressed.

4.4 Any immediate needs assessment report or documents associated with it that are obtained for the purposes of rehabilitation shall not be used in the litigation except by consent and shall in any event be exempt from the provisions of paragraphs 7.2 to 7.11 of this Protocol. Similarly, persons conducting the immediate needs assessment shall not be a compellable witness at court.

4.5 Consideration of rehabilitation options, by all parties, should be an on going process throughout the entire Protocol period.

5. LETTER OF CLAIM

5.1 Subject to paragraph 5.3 the claimant should send to the proposed defendant two copies of the Letter of Claim. One copy of the letter is for the defendant, the second for passing on to the insurers, as soon as possible, and, in any event, within 7 days of the day upon which the defendant received it.

5.2 The Letter of Claim should include the information described on the template at Annexe B1. The level of detail will need to be varied to suit the particular circumstances. In all cases there should be sufficient information for the defendant to assess liability and to enable the defendant to estimate the likely size and heads of the claim without necessarily addressing quantum in detail.

5.3 The letter should contain a clear summary of the facts on which the claim is based together with an indication of the nature of any injuries suffered, and the way in which these impact on the claimant's day to day functioning

[19.18] *Introduction to Civil Procedure*

and prognosis. Any financial loss incurred by the claimant should be outlined with an indication of the heads of damage to be claimed and the amount of that loss, unless this is impracticable.

5.4 Details of the claimant's National Insurance number and date of birth should be supplied to the defendant's insurer once the defendant has responded to the Letter of Claim and confirmed the identity of the insurer. This information should not be supplied in the Letter of Claim.

5.5 Where a claim no longer continues under either low value protocol, the CNF completed by the claimant under those protocols can be used as the Letter of Claim under this Protocol unless the defendant has notified the claimant that there is inadequate information in the CNF.

5.6 Once the claimant has sent the Letter of Claim no further investigation on liability should normally be carried out within the Protocol period until a response is received from the defendant indicating whether liability is disputed.

Status of Letters of Claim and Response

5.7 Letters of Claim and Response are not intended to have the same formal status as a statement of case in proceedings. It would not be consistent with the spirit of the Protocol for a party to 'take a point' on this in the proceedings, provided that there was no obvious intention by the party who changed their position to mislead the other party.

6. THE RESPONSE

6.1 Attached at Annexe B2 is a template for the suggested contents of the Letter of Response: the level of detail will need to be varied to suit the particular circumstances.

6.2 The defendant must reply within 21 calendar days of the date of posting of the letter identifying the insurer (if any). If the insurer is aware of any significant omissions from the letter of claim they should identify them specifically. Similarly, if they are aware that another defendant has also been identified whom they believe would not be a correct defendant in any proceedings, they should notify the claimant without delay, with reasons, and in any event by the end of the Response period. Where there has been no reply by the defendant or insurer within 21 days, the claimant will be entitled to issue proceedings. Compliance with this paragraph will be taken into account on the question of any assessment of the defendant's costs.

6.3 The defendant (insurer) will have a maximum of three months from the date of acknowledgment of the Letter of Claim (or of the CNF where the claim commenced in a portal) to investigate. No later than the end of that period, The defendant (insurer) should reply by no later than the end of that period, stating if liability is admitted by admitting that the accident occurred, that the accident was caused by the defendant's breach of duty, and the claimant suffered loss and there is no defence under the Limitation Act 1980.

6.4 Where the accident occurred outside England and Wales and/or where the defendant is outside the jurisdiction, the time periods of 21 days and three months should normally be extended up to 42 days and six months.

6.5 If a defendant denies liability and/or causation, their version of events should be supplied. The defendant should also enclose with the response, documents in their possession which are material to the issues between the parties, and which would be likely to be ordered to be disclosed by the court, either on an application for pre-action disclosure, or on disclosure during proceedings. No charge will be made for providing copy documents under the Protocol.

6.6 An admission made by any party under this Protocol may well be binding on that party in the litigation. Further information about admissions made under this Protocol is to be found in Civil Procedure Rules ("CPR") rule 14.1A.

6.7 Following receipt of the Letter of Response, if the claimant is aware that there may be a delay of six months or more before the claimant decides if, when and how to proceed, the claimant should keep the defendant generally informed.

7. DISCLOSURE

7.1 7.1.1 The aim of early disclosure of documents by the defendant is not to encourage 'fishing expeditions' by the claimant, but to promote an early exchange of relevant information to help in clarifying or resolving issues in dispute. The claimant's solicitor can assist by identifying in the Letter of Claim or in a subsequent letter the particular categories of documents which they consider are relevant and why, with a brief explanation of their purported relevance if necessary.

Documents

7.1.2 Attached at Annexe C are specimen, but non-exhaustive, lists of documents likely to be material in different types of claim.

7.1.3 Pre-action disclosure will generally be limited to the documents required to be enclosed with the Letter of Claim and the Response. In cases where liability is admitted in full, disclosure will be limited to the documents relevant to quantum, the parties can agree that further disclosure may be given. If either or both of the parties consider that further disclosure should be given but there is disagreement about some aspect of that process, they may be able to make an application to the court for pre-action disclosure under Part 31 of the CPR. Parties should assist each other and avoid the necessity for such an application.

7.1.4 The protocol should also contain a requirement that the defendant is under a duty to preserve the disclosure documents and other evidence (CCTV for example). If the documents are destroyed, this could be an abuse of the court process.

7.2 Experts

7.2.3 Before any party instructs an expert, they should give the other party a list of the name(s) of one or more experts in the relevant speciality whom they consider are suitable to instruct.

Save for cases likely to be allocated to the multi-track, the Protocol encourages joint selection of, and access to, quantum experts, and, on occasion liability experts e.g. engineers. The expert report produced is not a joint report for the purposes of CPR Part 35. The Protocol promotes the practice of the claimant obtaining a medical report, disclosing it to the defendant who then asks questions and/or agrees it and does not obtain their own report. The Protocol provides for nomination of the expert by the claimant in personal injury claims.

7.3 Before any party instructs an expert, they should give the other party a list of the name(s) of one or more experts in the relevant speciality whom they consider are suitable to instruct.

[19.18] *Introduction to Civil Procedure*

7.4 Some solicitors choose to obtain medical reports through medical agencies, rather than directly from a specific doctor or hospital. The defendant's prior consent to this should be sought and, if the defendant so requests, the agency should be asked to provide in advance the names of the doctor(s) whom they are considering instructing.

7.5 Where a medical expert is to be instructed, the claimant's solicitor will organise access to relevant medical records – see specimen letter of instruction at Annexe D.

7.6 Within 14 days of providing a list of experts the other party may indicate an objection to one or more of the named experts. The first party should then instruct a mutually acceptable expert assuming there is one (this is not the same as a joint expert). It must be emphasised that when the claimant nominates an expert in the original Letter of Claim, the defendant has a further 14 days to object to one or more of the named experts after expiration of the 21 day period within which they have to reply to the Letter of Claim, as set out in paragraph 6.2.

7.7 If the defendant objects to all the listed experts, the parties may then instruct experts of their own choice. It will be for the court to decide, subsequently and if proceedings are issued, whether either party had acted unreasonably.

7.8 If the defendant does not object to an expert nominated by the claimant, they shall not be entitled to rely on their own expert evidence within that expert's area of expertise unless—
(a) the claimant agrees;
(b) the court so directs; or
(c) the claimant's expert report has been amended and the claimant is not prepared to disclose the original report.

7.9 Any party may send to an agreed expert written questions on the report, via the first party's solicitors. Such questions must be put within 28 days of service of the expert's report and must only be for the purpose of clarification of the report. The expert should send answers to the questions simultaneously to each party.

7.10 The cost of a report from an agreed expert will usually be paid by the instructing first party: the costs of the expert replying to questions will usually be borne by the party which asks the questions.

7.11 If necessary, after proceedings have commenced and with the permission of the court, the parties may obtain further expert reports. It would be for the court to decide whether the costs of more than one expert's report should be recoverable.

8. NEGOTIATIONS FOLLOWING AN ADMISSION

8.1 8.1.1 Where a defendant admits liability which has caused some damage, before proceedings are issued, the claimant should send to that defendant—
(a) any medical reports obtained under this Protocol on which the claimant relies; and
(b) a schedule of any past and future expenses and losses which are claimed, even if the schedule is necessarily provisional. The schedule should contain as much detail as reasonably practicable and should identify those losses that are ongoing. If the schedule is likely to be updated before the case is concluded, it should say so.

8.1.2 The claimant should delay issuing proceedings for 21 days from disclosure of (a) and (b) above (unless such delay would cause his claim to become time-barred), to enable the parties to consider whether the claim is capable of settlement.

8.2 CPR Part 36 permits claimants and defendants to make offers to settle pre-proceedings. Parties should always consider if it is appropriate to make a Part 36 Offer before issuing. If such an offer is made, the party making the offer must always try to supply sufficient evidence and/or information to enable the offer to be properly considered.

The level of detail will depend on the value of the claim. Medical reports may not be necessary where there is no significant continuing injury and a detailed schedule may not be necessary in a low value case.

9. Alternative Dispute Resolution

9.1 9.1.1 Litigation should be a last resort. As part of this Protocol, the parties should consider whether negotiation or some other form of Alternative Dispute Resolution ("ADR") might enable them to resolve their dispute without commencing proceedings.

9.1.2 Some of the options for resolving disputes without commencing proceedings are—

(a) discussions and negotiation (which may or may not include making Part 36 Offers or providing an explanation and/or apology);
(b) mediation, a third party facilitating a resolution;
(c) arbitration, a third party deciding the dispute; and
(d) early neutral evaluation, a third party giving an informed opinion on the dispute.

9.1.3 If proceedings are issued, the parties may be required by the court to provide evidence that ADR has been considered. It is expressly recognised that no party can or should be forced to mediate or enter into any form of ADR but unreasonable refusal to consider ADR will be taken into account by the court when deciding who bears the costs of the proceedings.

9.2 Information on mediation and other forms of ADR is available in the Jackson ADR Handbook (available from Oxford University Press) or at—
- http://www.civilmediation.justice.gov.uk/
- http://www.adviceguide.org.uk/england/law_e/law_legal_system_ e/law _taking_legal_action_e/alternatives_to_court.htm

10. Quantification of Loss - Special damages

10.1 In all cases, if the defendant admits liability, the claimant will send to the defendant as soon as reasonably practicable a schedule of any past and future expenses and losses which he claims, even if the schedule is necessarily provisional. The schedule should contain as much detail as reasonably practicable and should identify those losses that are ongoing. If the schedule is likely to be updated before the case is concluded, it should say so. The claimant should keep the defendant informed as to the rate at which his financial loss is progressing throughout the entire Protocol period.

11. Stocktake

11.1 Where the procedure set out in this Protocol has not resolved the dispute between the parties, each party should undertake a review of its own

[19.18] *Introduction to Civil Procedure*

positions and the strengths and weaknesses of its case. The parties should then together consider the evidence and the arguments in order to see whether litigation can be avoided or, if that is not possible, for the issues between the parties to be narrowed before proceedings are issued. Where the defendant is insured and the pre-action steps have been taken by the insurer, the insurer would normally be expected to nominate solicitors to act in the proceedings and to accept service of the claim form and other documents on behalf of the defendant. The claimant or their solicitor is recommended to invite the insurer to nominate the insurer to nominate solicitors to act in the proceedings and do so 7 to 14 days before the intended issue date.

Note-Annexes are not reproduced here

[19.19A]

(A) TEXT OF THE PRACTICE DIRECTION TO THE PRE-ACTION PROTOCOLS

PRACTICE DIRECTION – PRE-ACTION CONDUCT AND PROTOCOLS

Introduction
1. Pre-action protocols explain the conduct and set out the steps the court would normally expect parties to take before commencing proceedings for particular types of civil claims. They are approved by the Master of the Rolls and are annexed to the Civil Procedure Rules (CPR). (The current pre-action protocols are listed in paragraph 18.)
2. This Practice Direction applies to disputes where no pre-action protocol approved by the Master of the Rolls applies.
3. Objectives of pre-action conduct and protocols
Before commencing proceedings, the court will expect the parties to have exchanged sufficient information to—
(a) understand each other's position;
(b) make decisions about how to proceed;
(c) try to settle the issues without proceedings;
(d) consider a form of Alternative Dispute Resolution (ADR) to assist with settlement;
(e) support the efficient management of those proceedings; and
(f) reduce the costs of resolving the dispute.
4. Proportionality
A pre-action protocol or this Practice Direction must not be used by a party as a tactical device to secure an unfair advantage over another party. Only reasonable and proportionate steps should be taken by the parties to identify, narrow and resolve the legal, factual or expert issues.
5. The costs incurred in complying with a pre-action protocol or this Practice Direction should be proportionate (CPR 44.3(5)). Where parties incur disproportionate costs in complying with any pre-action protocol or this Practice Direction, those costs will not be recoverable as part of the costs of the proceedings.
6. Steps before issuing a claim at court
Where there is a relevant pre-action protocol, the parties should comply with that protocol before commencing proceedings. Where there is no relevant pre-action protocol, the parties should exchange correspondence and informa-

tion to comply with the objectives in paragraph 3, bearing in mind that compliance should be proportionate. The steps will usually include—
(a) the claimant writing to the defendant with concise details of the claim. The letter should include the basis on which the claim is made, a summary of the facts, what the claimant wants from the defendant, and if money, how the amount is calculated;
(b) the defendant responding within a reasonable time - 14 days in a straight forward case and no more than 3 months in a very complex one. The reply should include confirmation as to whether the claim is accepted and, if it is not accepted, the reasons why, together with an explanation as to which facts and parts of the claim are disputed and whether the defendant is making a counterclaim as well as providing details of any counterclaim; and
(c) the parties disclosing key documents relevant to the issues in dispute.

7. Experts

Parties should be aware that the court must give permission before expert evidence can be relied upon (see CPR 35.4(1)) and that the court may limit the fees recoverable. Many disputes can be resolved without expert advice or evidence. If it is necessary to obtain expert evidence, particularly in low value claims, the parties should consider using a single expert, jointly instructed by the parties, with the costs shared equally.

8. Settlement and ADR

Litigation should be a last resort. As part of a relevant pre-action protocol or this Practice Direction, the parties should consider whether negotiation or some other form of ADR might enable them to settle their dispute without commencing proceedings.

9. Parties should continue to consider the possibility of reaching a settlement at all times, including after proceedings have been started. Part 36 offers may be made before proceedings are issued.

10. Parties may negotiate to settle a dispute or may use a form of ADR including—
(a) mediation, a third party facilitating a resolution;
(b) arbitration, a third party deciding the dispute;
(c) early neutral evaluation, a third party giving an informed opinion on the dispute; and
(d) Ombudsmen schemes.

(Information on mediation and other forms of ADR is available in the Jackson ADR Handbook (available from Oxford University Press) or at—
http://www.civilmediation.justice.gov.uk/
http://www.adviceguide.org.uk/england/law_e/law_legal_system_e/law_taking_legal_action_e/alternatives_to_court.htm)

11. If proceedings are issued, the parties may be required by the court to provide evidence that ADR has been considered. A party's silence in response to an invitation to participate or a refusal to participate in ADR might be considered unreasonable by the court and could lead to the court ordering that party to pay additional court costs.

12. Stocktake and list of issues

Where a dispute has not been resolved after the parties have followed a pre-action protocol or this Practice Direction, they should review their respective positions. They should consider the papers and the evidence to see

[19.19A] *Introduction to Civil Procedure*

if proceedings can be avoided and at least seek to narrow the issues in dispute before the claimant issues proceedings.

13. Compliance with this Practice Direction and the Protocols

If a dispute proceeds to litigation, the court will expect the parties to have complied with a relevant pre-action protocol or this Practice Direction. The court will take into account non-compliance when giving directions for the management of proceedings (see CPR 3.1(4) to (6)) and when making orders for costs (see CPR 44.3(5)(a)). The court will consider whether all parties have complied in substance with the terms of the relevant pre-action protocol or this Practice Direction and is not likely to be concerned with minor or technical infringements, especially when the matter is urgent (for example an application for an injunction).

14. The court may decide that there has been a failure of compliance when a party has—
(a) not provided sufficient information to enable the objectives in paragraph 3 to be met;
(b) not acted within a time limit set out in a relevant protocol, or within a reasonable period; or
(c) unreasonably refused to use a form of ADR, or failed to respond at all to an invitation to do so.

15. Where there has been non-compliance with a pre-action protocol or this Practice Direction, the court may order that
(a) the parties are relieved of the obligation to comply or further comply with the pre-action protocol or this Practice Direction;
(b) the proceedings are stayed while particular steps are taken to comply with the pre-action protocol or this Practice Direction;
(c) sanctions are to be applied.

16. The court will consider the effect of any non-compliance when deciding whether to impose any sanctions which may include—
(a) an order that the party at fault pays the costs of the proceedings, or part of the costs of the other party or parties;
(b) an order that the party at fault pay those costs on an indemnity basis;
(c) if the party at fault is a claimant who has been awarded a sum of money, an order depriving that party of interest on that sum for a specified period, and/or awarding interest at a lower rate than would otherwise have been awarded;
(d) if the party at fault is a defendant, and the claimant has been awarded a sum of money, an order awarding interest on that sum for a specified period at a higher rate, (not exceeding 10% above base rate), than the rate which would otherwise have been awarded.

17. Limitation

This Practice Direction and the pre-action protocols do not alter the statutory time limits for starting court proceedings. If a claim is issued after the relevant limitation period has expired, the defendant will be entitled to use that as a defence to the claim. If proceedings are started to comply with the statutory time limit before the parties have followed the procedures in this Practice Direction or the relevant pre-action protocol, the parties should apply to the court for a stay of the proceedings while they so comply.

4. THE OVERRIDING OBJECTIVE

CPR 1.2 – APPLICATION BY THE COURT OF THE OVERRIDING OBJECTIVE

[19.33A]
1.2 Application by the court of the overriding objective
The court must seek to give effect to the overriding objective when it –
(a) exercises any power given to it by the Rules; or
(b) interprets any rule subject to rules 76.2, 79.2 and 80.2, 82.2 and 88.2.

5. CASE AND COST MANAGEMENT

(A) COURT'S POWERS

CPR 3.1 – THE COURT'S GENERAL POWERS OF CASE MANAGEMENT

[19.61A] CPR 3.1 (2)(m) take any other step or make any other order for the purpose of managing the case and furthering the overriding objective, including hearing an Early Neutral Evaluation with the aim of helping the parties settle the case.

(D) SANCTIONS

CPR 3.7 – SANCTIONS FOR NON-PAYMENT OF CERTAIN FEES

[19.68AA] CPR 3.7(1)(e). (Rule 26.3 provides for the court to dispense with the need for a directions questionnaire and rules 28.5 and 29.6 provide for the court to dispense with the need for a pre-trial check list) (Rule 54.12 provides for the service of the order giving permission to proceed with a claim for judicial review)
CPR 3.7(4)(b)(ii). (Rule 44.9 provides for the basis of assessment where a right to costs arises under this rule and contains provisions about when a costs order is deemed to have been made and applying for an order under s 194(3) of the Legal Services Act 2007).

[19.68AB]   Walsham Chalet Park Ltd (t/a Dream Lodge Group) v Tallington Lakes Ltd
[2014] EWCA Civ 1607, [2015] 1 Costs LO 157

It was held, on appeal, that in hearing an application for strike out following non-compliance with a court's case management order, the court had correctly applied the principles in *Mitchell v News Group Newspapers Ltd* [2013] EWCA Civ 1537, [2014] 2 All ER 430, [2014] 1 WLR 795 and the three stage test in *Denton v TH White Ltd* [2014] EWCA Civ 906, [2015] 1 All ER 880, [2014] 1 WLR 3926 in deciding whether or not to impose a sanction for non-compliance, even though those cases largely concern whether relief from sanctions should be granted.

[19.94A] *Introduction to Civil Procedure*

(E) APPLYING FOR RELIEF FROM SANCTIONS

(iii) Relief from sanctions

[19.94A] Riff Trading Ltd (in liq), Timothy James Bramston v John Saunders (dec'd), Paul Oliver Saunders, John Gerrard Saunders, Waterleaf Ltd (a company registered in the British Virgin Islands) and Prestwood Property Ltd (a company registered in the British Virgin Islands)

[2014] EWHC 2116 (Ch)

The defendants applied for relief from sanction after they failed to comply with orders requiring them to file and serve witness evidence, including an unless order.

The court said discipline did not necessarily mean refusal to grant relief, as long as a sufficiently harsh sanction was imposed. The court granted relief from the unless order so the defendants could rely on witness evidence on the basis that they served their evidence and paid the claimant's costs of the application within a specific period, and even if successful at trial, they would not recover any costs whatsoever from the claimants.

[19.94B] Matthew Chadwick (trustee in bankruptcy of Anthony Burling) v Linda Burling

[2015] EWHC 1610 (Ch), [2015] 3 Costs LR 589, [2015] BPIR 1019

In deciding an application for a relief from sanction by a litigant in person, a district registrar had erred in not properly following the third stage of the test in *Denton v TH White Ltd* [2014] EWCA Civ 906, [2015] 1 All ER 880, [2014] 1 WLR 3926, ie he had not taken into account any factors other than CPR r 3.9(i)(a) and (b), which he expressly mentioned. His reference to 'looking at all of the circumstances' could not be taken as a statement that all relevant factors had been taken into account and irrelevant factors left out of account. Nevertheless, the application was not made promptly and it was determined that relief from sanction should not be granted.

It cannot be right that a court must enquire into the state of knowledge and intellectual capacity of a litigant in person who says that he or she did not understand the process. This may be a relevant issue where there is some extremely complex factor or complicated order which a lay person would find it difficult to understand. In this instance, the relevant orders were straightforward and easy to understand.

[19.94C] Viridor Waste Management Ltd v Veolia Es Ltd

[2015] EWHC 2321 (Comm), [2015] All ER (D) 99 (Oct)

The claimant, C, made a claim for unjust enrichment against the defendant, D (both parties were waste management companies that used each other's facilities). C served its claim form four days prior to the expiry of the four month service period and the parties agreed to a 28 day extension for service of the particulars of claim and agreed a stay to allow for settlement. C then served its particulars of claim one day after the new deadline for service, because its firm of solicitors served the particulars by second class post, contrary to its usual procedures. D complained that service was not effective as second class post is not a recognised method of service. C re-effected service four days later and D refused an extension of time for service of particulars and made an application to strike out C's application.

D submitted that the delay was significant and serious as a generous period had already been allowed for service of the particulars, an important document in allowing D to identify the grounds of the claim against it.

In considering the cases of *Mitchell* and *Denton*, the Court found that it was not necessary to resolve which date service was actually effected, and that although there were formal rules to be complied with, in practical terms D's solicitors had received C's particulars only one day after the agreed date for service. In assessing the seriousness and significance of the default, it was important to focus on the rule's purpose, which in this case was to bring the document to the attention of the other party. This had been done and the default would not have any real impact on the course of the litigation or on other court users. No delay or inefficiency had been caused, the breach was immaterial and *Denton* was followed. The submission that the delay was serious and significant was unrealistic and the application for an extension of time was granted.

It was also held that D had sought to take unreasonable advantage of C's default in the hope of obtaining a lucrative strike out when it was clear that relief from sanctions was suitable. It was held as appropriate to award C costs on the indemnity basis due to the fact that the application had been made unreasonably.

[19.94D] Mishcon De Reya (a firm) and Mishcon De Reya LLP v Antonio Caliendo and Barnaby Holdings Ltd

[2015] EWCA Civ 1029, [2015] All ER (D) 99 (Oct)

The defendants appealed against the order of Mr Justice Hildyard ('judge'), dated 21 October 2014 ([2014] EWHC 3414), which granted the claimant relief from sanctions pursuant to CPR r 3.9(1). In that hearing, the claimant had made an application for relief from sanctions for failure to serve a notice of funding on the defendants within the seven day time limit provided by the CPR. The notice was served three and a half months out of time. The application was granted with the court finding that whilst complying with the court rules ought to be encouraged the delay had not caused any undue prejudice to the defendant nor had any significant effect on the progress of the claim as a whole.

The defendants appealed this decision and argued firstly pursuant to the first test in *Denton* the judge had concluded wrongly that they had not suffered prejudice. Secondly, it was argued that the judge had wrongly failed to attach any weight to the default under stage two of *Denton* due to the fact that no good reason had been given for the delay. They also argued that in applying stage 3 of *Denton* the judge had failed to adequately consider the significant impact on them if relief from sanction was granted. Finally, the defendant argued the judge had held wrongly that CPR r 3.9(1)(a) required consideration of the need for litigation to be conducted at a proportionate cost and efficiently in relation to the delay in serving the notice of funding.

The appeal was unanimously dismissed. The Court of Appeal held that it should not interfere with the original judge's decision as they found the judge's analysis of the *Denton* test to be correct. The judge had clearly taken into consideration the failure on the claimant's part and there was no good reason to suggest the defendants would have changed their position had they been aware of the claimant's funding arrangements earlier. Further, the judge's failure to attach any weight to the fact that no good reason was given for the delay in serving the notice of funding was not sufficient to hold that the judge wrongly exercised his discretion flawed. The absence of a good reason did not mean that relief from sanction would automatically be refused. *Denton* expressly stated that the courts were to consider prejudice in all the circumstances, and in this case the claimant could have been at risk of covering the ATE premiums as a consequence of losing the application for relief. Finally, in consideration of the third test in *Denton*, the correct approach in CPR r 3.9(1)(a) is to concentrate on the impact of breaching of procedural rules rather than considering the impact of granting relief.

[19.94E] Barbara Pipe v Spicer Haart Estate Agents Ltd (t/a Haart)

[2016] EWHC 61 (QB), [2016] All ER (D) 152 (Jan)

The court considered stage 3 of the *Denton* test in the context of an application for a 48 day extension of time to file a respondent's notice. The failure to file the notice was a serious or significant breach and there was no good reason for it. Stage 3 of the test was to consider all the circumstances of the case. The respondent's conduct had prevented the parties from conducting the litigation at proportionate cost. The appellant had tried on many occasions to correspond with the respondent to proceed with this matter but the respondent had continually failed to respond until it was too late. The judge rejected the respondent's argument that the consequences of granting the application would be minimal. Application refused.

[19.94F] British Gas Trading Ltd v Oak Cash & Carry Ltd
[2016] EWCA Civ 153, 166 NLJ 7692

In a debt claim, the parties were ordered to file pre-trial checklists by 3 February 2014. The defendant failed to do so. The judge ordered that the defendant's defence would be struck out if it did not file a pre-trial checklist by 19 February 2014; it was filed on 21 February 2014. Judgment in default was granted for the claimant on 18 March 2014. The defendant successfully applied for relief from sanctions on 24 March 2014. The claimant appealed against this and the decision was overturned: [2014] EWHC 4058.

The defendant appealed. The Court of Appeal considered that the breach by the defendant had been serious. In coming to this conclusion the Court of Appeal considered it had to look at the underlying breach as well as the breach of the unless order. The failure to comply with both was deemed to be significant. It considered the defendant's excuse that the solicitor handling the case had to pass the file to a trainee during February 2014 because of his wife's health problems was not a good reason for the default. Finally the court considered the delay in applying for relief from sanction was fatal to the defendant's application.

In the circumstances the appeal was dismissed on the basis that relief from sanction should not have been granted had the three stage test in *Denton* been applied correctly.

[19.94G] Murray v BAE Systems PLC
(2016) unreported

The claimant had filed his costs budget with the court on 24 August 2015. This was seven days after the deadline, with this delay being described as a breakdown in communication whilst the case was being transferred to another fee earner. In the original decision, the judge had refused to grant relief from sanction. The claimant appealed this decision.

It was held on appeal that even though the costs budget had been filed seven days late it did not have serious impact on the court timetable and it was found that the judge had wrongly held that the breach was 'serious and significant' under the 3-stage test laid down in *Denton v TH White Ltd*.

CHAPTER 20

The MOJ Process

1. INTRODUCTION

(IV) EXIT FROM THE MOJ PROCESS

[20.8A]   Tennant v W Cottrell Ltd

(11 December 2014, unreported) LIVERPOOL COUNTY COURT

The claimant's solicitors gave notice by way of a letter dated 23 August 2013 that they were removing this case from the RTA portal as the defendant had, as part of their stage 2 counter-offer, made nil offers. The matter subsequently progressed to Part 7 proceedings and the defendant filed a defence and suggested that the matter be tracked. The parties settled the claim and on the issue of costs the defendant argued that the claimant had unreasonably removed the claim from the portal and should be restricted to portal costs. In replying to the Points of Dispute the claimant argued that the removal was due to the claim being too complex and therefore unsuitable for the process.

HELD: The court held that it was necessary to look at whether or not the claimant's solicitors acted reasonably in giving the notice to remove the matter at the time that they did so, rather than imputing hindsight. It seemed to the district judge that the letter removing the matter from the portal made the reason clear – the defendants had not made offers. The court held the defendant had made offers – they were nil offers. It was held that it would be wrong to look at the course which the case followed once it entered a different costs regime as defendants often do behave differently when they are seeking to defend a full Part 7 claim, as opposed to one proceeding within the fixed costs regime of the portal. For this reason the court held that the exit from the portal was unreasonable and the claimant should be awarded no more than the fixed costs that would have applied had the matter proceeded within the portal.

[20.8B]   Modhwadia v Modhwadia

(20 January 2015, Unreported) Leicester County Court

Following a road traffic accident on 20 November 2011 the claimant issued proceedings via the portal and liability was admitted at stage 1. The claimant provided a stage 2 pack and the defendant made a counter-offer within the requisite time scale. The claimant subsequently made a further offer. At the end of the negotiation period the claimant treated the claim as having dropped out of the portal and issued Part 7 proceedings. The parties negotiated settlement and the matter came before the court on the issue of costs. The claimant argued that the counter-offer made by the defendant did not comply with the requirements in para 7.3.4 which are mandatory. This stated that in making a counter offer the defendant must explain why a particular head of loss has been reduced. The claimant argued that by not including a reason as to why the PSLA offer had been reduced the matter had automatically dropped out of the portal. At first instance the judge held that the claimant was justified in proceeding down the Part 7 route due to the defendant's breach. However,

[20.8B] *The MOJ Process*

on oral review DJ Atkinson reversed his original decision finding that the claim had continued in the portal beyond the defendant's breach, with the claimant being able to make a further offer without the need to know the reason for the reduction. It was noted that an explanation as to the reduction of PSLA is of limited value in any event as it is not a matter that can be precisely calculated. The claimant appealed.

HELD, ON APPEAL. In dismissing the appeal Her Honour Judge Hampton accepted that the protocol makes no express provision for what should happen if there is non-compliance with para 7.3.4 – no sanction being provided. The defendant's failure was therefore no more than a technical breach and the claimant's removal from the process was therefore elective. Having considered the circumstances she agreed that the claimant had acted unreasonably in removing the matter from the portal and restricted them to portal costs.

[20.8C] Payne v Scott

(19 August 2015, unreported), LTL

The matter proceeded in the portal and the stage 2 pack included a loss of earnings claim of £4325. The defendant requested documentation in support and on the morning of the stage 3 hearing the claimant confirmed that they were not going to rely on any further evidence. The matter came before DDJ Hennessy and at that hearing the claim exited the portal and directions were given for further witness statements. The matter was compromised by the parties with the defendant making an increased offer. In relation to costs however the defendants argued that the claim had been removed from the portal inappropriately by the claimant and accordingly the claimant should be restricted to portal costs. The claimant argued that the matter was taken out of the portal as a result of a case management decision made by the deputy district judge.

HELD: Judge Smedley held that it was the claimant who had caused the matter to come out of the portal, as they, as a result of the request by their counsel, had asked the judge to remove it. It was also held that this elected removal was unreasonable and the claimant was restricted to portal costs.

2.   STAGE 1

(II) CLAIM NOTIFICATION FORM (CNF)

[20.12A]   Rafiania v All Type Scaffolding Ltd

(14 October 2015, unreported), Manchester County Court

The claimant's solicitors failed to use the portal at all because the defendant insurers had written to them denying liability. The claimant's solicitors had also received denials of liability through the portal for other people in the same vehicle as the claimant. The defendant insurers argued that the claimant's failure to use the portal meant that their costs were restricted to fixed MOJ costs. The matter proceeded to detailed assessment.

HELD: The claim should have been submitted in the normal manner under the portal scheme. It is not for the claimant to argue that this was pointless. If the claim subsequently exited the process so be it.

CPR r 45.24(2)(c) applied as the claimant did not comply with the protocol at all. There is no test of reasonableness and the sanction is a restriction on costs. This contrasts with r 45.24(2)(b) which applies where a party exits the process and the court considers whether they have acted unreasonably.

Stage 1 **[20.18A]**

The claimant was awarded portal costs only.

[20.12B] Raja v Day and MIB

(2 March 2015, unreported) Birkenhead County Court

The matter arises out of a road traffic accident that occurred on 24 April 2012. The matter gave rise to a claim that should, and which was accepted by both parties, have been piloted through the MOJ portal. Attempts were made by the claimant to instigate via the portal with a number of potential defendants. They had sent the CNF to a variety of insurers, all of whom had denied responsibility. A portal claim was never however served on the MIB who eventually ended up settling the claim and compensating the claimant. The matter came before DJ Peake who made a provisional assessment of costs and thereafter it was pursued before him by way of oral hearing. DJ Peake in assessing costs held that due to the value of the claim the matter was destined to exit the portal process in any event. This view was fundamental to his decision when finding that although there was a breach of the protocol the claimant had acted reasonably. The defendants appealed.

HELD ON APPEAL: HHJ Gregory found that the lower court had erred by considering whether the matter would have exited the portal in any event. This decision was based on the claim settling for more than the upper portal limit. By considering the value of the damages the judge had used hindsight – which he ought not to have done. By not bringing the matter within the portal there was a clear breach of the protocol and there was nothing in the reasoning of the district judge that explains why he felt the claimant's solicitors to have acted reasonably. Once the court had found that the claimant had acted unreasonably in leaving the portal the burden shifted to the claimant to show that they had acted reasonably. This it was held they did not do. The claimant was therefore restricted to portal costs and the defendant recovered their costs of defending the Part 7 proceedings.

(IV) ADMISSION OF LIABILITY

[20.18A] Malak v Nasim

[2015] LTLPI

Following a road traffic accident between Nasim and Malak, Nasim brought a claim in the portal. Malak's insurers admitted liability and dealt with Nasim's claim. Subsequently Malak made a claim through the portal which exited and Part 7 proceedings were defended. Nasim filed a defence contending that Malak was bound by his insurers' admission of liability and the case was struck out.

Malak then applied to resile from the admission of liability made by his own insurers and for the strike out order to be set aside.

Malak submitted that:
(1) An admission within the portal related solely to the subject matter of that portal claim and did not bind a driver in relation to his own personal injury claim arising out of the same accident.
(2) The determining factor was the protocol that the admission had been made under and his insurers admission had been made under the RTA protocol: CPR r 14.1B.

HELD: The insurers admission was binding between the insurer and the claimant to whom it was addressed (in this case Nasim). As CPR r 14.1B provided for withdrawal of an admission after the commencement of proceedings this implied that the admission continued to be binding after the claim had exited the portal and remained binding on a defendant personally if not withdrawn.

[20.18A] *The MOJ Process*

However, an admission made under the RTA protocol was binding only in relation to the claim within which it was made and not, as here, in relation to a potential counterclaim. The strike out order was set aside.

3. STAGE 2

(IV) OFFERS – MAKING AND ACCEPTANCE OF

[20.33A] **Bushell v Parry**

(27 March 2015, Unreported), Liverpool County Court

The claim proceeded through the RTA process to stage 2. The claimant made an offer of £11,118 including £2,950 for general damages. The defendant insurers made a counter offer of £5,152.10. This included £2,950 in respect of general damages.

The claimant served notice under Part 7.67 of the RTA protocol that the claim was unsuitable for the protocol due to the hire claim; withdrew all previous offers and issued Part 7 proceedings.

The defendant served a defence putting the claimant to strict proof in respect of the injury claim. The defendant's solicitors subsequently sent a cheque for £2,950 in respect of the general damage claim arguing that this had been compromised and the defendant's solicitors requested the matter be allocated to the small claims track.

At an allocation hearing, the matter was re-allocated to the small claims track on the basis that the general damage claim had been compromised. The claimant appealed, submitting that the protocol allowed for global offers to be made and did not provide for the compromise of individual heads of claim.

HELD: The scheme under the RTA protocol does not allow for the agreement of discreet heads of claim. If this is wrong and *Berwick Copley v Ibeh* (5 June 2014, unreported) Oxford County Court) is correct, this case can be distinguished. A full defence to the entire claim has been filed with no reference to any compromise. The defendant at no time has asked the court to enter judgment for damages and appropriate portal costs in relation to the injury claim.

On the basis of the ongoing general damage claim, the order allocating to the small claims track was set aside and the case was reallocated to the fast track.

[20.33B] **Maddocks v Lyne**

(22 January 2016, unreported), Appeal No 80/2015, Chester County Court

The claimant submitted a stage 2 pack with an offer of £2,725. This allowed £2,300 for general damages and £425 for special damages. The defendant's insurers responded with a counter offer of £1,905 for general damages and disputing all special damages. The claimant's next offer repeated the special damage claim but included the defendant's offer of £1,905 for special damages. The total figure of £2,330 was included within the Court Proceedings Pack A as against the defendant's offer of £1,905. In the Court Proceedings Pack B the claimant had inserted the original offer of £2,725. It is likely that the claimant's last offer of £1,905 for general damages at Stage 2 was made in error.

The matter proceeded to a stage 3 hearing and the defendant argued that general damages had been agreed and the hearing should be limited to the heads of claim in dispute. The district judge, following *Bushell v Parry* held that unless everything had settled at stage 2 there could be no individual agreement on a head of claim which was binding. He awarded £2,500 for general damages and £400 for special damages plus penalty interest. The defendant appealed.

In cases remaining in the protocol and proceeding to a stage 3 hearing, courts will not reconsider a compromised figure within the Court Proceedings Pack A, save in exceptional circumstances.

HELD ON APPEAL: If a claim exits the process, any offer at stage 2 is not binding in Part 7 proceedings but will be considered if appropriate in relation to costs.

In the circumstances of this case the appeal judge was not prepared to interfere with the original decision. However, he generally supported the stepped approach restricting the areas in dispute at stage 2 as advocated in *Berwick Copley v Ibeh*.

[20.34A]   Akinrodoye v Esure Services Ltd

(16 February 2015, unreported), Romford County Court

Following a road traffic accident the insurer received a CNF from the claimant's solicitor and liability was admitted in the portal. A stage 2 pack was submitted on 16 May 2014, together with an offer at that stage at £19,672.57. The defendant's insurers had issues with the medical evidence submitted and wished for medical records to be obtained with a possibility that Part 35 questions may be required. The matter therefore fell out of the portal and Part 7 proceedings were issued. As part of those Part 7 proceedings the claimant obtained further medical evidence. The matter progressed through Part 7 and negotiating offers were made. On 19 December 2014 the defendant sent an email to the claimant's solicitor accepting the 'first offer' of £19,672.57 (made at the beginning of stage 2). The claimant argued that the offer was no longer open for acceptance. The matter had fallen out of the portal since the offer had been made, and the parties had been in negotiations which, it was argued, had resulted in a 'contractual alteration of position' arguably some sort of estoppel preventing the defendant from going back to the first offer. The defendant applied for summary judgment for £19,672.57, accepting that in doing so they would be responsible for the costs of late acceptance. The claimant opposed.

HELD: In granting the defendants application for summary judgment the district judge held that a portal offer is not automatically or otherwise withdrawn simply by the matter falling out of the portal and proceeding under Part 7. The district judge was persuaded by the case of *Purcell v McGarry* at para **[20.36]**.

(VI) SETTLEMENT IN STAGE 2

[20.38A]   Budd v Abayle

(2015, unreported), Oxford County Court

The claimant served a Court Proceedings Pack before the end of stage 2. As the defendant could not make a counter-offer since it was not their turn, they uploaded a letter with an offer on to the portal. The offer was accepted and the claim settled. The claimant sought stage 3A costs and argued that the way in which the defendant's offer had been made meant that it was not a valid offer made within stage 2.

HELD: There is no rule that offers must be made sequentially and through the portal. On the facts the claimant was not entitled to stage 3A costs.

[20.57A] *The MOJ Process*

4. STAGE 3

(III) STAGE 3 HEARING

[20.57A]   Phillips v Willis
[2016] EWCA Civ 401, [2016] All ER (D) 149 (Apr)

The claimant's solicitors submitted a stage 2 pack detailing hire charges at £3,486, physiotherapy at £571 and general damages at £2,500. Full hire details were provided and a statement including a schedule of comparable hire figures.

The defendant insurers responded agreeing the claims for general damages and treatment and making a counter-offer of £2,334 for hire. Following further exchanges the amount in dispute was narrowed down to £462 and the matter proceeded to Stage 3. At the stage 3 oral hearing the district judge noted only hire was in issue. Neither party sought to rely on further evidence or to have the case transferred. However, the district judge ordered the action to proceed under CPR Part 7 on the small claims track. He ordered standard hire directions including the provision of witness evidence and financial documentation to support impecuniosity.

The claimant appealed to a circuit judge who upheld the district judge's case management decision under PD 8b paragraph 7.2. This allows for cases to continue under Part 7 where:
(1)   Further evidence must be provided by a party.
(2)   The claim is not suitable to continue under the stage 3 procedure.

The claimant appealed to the Court of Appeal. The defendant argued that the district judge was entitled to decide further evidence was needed. In addition, the RTA process applied when there was a personal injury claim but this element had been resolved.

HELD, ON APPEAL, TO THE COURT OF APPEAL: The issue was how the court should deal at Stage 3 when the personal injury claim had settled and a modest hire dispute remained.

On the facts there was no need for further evidence and the district judge's decision was 'irrational'. The case did not fall within CPR 7.2 of PD 8b.

CPR 8.1(3) was considered which states *'The court may at any stage order the claim to continue as if the claimant had not used the Part 8 procedure and, if it does so, the court may give any directions it considers appropriate'*.

Although the language was wider, this section should not be used to circumvent the RTA process.

The defendant chose not to submit hire evidence and at the hearing counsel were not given the opportunity to make submissions as to rates. The amount in dispute was £462 and the district judge's decision would cause disproportionate costs including a listing fee of £355.

When a personal injury claim is settled a case does not exit the RTA process. Parties are expected to resolve disputes as they go through the various stages.

The Court of Appeal did not specifically consider when 7.2 should operate but accepted that with very high car hire claims there might be complex issues making them unsuitable for the Stage 3 process.

CHAPTER 21

Parties

1. **CLAIMANTS**

(A) CHILDREN AND PROTECTED PARTIES

[21.1]

CPR 21 — CHILDREN AND PROTECTED PARTIES: THE LITIGATION FRIEND

'21.1

(1) This Part –

(a) contains special provisions which apply in proceedings involving children and protected parties;

(b) sets out how a person becomes a litigation friend; and

(c) does not apply to—

(i) proceedings under Part 75;

(ii) enforcement of specified debts by taking control of goods; or

(iii) applications in relation to enforcement of specified debts by taking control of goods,

where one of the parties to the proceedings is a child.

(2) In this Part –

(a) 'the 2005 Act' means the Mental Capacity Act 2005;

(b) 'child' means a person under 18;

(c) 'lacks capacity' means lacks capacity within the meaning of the 2005 Act;

(d) 'protected party' means a party, or an intended party, who lacks capacity to conduct the proceedings;

(e) 'protected beneficiary' means a protected party who lacks capacity to manage and control any money recovered by him or on his behalf or for his benefit in the proceedings.

(f) 'specified debts' has the same meaning as in rule 75.1(2)(e); and

(g) 'taking control of goods' means using the procedure to take control of goods contained in Schedule 12 to the Tribunals, Courts and Enforcement Act 20071.

21.12

(1) Subject to paragraph (1A), in proceedings to which rule 21.11 applies, a litigation friend who incurs costs or expenses on behalf of a child or protected

[21.1] *Parties*

party in any proceedings is entitled on application to recover the amount paid or payable out of any money recovered or paid into court to the extent that it –

(a) has been reasonably incurred; and

(b) is reasonable in amount.

(1A) Costs recoverable under this rule are limited to—

(a) costs incurred by or on behalf of a child and which have been assessed by way of detailed assessment pursuant to rule 46.4(2); or

(b) costs incurred by or on behalf of a child by way of success fee under a conditional fee agreement or sum payable under a damages based agreement in a claim for damages for personal injury where the damages agreed or ordered to be paid do not exceed £25,000, where such costs have been assessed summarily pursuant to rule 46.4(5).

(2) Expenses may include all or part of –

(a) a premium in respect of a costs insurance policy (as defined by section 58C(5) of the Courts and Legal Services Act 1990); or

(b) interest on a loan taken out to pay a premium in respect of a costs insurance policy or other recoverable disbursement.

(3) No application may be made under this rule for costs or expenses that –

(a) are of a type that may be recoverable on an assessment of costs payable by or out of money belonging to a child or protected party; but

(b) are disallowed in whole or in part on such an assessment.

(Costs and expenses which are also "costs" as defined in rule 44.1(1) are subject to rule 46.4(2) and (3).)

(4) In deciding whether the costs or expenses were reasonably incurred and reasonable in amount, the court will have regard to all the circumstances of the case including the factors set out in rule 44.4(3) and 46.9.

(5) When the court is considering the factors to be taken into account in assessing the reasonableness of the costs or expenses, it will have regard to the facts and circumstances as they reasonably appeared to the litigation friend or to the child's or protected party's legal representative when the cost or expense was incurred.

(6) Subject to paragraph (7), where the claim is settled or compromised, or judgment is given, on terms that an amount not exceeding £5,000 is paid to the child or protected party, the total amount the litigation friend may recover under paragraph (1) must not exceed 25% of the sum so agreed or awarded, unless the court directs otherwise. Such total amount must not exceed 50% of the sum so agreed or awarded.

(7) The amount which the litigation friend may recover under paragraph (1) in respect of costs must not (in proceedings at first instance) exceed 25% of the amount of the sum agreed or awarded in respect of—

(a) general damages for pain, suffering and loss of amenity; and

(b) damages for pecuniary loss other than future pecuniary loss, net of any sums recoverable by the Compensation Recovery Unit of the Department for Work and Pensions.

(8) Except in a case in which the costs payable to a child or protected party are fixed by these rules, no application may be made under this rule for a payment out of the money recovered by the child or protected party until the costs payable to the child or protected party have been assessed or agreed.'

(D) VEXATIOUS LITIGANTS

COURT'S POWERS TO IMPOSE RESTRAINT ORDERS

[21.17AA] Sheikh v Beaumont

[2015] EWHC 1923 (QB), [2015] All ER (D) 68 (Jul)

The claimant brought unsuccessful professional negligence proceedings against her barrister and then against a further five lawyers who had acted for her in her case against the barrister. Those claims were stayed and the claimant brought claims against a total of 16 defendants, which were struck out on the basis that there was no reasonable cause of action.

A general civil restraint order was issued against the claimant, which was extended for two years after its cessation. During the operation of the restraint order, a claim was brought in the claimant's mother's name against two further barristers who had acted against the claimant in the litigation. The restraint order was further extended against the claimant and a similar order was made against her mother, on the basis that she was being used to make further claims on behalf of the claimant in an attempt to bypass the order.

Allowing the barristers' application for a further extension of the order, the court held that there was a realistic prospect that further proceedings would be issued in the claimant's mother's name. In the circumstances, renewal of the civil restraint orders to prevent further vexatious litigation was necessary and proportionate.

CHAPTER 22

Issuing Proceedings

3. PARTICULARS OF CLAIM

(B) MATTERS WHICH MUST BE INCLUDED IN THE PARTICULARS OF CLAIM IN CERTAIN TYPES OF CLAIM

[22.16A]

'4.3A

(1) In a soft tissue injury claim, the claimant may not proceed unless the medical report is a fixed cost medical report. Where the claimant files more than one medical report, the first report obtained must be a fixed cost medical report from an accredited medical expert selected via the MedCo Portal (website at: www.medco.org.uk) and any further report from an expert in any of the following disciplines must also be a fixed cost medical report:

(a) Consultant Orthopaedic Surgeon;

(b) Consultant in Accident and Emergency Medicine;

(c) General Practitioner registered with the General Medical Council;

(d) Physiotherapist registered with the Health and Care Professions Council.

(1A) The cost of obtaining a further report from an expert not listed in paragraph (1)(a) to (d) is not subject to rule 45.29(2A)(b), but the use of that expert and the cost must be justified

(2) In this paragraph, 'accredited medical expert', 'fixed costs medical report', 'MedCo' and 'soft tissue injury claim' have the same meaning as in paragraph 1.1(A1), (10A), (12A), and (16A), respectively, of the RTA Protocol.'

CHAPTER 23

Service

1. SERVICE GENERALLY

(B) ADDRESS FOR SERVICE

CPR 6.8 & 6.9 — (Claim form)

[23.13A]   Chopra (Renu) and Vivek Rattan v Bank of Singapore Ltd and Oversea-Chinese Banking Corpn Ltd

[2015] EWHC 1549 (Ch), [2015] All ER (D) 42 (Jun)

The claimants brought proceedings in respect of alleged mis-sold bonds against the first defendant, a Singapore bank and the second defendant, their Chinese parent company. They served upon both defendants on the second defendant's premises in London. The court held they had not validly served the claim form on the first defendant in accordance with CPR r 6.9(2). The evidence did not establish that the bank was carrying on its activities or had a place of business in England. The court declined to dispense with service of the claim form under CPR r 6.16 as it was not an exceptional case. The appropriate forum for the claim was Singapore. The claim against the second defendant was struck out pursuant to CPR r 3.4(2)(a) on the ground the particulars of claim disclosed no reasonable grounds for bringing the claim.

Service on a solicitor

[23.22A]   American Leisure Group Ltd v Sir David Eardley Garrard

[2014] EWHC 2101 (Ch), [2014] 1 WLR 4102, 164 NLJ 7613

The claim was issued on 7 August 2013 with two addresses for the first defendant: one in Switzerland and one in England. The claimant made no attempt to serve it on any of the seven defendants within the following four months. On 9 January 2014 the first defendant received a court order permitting the claimant to serve outside of the jurisdiction. He instructed solicitors who informed the claimant he lived in London and they had instructions to accept service. After receiving the claim form, they applied for a declaration that service was not valid. The claimant applied for either an order that steps already taken constituted valid service, or an extension of time for service.

The claimant said that the six-month period for service should apply, because the claim form was being served outside of the jurisdiction. The court rejected that submission and said the four-month period applied as it was being served within the UK. The claimant had taken no steps to effect service within that period, when simple enquiries or attempted service in Switzerland would have revealed it should be served in England. A declaration would be made that service on the first defendant was not valid.

[23.22B] *Service*

[23.22B]   Edward Power v Meloy Whittle Robinson Solicitors
[2014] EWCA Civ 898

One month before limitation expired, the claimant sent the claim form to the court to issue, asking for it to be returned to them to serve (on the defendant's solicitors, who were nominated to accept service). In error, the court sent it to the defendant direct and did not send the claimant notice of deemed service. Correspondence was ongoing between the parties but the claimant did not serve the proceedings on the defendant's solicitors. Limitation expired and so did the four-month period for service of the claim form. The claim was struck out and the claimant appealed.

The purpose of the claim form was to demonstrate the claimants' intension to convert a potential claim into an existing claim, as the defendant already knew the nature of the case.

The relevant focus was on why the claim form could not have been served in the ordinary way during the period for its validity for service and whether steps taken to bring the claim form to the defendant's attention constituted good service. The court of appeal took into account that correspondence between the parties during that period suggested both parties considered the claim was live, and found the claim had been served effectively.

[23.22C]   Gee 7 Group Ltd v Personal Management Solutions
[2016] EWHC 891 (Ch)

Service of a claim form on solicitors who had not specifically stated that they were authorised to accept service on their client's behalf had rendered the service ineffective and it was not appropriate to order service by alternative means under r 6.15.

3.   SERVICE BY AN ALTERNATIVE METHOD

CPR 6.15 (CLAIM FORM) & 6.27 (GENERAL) – SERVICE BY AN ALTERNATIVE METHOD OR AT AN ALTERNATIVE PLACE

[23.36B]   Dunbar Assets plc v BCP Premier Ltd
[2015] EWHC 10 (Ch), [2015] All ER (D) 64 (Jan)

The respondent served a claim form on the appellant by email on the last day of service. The appellant argued that this method of service did not comply with CPR and the respondent was out of time for service.

The respondent applied to the court for an extension of time for service and/or relief from sanctions and a deputy master allowed the application and ordered that there had been good service.

The appellant appealed against the order and the appeal was allowed. The deputy master had been wrong to conclude on the facts that there was a good reason to make an order under CPR r 6.15. The court would not exercise its discretion in favour of granting the order as the respondent had not explained why the claim form was not served in accordance with the CPR and it would prejudice the appellant by denying it a limitation defence.

[23.36C]   Barton v Wright Hassall LLP
[2016] EWCA Civ 177, [2016] All ER (D) 202 (Mar)

Paragraph 4.1 of CPR PD 6A provides that email is not a permitted method of service unless the defendant (or its solicitor) has supplied an email address, and has stated that the e-mail address may be used for service. The court would not validate service by an alternative method (ie email) by reason only that the claimant was a litigant in person and had brought the claim form to the attention of the defendant by email prior to expiry of the period for service. This would not amount to 'a good reason to authorise service' in accordance with CPR r 6.15(1), which would inevitably include focus on why the claim form could not be served within the period of its validity, absent any 'technical game playing' by a defendant.

The first instance judge found there was no obligation on a defendant's solicitor to notify a litigant in person before the claim form expired of their intention to challenge service (in the instant case, the period expired on 25 June 2013 and proceedings were emailed by way of purported service on 24 June 2013).

Where the claimant had:
(a) received correspondence with the correct address for service;
(b) been advised that an extension of time would not be agreed; and
(c) been reminded after issue but prior to expiry that service remained awaited, no indulgences would be granted to a litigant in person by virtue only of their absence of legal representation.

5. EXTENDING TIME FOR SERVICE

(B) EXTENDING TIME FOR SERVICE OF THE CLAIM FORM

THE REASON FOR THE APPLICATION TO EXTEND THE TIME HAS TO BE EX-PLAINED TO THE COURT'S SATISFACTION

[23.59BA]   Hallam Estates Ltd and Michael Stainer v Baker
[2014] EWCA Civ 661, 164 NLJ 7608, [2014] 4 Costs LR 660

Following the first appeal decision (see para **[23.59B]**), this is the claimant's appeal to the Court of Appeal, arguing that the judge was wrong to determine that its application for an extension of time was an application for relief from sanctions and that as a result the judge should not have interfered with the costs judge's case management decisions.

It was held that the application for an extension was made before the expiry of the time period for filing points of dispute, as it was filed on that day but not stamped by court staff until the following day, which was immaterial. The court found that an application for an extension of time to take any particular step in litigation was not an application for relief from sanctions provided the applicant filed his application notice before the expiry of the permitted time period, even if the court dealt with the application after the expiry of the relevant time period. Accordingly the costs judge was dealing with a straightforward application for an extension of time and the principles concerning relief from sanctions in *Mitchell v News Group Newspapers Ltd* [2013] EWCA Civ 1537, [2014] 2 All ER 430, [2014] 1 WLR 795 did not apply.

It was also held that when H asked B to agree an extension of time, they had given sensible reasons for the request and B should have agreed given its own delays. Given r 3.8 of the CPR was soon to be amended, parties would be able to agree a time extension of up to 28 days without reference to the court provided that it did not put at risk any hearing date. Under r 1.3 parties had a duty to help the court in furthering the overriding objective and legal representatives were not in breach of any duty to their client when they agreed to a reasonable extension of time which did not affect future hearing dates or disrupt the litigation. The court also should not refuse to grant reasonable extensions of time in such circumstances.

[23.59F] *Service*

[23.59F]   OOO Abbott and Godfrey Victor Chasmer v Econowall UK Ltd, Project Consultancy and Construction Ltd, Smith Brewer Ltd and Retail Display Connections Ltd
[2016] EWHC 660 (IPEC), [2016] All ER (D) 41 (Apr)

In proceedings concerning breach of an alleged licence agreement, the defendant granted the claimant an extension to serve the signed claim form and the particulars of claim by 15 November 2015; the original date for service was 3 November 2015. The claimant's solicitors misread the letter granting the extension and thought they had an extension until 3 December 2015. The claim form and particulars were served on 25 November 2015 and the defendant applied to strike the claim out. The claimant sought to establish that there had been good service.

The court held that the claim form was served out of time because the claimant's solicitors made an honest mistake; however a reasonable reader of their response would have known that and the defendant made a decision to take no steps to clear up the misunderstanding. The court acknowledged that each party to a litigation has to look after itself, and there was no obligation to inform the opposing side of its mistake. However, this is subject to the overriding objective which requires parties to take reasonable steps to ensure there is a clear and common understanding as to the identity of the substantive and procedural issues. To do otherwise would waste money and court resources. Accordingly, the defendant should have informed the claimant's solicitors of their mistake and the court exercised its discretion to authorise service retrospectively on the basis that the defendant's conduct fell short of the overriding objective. Further, the claimant's solicitors had provided an unsigned photocopy of the claim form to the defendant shortly after the issue of proceedings, so the defendant knew the contents of the claim form in any event. Good service was deemed to have been achieved by delivery of the photocopied unsigned claim form on 6 July 2015 and time for service of the particulars of claim was extended.

(C) EXTENDING TIME FOR SERVICE OF PARTICULARS OF CLAIM

CPR 7.4 – PARTICULARS OF CLAIM

[23.61]

'CPR 7.4 - Particulars of claim

(1) Particulars of claim must –

(a) be contained in or served with the claim form; or

(b) subject to paragraph (2) be served on the defendant by the claimant within 14 days after service of the claim form.

(2) Particulars of claim must be served on the defendant no later than the latest time for serving a claim form.

(Rule 7.5 sets out the latest time for serving a claim form)

(3) Where the claimant serves particulars of claim, then unless a copy of the particulars has already been filed, the claimant must, within 7 days of service on the defendant, file a copy of the particulars except where –

(a) paragraph 5.2(4) of Practice Direction 7C applies; or

(b) paragraph 6.4 of Practice Direction 7E applies.'

CHAPTER 24

Defence

1. RESPONDING TO PARTICULARS OF CLAIM

(B) ACKNOWLEDGEMENT OF SERVICE

CPR 10.3 – THE PERIOD FOR FILING AN ACKNOWLEDGEMENT OF SERVICE

[24.7A] Sharon Hockley v North Lincolnshire & Goole NHS Foundation Trust
(2014) unreported, HC

The claimant issued proceedings due to limitation and the defendant filed the acknowledgment of service 13 days out of time, meanwhile the claimant applied for default judgment which was granted the day after the acknowledgment was filed. The claimant then appealed against a decision to set the default judgment aside.

HELD: Granted. The court stressed the importance of filing an acknowledgment of service of proceedings in time when it allowed the claimant's appeal against the decision to set aside the default judgment. Failure to acknowledge the particulars of claim was a serious default.

2. DEFAULT JUDGMENT

(B) PROCEDURE

CPR 12.10 – CIRCUMSTANCES WHERE AN APPLICATION MUST BE MADE

[24.13]

'The claimant must make an application in accordance with Part 23 where–

(a) the claim is–

(i) a claim against a child or patient; or

(ii) a claim in tort by one spouse or civil partner against the other.

(b) the claimant wishes to obtain a default judgment where the defendant has failed to file an acknowledgment of service–

(i) against a defendant who has been served with the claim out of the jurisdiction under rule 6.32(1), 6.33(1), 6.33(2) or 6.33(2B); (service where permission of the court is not required under the Civil Jurisdiction and Judgments Act 19824);

(ii) against a defendant domiciled in Scotland or Northern Ireland or in any other Convention territory or Regulation State;

(iii) against a State;

[24.13] *Defence*

(iv) against a diplomatic agent who enjoys immunity from civil jurisdiction by virtue of the Diplomatic Privileges Act 1964(5); or

(v) against persons or organisations who enjoy immunity from civil jurisdiction pursuant to the provisions of the International Organisations Acts 1968 and 1981.'

(C) SUBSEQUENT PROCEDURAL STEPS

CPR 12.7 – PROCEDURE FOR DECIDING AN AMOUNT OR VALUE

[24.17A]   Timothy Symes v St George's Healthcare NHS Trust
[2014] EWHC 2505 (QB), 140 BMLR 171, [2014] All ER (D) 292 (Jul)

The defendant appealed against a decision preventing it from raising causation as an argument after judgment in default had been entered. It was argued that default judgment related to liability and it would be inappropriate to assume that a defendant should automatically be held liable for all losses claimed as a result of judgment being entered.

HELD: Granted. It was held that default judgment established some loss only. The CPR did not stop causation arguments being raised at a quantum hearing, particularly where causation had been disputed in pre-action correspondence.

3.   SETTING ASIDE OR VARYING DEFAULT JUDGMENT

(B) THE COURT'S DISCRETION TO SET ASIDE OR VARY DEFAULT JUDGMENTS

JUDGMENT WHERE THE DEFENDANT HAS NO NOTICE OF PROCEEDINGS IS A REGULAR JUDGMENT

[24.21A]   Khalid Hussain v Robert Parry
(2014) unreported

The claimant elected to exit the RTA portal by giving notice to the defendant's insurer that they would be issuing Part 7 proceedings. Despite being contacted by the defendant insurer's solicitors who confirmed that they were nominated to accept service of proceedings, no contact was made with the claimant's solicitors. It transpired that the claimant's solicitors had already issued directly against the defendant insured at his last known address.

The matter proceeded to a disposal hearing where damages were to be assessed. The claimant's solicitor faxed a trial bundle to the defendant's insurer at 4:26pm the day before the hearing and was subsequently awarded damages and costs at the hearing. The defendant's insurer applied to have the judgment set aside however this was refused. The defendant's insurer appealed.

HELD: Granted. It was wrong not to consider the position of the insurers who plainly would have attended had they known of the trial. The judge was also wrong to find that the insurers had known of the trial the day before. It was quite unrealistic to expect the insurers to deal with the fax or to understand the details of it at the end of the afternoon or the following morning in order for them to arrange representation. Judgment set aside.

Admissions **[24.32]**

THE TEST (2) – DEFENDANT MUST SHOW 'SOME OTHER GOOD REASON'

[24.25A]   Sharon Hockley v North Lincolnshire & Goole NHS Foundation Trust
(2014) unreported, HC

The defendant filed the acknowledgment of service 13 days out of time, meanwhile the claimant applied for default judgment which was granted the day after the acknowledgment was filed. The defendant applied to have the judgment set aside which was dealt with by telephone hearing where the application was granted. The judge held that 'fairness and justice' was good enough reason to set the judgment aside. The claimant then appealed against a decision to set the default judgment aside.

HELD: Granted. The failure to acknowledge the particulars of claim was a serious default and the claimant was entitled to take advantage and apply for default judgment, as this would save her costs in not having to prove her case. The procedural advantage would also save court time. The assertion that it is preferable for cases to be decided on evidence will not suffice. In addition, the judge said that telephone hearings are not suitable where there is a difficult factual matrix.

4.   ADMISSIONS

(A)   CPR PT 14

CPR 14.1 – ADMISSIONS MADE BEFORE COMMENCEMENT OF PROCEEDINGS

[24.32]

'(1) A party may admit the truth of the whole or any part of another party's case.

(2) The party may do this by giving notice in writing (such as in a statement of case or by letter).

(3) Where the only remedy which the claimant is seeking is the payment of money, the defendant may also make an admission in accordance with–

(a) rule 14.4 (admission of whole claim for specified amount of money);

(b) rule 14.5 (admission of part of claim for specified amount of money);

(c) rule 14.6 (admission of liability to pay whole of claim for unspecified amount of money); or

(d) rule 14.7 (admission of liability to pay claim for unspecified amount of money where defendant offers a sum in satisfaction of the claim).

(4) Where the defendant makes an admission as mentioned in paragraph (3), the claimant has a right to enter judgment except where–

(a) the defendant is a child or protected party ; or

(b) the claimant is a child or protected party and the admission is made under rule 14.5 or 14.7.

(5) The permission of the court is required to amend or withdraw an admission.'

[24.41E] *Defence*

(C) APPLICATIONS TO WITHDRAW AN ADMISSION

TEST TO BE APPLIED

[24.41E]   Philip Cavell v Transport for London

[2015] EWHC 2283 (QB), [2015] All ER (D) 36 (Aug)

The claimant fell from his bicycle due to uneven ground, in particular a pothole. He notified the defendant and attached a clear digital image of the accident scene. The defendant instructed a claims handling firm to investigate who issued a denial of liability on the basis of regular inspection with no defects being identified. The claimant sent further images 1½ years later which showed the pothole was still present. After the claimant instructed solicitors, the claims handling firm made an admission within 24 hours. The defendant then sought to withdraw this pre-action admission.

HELD: Refused. The admission had been made by competent professional advisers with experience in the type of claim being pursued. There was no new evidence to undermine the admission and as such it was not in the interests of justice to permit the withdrawal.

It should be noted that this admission did not prevent the defendant claiming a contribution or indemnity from the contractor responsible for inspection and repair of the road.

[24.41F]   S E Wood v Days Health UK Ltd

[2016] EWHC 1079 (QB), [2016] All ER (D) 85 (May)

The claimant asserted that her wheelchair's seat riser unit had malfunctioned, propelling her forwards and causing her significant injury. She had been supplied with the chair with the seat riser as an add-on unit by her local care trust, D2, which had bought the chair and riser from D5 which had obtained them from another supplier, D1. The riser had been supplied by a manufacturer, D4. After the accident, the claimant brought proceedings in contract, under statute and in tort against all those involved in the production and supply o the chair. D1 made a pre-action admission but when it realised that D2 had fitted new components, it sought to withdraw the admission on the basis that the chair was no longer the one it had supplied.

HELD: Refused. D1 would not be permitted to withdraw its admission. The admission had been made following an inspection of the chair by D1 and reasonable steps had been taken to investigate and D1 would have discovered the post-supply modifications at that time. The fact that the potential value of the claim had increased was no justification to permit a withdrawal of the admission. There had also been considerable delay by D1 before indicating its intention to resile from the admission and both the claimant and D2 would be prejudiced by the withdrawal. On the other hand, D1 had reasonable prospects of defending a claim and could claim a contribution from D2 and D4.

The claimant had reasonably issued proceedings against D1, D2 and D4 and had concurrent causes of action against all three. The entry of summary judgment against D2 was not a reason for allowing D1 to withdraw the admission as the liability of one defendant did not extinguish that of another in respect of a different cause of action.

8. AMENDMENTS TO THE DEFENCE

[24.62] LBI HF (formerly Landsbani Island HF) v Kevin Gerald Stanford & Landsbanki Luxembourg SA

[2014] EWHC 3273 (Comm)

The defendant made an application on the 2nd day of the trial to serve a third amendment to his additional defence and counter claim. The said application was made shortly before the claimant's witnesses were due to give evidence.

HELD: Refused. The application had been much too late and would cause significant prejudice to the claimant were it to be allowed. There was no reason why the issues in question could not have been dealt with at an earlier stage.

CHAPTER 25

Summary Judgment

1. SUMMARY JUDGMENT

(B) THE TEST – 'NO REAL PROSPECT OF SUCCESS'

Meaning of 'real prospect of success'

[25.6D] PM Law Ltd v Motorplus Ltd and Members of Equity 218 at Lloyds (t/a Equity Red Star)
[2016] EWHC 193 (QB), [2016] All ER (D) 89 (Feb)

The claimants, a firm of solicitors, had entered into a referral agreement with an insurance agent in relation to legal expenses insurance policies. When the agent ceased making referrals, the solicitors sued for lost profits together with monies allegedly due to them under the policies issued to their clients.

HELD: The solicitors were unable to recover from the agent, whether contractually or by way of restitution, monies allegedly due under the policies. The policies had been issued in favour of their clients and the solicitors were not a party to them. As such, the court struck out parts of the solicitors' claim against the agent and awarded summary judgment to the first defendant as the claimant had no real prospect of succeeding with his claim.

2. PROCEDURE

(A) WHEN AN APPLICATION CAN BE MADE

CPR 24.4 – Procedure

[25.12B] Greig v Anthony Francis Stirling and Anthony Tomas Etridge
[2014] EWHC 4017 (QB), [2014] All ER (D) 20 (Dec)

The claimant applied to set aside an order striking out his claim against the second defendant and an order to pay the second defendant's costs. The second defendant applied to strike out the claim on the basis that the claimant was guilty of unreasonable delay in progressing the claim and had failed to comply with an order to substitute the first defendant's executors for the first defendant. The application was dealt with on paper without a hearing.

HELD: It would be unjust and disproportionate to deny the claimant the opportunity to apply to set aside an order which had put an end to his entire claim against the second defendant when that order was made without a hearing and without the claimant having submitted evidence or representations. Dismissal of the claim without investigation of its merits would be an excessive sanction for a procedural default.

[25.12C] *Summary Judgment*

[25.12C] Lewis v Ward Hadaway (A Firm)

[2015] EWHC 3503 (Ch), [2016] 4 WLR 6

The claimants issued proceedings very close to the end of the limitation period and deliberately understated the value of their claims in order to pay reduced issue fees and to stop the limitation period from running. The defendant applied for the striking out of claims brought against it on the ground of alleged abuse of process. Alternatively, the defendant applied for summary judgment on limitation grounds.

HELD: Application granted. The claimants' conduct was found to be an abuse of process and they had not done all that was in their power to set the wheels of justice in motion and bring the matter before the court. Since the appropriate fee had not been paid in time, the defendant's application for summary judgment succeeded.

(B) CONTENT OF THE APPLICATION NOTICE

Practice Direction to CPR 24 – Procedure for making an application

[25.13A] Bhatti v Ashgar

[2016] EWHC 1049 (QB)

The defendant applied for summary judgment or to strike out the claimant's claim due to failure to pay the correct fees and the resultant expiry of the limitation period.

HELD: Application refused. The limitation period had never been pleaded as a defence, nor had it been mentioned in the summary judgment application. There was no excuse for raising it at a late stage and the claimant's had been denied a reasonable opportunity to address the defendant's arguments.

CHAPTER 26

Additional Claims

5. PROCEDURAL MATTERS COMMON TO ALL ADDITIONAL CLAIMS

(B) APPLICATION FOR PERMISSION TO MAKE AN ADDITIONAL CLAIM

Practice Direction to CPR 20, paragraph 2

[26.16A]   XYZ v Various (Including Transform Medical Group (CS) Ltd and Spire Healthcare Ltd)

[2014] EWHC 4056 (QB), [2014] All ER (D) 85 (Dec)

A defendant in group litigation applied pursuant to CPR rr 19.2 & 3.1(2), 20.96, to join a non-party insurer to proceedings, or alternatively, to obtain a declaration from them as to the limit of indemnity applicable to the policy of insurance held by defendant in the action.

The court refused the application to join the non-party insurer. All of the matters in the litigation were capable of being resolved without adding them in to the proceeding. Furthermore, the rules were not available to claimants in personal injury cases to establish the depths of another party's pockets and to permit the application would be to set a dangerous precedent. Establishing in advance how much money a defendant potentially had was not a matter of case management.

6. COSTS OF A PART 20 CLAIM WHERE THE MAIN ACTION FAILS

(A) WHEN AN APPLICATION CAN BE MADE

[26.25A]   Wagenaar v Weekend Travel Ltd (t/a Ski Weekend)

[2014] EWHC Civ 1105, [2016] 1 All ER 643, [2015] 1 WLR 1968

The claimant had been injured in a skiing accident whilst on a package holiday arranged by D. D denied negligence and joined the ski instructor as a third party. The judge dismissed C's claim against D and D's claim against the third party. He ordered that C should pay D's costs and that D should pay the third party's costs. Applying the rules of QOCS, the judge ordered that neither costs order was to be enforced. As such, the judge held that the QOCS rules applied to Part 20 claims in the same way as they applied to primary claims between claimant and defendant.

The third party submitted that the judge had erred in holding that the QOCS rules applied to Part 20 proceedings.

HELD: The judge had erred in holding that the QOCS rules applied to the Part 20 claim against the third party. As a result, the third party's application was allowed and the defendant was ordered to pay the third party's costs to be assessed

[26.25A] *Additional Claims*

on the standard basis if not agreed.

CHAPTER 27

Allocation

1. **GENERALLY**

(B) PRELIMINARY MATTERS

CPR 26.2A – Transfer of money claims within the County Court

[27.3A]

'(1) This rule applies where the claim is for an amount of money in the County Court, specified or unspecified.

(2) If at any time a court officer considers that the claim should be referred to a judge for directions, the court officer may send the proceedings to the preferred court or the defendant's home court or such other court as may be appropriate.

(3) Subject to paragraph (5), if the defendant is an individual, at the relevant time the claim will be sent to the defendant's home court (save that where there are two or more defendants, one or more of whom are individuals, the claim will be sent to the home court of the defendant who first files their defence).

(4) Subject to paragraph (5), in any other claim to which this rule applies, the court will, at the relevant time, send the claim to the preferred court.

(5) If, on their directions questionnaire—

(a) a defendant under paragraph (3) has specified a hearing centre other than the defendant's home court; or

(b) a claimant under paragraph (4) has specified a hearing centre other than the preferred hearing centre,

(6) The relevant time for the purposes of this rule is when –

(a) all parties have filed their directions questionnaires;

(b) any stay ordered by the court or period to attempt settlement through mediation has expired; or

(c) if the claim falls within Practice Direction 7D –

(i) the defence is filed; or

(ii) enforcement of a default judgment other than by a warrant of control is requested, whichever occurs first.'

[27.11B] *Allocation*

CPR 26.8 – Matters relevant to allocation to a track

[27.11B]   Cammack v Naqvi

(2015) unreported, CC

In a claim concerning vehicle repair-related damages, the court allocated the matter to the fast track, applying CPR 26.8, notwithstanding the fact that the sum in dispute was just over £9,200 and the matter would normally have fallen within the Small Claims Track. The defendant had raised complex agency arguments which increased the importance of the case in terms of its general applicability which removed the matter from the remit of the Small Claims Track.

CPR 26.10 – Re-allocation

[27.17A]   Edward Williams v Santander UK Plc

(2015) unreported, CC

The claimant sought to have the matter re-allocated to the Fast Track, referring to a request to rely on expert evidence while also considering the alleged complexity of the facts and the law and the evidence that would be required.

HELD: The original judge had given considered allocation, having provided detailed reasoning for his decision at the start of the Order. In particular, the judge had stated that the costs likely to be incurred by allocation to any other track would be wholly disproportionate to the sums in issue. It was conceded by the claimant that the matter was a small value claim, at best in the region of £7,500. No new information had come to light since the original judge's allocation, nor had there been any change in circumstance. As such, there was no good reason why the claim should be re-allocated.

CHAPTER 28

Disclosure

1. PRE-ACTION DISCLOSURE

(A) TEXT OF THE PRE-ACTION PROTOCOL FOR PERSONAL INJURY CLAIMS RELEVANT TO DISCLOSURE

NOTES OF GUIDANCE

[28.1]

6. The Response

6.5 If a defendant denies liability and/or causation, their version of events should be supplied. The defendant should also enclose with the response, documents in their possession which are material to the issues between the parties, and which would be likely to be ordered to be disclosed by the court, either on an application for pre-action disclosure, or on disclosure during proceedings. No charge will be made for providing copy documents under the Protocol.

7.1 Documents

7.1.1 The aim of early disclosure of documents by the defendant is not to encourage 'fishing expeditions' by the claimant, but to promote an early exchange of relevant information to help in clarifying or resolving issues in dispute. The claimant's solicitor can assist by identifying in the Letter of Claim or in a subsequent letter the particular categories of documents which they consider are relevant and why, with a brief explanation of their purported relevance if necessary.

7.1.2 Attached at Annexe C are specimen, but non-exhaustive, lists of documents likely to be material in different types of claim.

7.1.3 Pre-action disclosure will generally be limited to the documents required to be enclosed with the Letter of Claim and the Response. In cases where liability is admitted in full, disclosure will be limited to the documents relevant to quantum, the parties can agree that further disclosure may be given. If either or both of the parties consider that further disclosure should be given but there is disagreement about some aspect of that process, they may be able to make an application to the court for pre-action disclosure under Part 31 of the CPR. Parties should assist each other and avoid the necessity for such an application.

7.1.4 The protocol should also contain a requirement that the defendant is under a duty to preserve the disclosure documents and other evidence (CCTV for example). If the documents are destroyed, this could be an abuse of the court process.

Note – Annex C is not reproduced here – reference should be made to *The Civil Court Practice*, published by LexisNexis Butterworths.

[28.5B] *Disclosure*

(B) APPLICATION TO THE COURT FOR PRE-ACTION DISCLOSURE

GENERALLY

[28.5B]   Bromley London Borough Council v Stephen Heckel
[2015] EWHC 3606 (TCC), [2015] All ER (D) 117 (Dec)

The claimant applied for disclosure of documents together with an extension of time for service of the Particulars of Claim. The court dismissed the application for disclosure because the defendant was not in possession of them and it was likely that the claimant would have copies of the documents in any event.

MEANING OF 'LIKELY TO BE A PARTY TO SUBSEQUENT PROCEEDINGS'

[28.6E]   Jet Airways (India) Ltd v Barloworld Handling Ltd
[2014] EWCA Civ 1311, [2014] All ER (D) 133 (Oct)

The respondent applied for pre-action disclosure of maintenance documents relating to forklift trucks which were supplied and maintained by the appellant and an associated company after the respondent's cargo handling depot was destroyed by fire which was started by a forklift truck. The appellant opposed the application as speculative. The judge at first instance disagreed with the appellant and made the order for disclosure which was subsequently appealed.

HELD, ON APPEAL: CPR, r 31.16 required no more than that the parties to the application would be likely to be involved in proceedings if any were started. Since the appellant had undertaken routine maintenance of the trucks, which had been the source of the fire resulting in the loss, if the respondent started proceedings, the appellant was likely to be a party to them. There was also sufficient evidence to suggest that the case was not merely speculative.

2.   STANDARD DISCLOSURE

(A) WHAT IS STANDARD DISCLOSURE?

CPR 31.6 – STANDARD DISCLOSURE – WHAT DOCUMENTS ARE TO BE DISCLOSED

[28.14B]   Euro-Asian Oil SA v Abilo (UK) Ltd, Credit Suisse AG and Dan Igniska
[2015] EWHC 1741 (Comm), [2015] All ER (D) 239 (Jun)

The parties had agreed by consent to provide standard disclosure and inspection. In the event that the defendants did not comply with this order, it was agreed that their defences would be struck out and judgment entered against them.

The defendants disclosed a 'few documents' which the claimant concluded did not comply with the unless order. The claimant alleged that the defendants' attempts at disclosure had not been made in good-faith and subsequently requested judgment, which the court granted.

The first and third defendants sought to set aside the judgment.

HELD: The court found that the claimant had not shown there was an 'illusory' list of documents, or they had been served in bad faith. The test had not been met and therefore judgment was set aside.

3. SPECIFIC DISCLOSURE

CPR 31.12 – SPECIFIC DISCLOSURE OR INSPECTION

[28.29D] Luftu Ali v CIS General Insurance
(2015) Unreported, CA

The claimant was involved in a road traffic accident after which she sought the cost of damage to her vehicle, recovery, storage and credit hire charges. The following week she sustained another accident whilst driving another family car. The day after the 2nd accident, a credit hire vehicle in respect of the 1st accident was delivered to the claimant.

The defendant doubted whether there was any need for a hire vehicle or, if so, whether this related to the 1st accident. As such, the defendant obtained an order for specific disclosure as to details of all accidents the claimant had been involved in within five years prior to and subsequent to the index accident, which should include medical reports and details of special damages. The claimant failed to comply and the claim was subsequently struck out.

The claimant later appealed against the strike out but the court held that there was no good reason for non-compliance.

CHAPTER 29

Witnesses

1. WITNESS STATEMENTS

(D) USE OF WITNESS STATEMENTS AT TRIAL

CPR 32.5 – USE AT TRIAL OF WITNESS STATEMENTS WHICH HAVE BEEN SERVED

[29.7A] Donald MacLeod (a protected party by his litigation friend Barbara Macleod) v Metropolitan Police Comr

[2015] EWCA Civ 688, [2015] All ER (D) 98 (Jul)

The claimant was a cyclist who suffered a serious head injury after being hit by a police car responding to an emergency call at a junction. The dispute as to who caused the accident centred on the direction the cyclist was travelling in, however, the claimant's head injury rendered him unable to give evidence.

The judge at first instance relied upon two independent witnesses in drawing an inference that the claimant had been travelling in the same direction as the police car and was hit from behind, meaning that the accident had been caused by the negligence of the police driver. The decision was appealed.

HELD: Appeal dismissed. The judge had been entitled to rely upon the two independent witnesses and to apply his common sense and experience when evaluating the totality of the evidence.

CPR 32.10 – PERMISSION REQUIRED TO RELY UPON WITNESS STATEMENT SERVED LATE

[29.9A] Riff Trading Ltd (in liq) and Timothy James Bramston v John Saunders (dec'd)

[2014] EWHC 2116 (Ch)

The defendants applied for relief from sanction after they failed to comply with orders requiring them to file and serve witness evidence, including an unless order.

HELD: The court granted relief so the defendants could rely on witness evidence on the basis that they served their evidence and paid the claimant's costs of the application within a specific period and ordered that, even if the defendants were successful at trial, they would not recover any costs whatsoever from the claimants.

CHAPTER 30

Evidence and Admissibility

1. THE COURT'S GENERAL POWER TO CONTROL EVIDENCE

POWER MUST BE EXERCISED IN ACCORDANCE WITH THE OVERRIDING OBJECTIVE

[30.7B] Stobart Group Ltd, William Andrew Tinkler, William Stobart, Eddie Stobart Ltd, WA Developments International Ltd v Peter Elliott

[2015] EWCA Civ 449, [2015] All ER (D) 121 (May)

The claimant served an expert psychiatric report two months late and, despite being given permission by the court to apply for an extension of time to vary the order made at the CMC, the claimant failed to do so. The claimant subsequently appealed against a decision dismissing his application for an extension of time for service of the report.

HELD: Appeal dismissed. The Court of Appeal held that the judge had properly exercised his discretion in refusing to give the claimant a further extension to serve the psychiatric report.

[30.7C] Desmond Atkins v Co-Operative Group Ltd

[2016] EWHC 80 (QB), [2016] All ER (D) 205 (Jan)

The court decided that the defendant should be permitted to adduce fresh evidence in the form of a report by an expert in cardio thoracic radiology in which it was concluded that the claimant had not developed asbestosis. This new evidence could not have previously been obtained by reasonable diligence.

3. SURVEILLANCE EVIDENCE

[30.12D] Watson v Ministry of Defence

(8 April 2016, unreported, QBD), Yelton J

The claimant brought a claim for injury including a hip problem which left her unable to work, permanently crippled and in severe pain.

The claimant's expert found in November 2015 that the level of restriction displayed by the claimant was disproportionate. The defendant's expert had seen a video of the claimant and concluded in his February 2016 report that her inability to bend over and pick things up was either through fear or conscious exaggeration.

The defendant decided that video surveillance of the claimant was necessary and she was observed picking things up from the floor.

The surveillance was obtained in March 2016 and disclosed to the claimant the following week.

HELD: The surveillance was of clear significance, especially given the observations of the claimant's expert about checking the claimant's behaviour in the examination room against her behaviour in day-to-day life.

[30.12D] *Evidence and Admissibility*

The claimant's submission that the defendant should have obtained surveillance evidence in November 2015 following the claimant's expert's report was wrong. The defendant was entitled to obtain its own expert report first. Its application did not amount to an ambush of the claim, albeit late in the day. It was in the interests of justice to admit the surveillance.

[30.12E]   Hayden v Maidstone & Tunbridge Wells NHS Trust
[2016] EWHC 1121 (QB), [2016] All ER (D) 108 (May)

The defendant NHS trust admitted liability but later applied to rely on surveillance evidence relating to the severity of the claimant's alleged injuries.

The surveillance evidence was obtained in February and March 2016 close to the start of the trial window.

The evidence had been seen by the defendant's pain medicine expert and had produced a supplemental report starting that the footage was supportive of his view. Consequently, the trial date was vacated to give the claimant an opportunity to consider her position.

The defendant contended that once the evidence was available, it was in the interests of justice that it remain in play.

HELD: The judge was highly critical of the fact that there had been every reason for the defendant to commission surveillance evidence at least from May 2015. The delay in obtaining the evidence was unexplained and unreasonable. That being said, the overall interests of justice required that the surveillance evidence be considered in the round at trial.

A very significant factor in deciding whether to accede to a late application was the time when a defendant should reasonably commission such evidence. Once the claimant's case had been clearly articulated and the defendant had an opinion from an expert that the claim was suspect, the obligation actively to obtain surveillance evidence arose if it was considered a proportionate approach to adopt in the particular case.

CHAPTER 31

Expert Evidence

1. PROTOCOL FOR THE INSTRUCTION OF EXPERTS TO GIVE EVIDENCE IN CIVIL CLAIMS

(B) GUIDANCE FOR THE INSTRUCTION OF EXPERTS TO GIVE EVIDENCE IN CIVIL CLAIMS

[31.1] Any instruction issued to an expert after 5 September 2005 is governed by a Code of Practice introduced by the Civil Justice Council, the Protocol for the Instruction of Experts to give evidence in civil claims. The Protocol was amended in October 2009 and replaced in 2012 by the Civil Justice Council's 'Guidance for the Instruction of Experts to Give Evidence in Civil Claims'. This guidance was then further updated in August 2014 and should be referred to when considering instruction of experts.

The Civil Justice Council's guidance for the instruction of experts in civil claims (which replaced the protocol that was annexed to Practice Direction 35 of the Civil Procedure Rules) entered into force on 1 December 2014 and may be accessed at: https://www.judiciary.gov.uk/related-offices-and-bodies/advisory-bodies/cjc/cjc-publications/guidance-for-the-instruction-of-experts-in-civil-claims/

2. INSTRUCTING EXPERTS UNDER THE PERSONAL INJURY PRE-ACTION PROTOCOL

(A) TEXT OF THE PROTOCOL RELEVANT TO INSTRUCTING EXPERTS

[31.3] Experts

7.2 Save for cases likely to be allocated to the multi-track, the Protocol encourages joint selection of, and access to, quantum experts, and, on occasion liability experts e.g. engineers. The expert report produced is not a joint report for the purposes of CPR Part 35. The Protocol promotes the practice of the claimant obtaining a medical report, disclosing it to the defendant who then asks questions and/or agrees it and does not obtain their own report. The Protocol provides for nomination of the expert by the claimant in personal injury claims.

7.3 Before any party instructs an expert, they should give the other party a list of the name(s) of one or more experts in the relevant speciality whom they consider are suitable to instruct.

7.4 Some solicitors choose to obtain medical reports through medical agencies, rather than directly from a specific doctor or hospital. The defendant's prior consent to this should be sought and, if the defendant so requests,

[31.3] *Expert Evidence*

the agency should be asked to provide in advance the names of the doctor(s) whom they are considering instructing.

7.5 Where a medical expert is to be instructed, the claimant's solicitor will organise access to relevant medical records – see specimen letter of instruction at Annexe D.

7.6 Within 14 days of providing a list of experts the other party may indicate an objection to one or more of the named experts. The first party should then instruct a mutually acceptable expert assuming there is one (this is not the same as a joint expert). It must be emphasised that when the claimant nominates an expert in the original Letter of Claim, the defendant has a further 14 days to object to one or more of the named experts after expiration of the 21 day period within which they have to reply to the Letter of Claim, as set out in paragraph 6.2.

7.7 If the defendant objects to all the listed experts, the parties may then instruct experts of their own choice. It will be for the court to decide, subsequently and if proceedings are issued, whether either party had acted unreasonably.

7.8 If the defendant does not object to an expert nominated by the claimant, they shall not be entitled to rely on their own expert evidence within that expert's area of expertise unless—
(a)   the claimant agrees;
(b)   the court so directs; or
(c)   the claimant's expert report has been amended and the claimant is not prepared to disclose the original report.

7.9 Any party may send to an agreed expert written questions on the report, via the first party's solicitors. Such questions must be put within 28 days of service of the expert's report and must only be for the purpose of clarification of the report. The expert should send answers to the questions simultaneously to each party.

7.10 The cost of a report from an agreed expert will usually be paid by the instructing first party: the costs of the expert replying to questions will usually be borne by the party which asks the questions.

7.11 If necessary, after proceedings have commenced and with the permission of the court, the parties may obtain further expert reports. It would be for the court to decide whether the costs of more than one expert's report should be recoverable.

3.   INSTRUCTION OF EXPERTS AFTER PROCEEDINGS

(A) THE EXPERT'S OVERRIDING DUTY TO THE COURT

DUTIES AND RESPONSIBILITIES OF EXPERT WITNESSES

[31.6A]   Kennedy v Cordia (Services) LLP
[2016] UKSC 6, [2016] 1 WLR 597, [2016] ICR 325

The Supreme Court provided guidance in the immediate case, at [38]–[61], on the use of expert evidence in civil cases, including:
(a)   the admissibility of expert evidence;

(b) the responsibility of each party's legal representatives to ensure their expert(s) assisted the court;
(c) the court's role in policing the performance of an expert's duties; and
(d) the considerations of economy in litigation.

The Supreme Court, with reference to an expert's duty to assist the court, restated Lord Prosser's judgment in *Dingley v Chief Constable*, Strathclyde Police 1998 SC 548: 'As with judicial or other opinions, what carries weight is the reasoning, not the conclusion'.

INDEPENDENCE

[31.8B]   EXP v Barker

[2015] EWHC 1289 (QB), 165 NLJ 7656

During cross-examination, it emerged that the defendant's expert had been a consultant at the same hospital where the defendant himself was a senior registrar, and that the connection between the two was quite extensive, yet neither had actually revealed the extent or indeed existence of any connection prior to trial.

HELD: The parties were under an obligation to state openly and with adequate particulars the extent of any connection between themselves and their expert. Otherwise, they risked a finding that the expert's objectivity was compromised, and their evidence being deemed either inadmissible or such that only limited weight should be attached.

It was desirable that an expert should have no actual or apparent interest in the outcome of the proceedings in which they were giving evidence, however, where there was a degree of conflict, early disclosure was imperative.

(B) RESTRICTING EXPERT EVIDENCE

CPR 35.4 – COURT'S POWER TO RESTRICT EXPERT EVIDENCE

[31.12]

'35.4

(1) No party may call an expert or put in evidence an expert's report without the court's permission.
(2) When parties apply for permission they must provide an estimate of the costs of the proposed expert evidence and identify –
    (a) the field in which expert evidence is required and the issues which the expert evidence will address; and
    (b) where practicable, the name of the proposed expert.
(3) If permission is granted it shall be in relation only to the expert named or the field identified under paragraph (2). The order granting permission may specify the issues which the expert evidence should address.
(3A) Where a claim has been allocated to the small claims track or the fast track, if permission is given for expert evidence, it will normally be given for evidence from only one expert on a particular issue.
(3B) In a soft tissue injury claim, permission—
    (a) may normally only be given for one expert medical report;
    (b) may not be given initially unless the medical report is a fixed cost medical report. Where the claimant seeks permission to obtain a further medical report, if the report is from a medical expert in any of the following disciplines—
        (i) Consultant Orthopaedic Surgeon;

[31.12] *Expert Evidence*

    (ii) Consultant in Accident and Emergency Medicine;
    (iii) General Practitioner registered with the General Medical Council; or
    (iv) Physiotherapist registered with the Health and Care Professions Council, the report must be a fixed cost medical report.

(3C) In this rule, 'fixed cost medical report' and 'soft tissue injury claim' have the same meaning as in paragraph 1.1(10A) and (16A), respectively, of the RTA Protocol.

(Paragraph 7 of Practice Direction 35 sets out some of the circumstances the court will consider when deciding whether expert evidence should be given by a single joint expert.)

(4) The court may limit the amount of a party's expert's fees and expenses that may be recovered from any other party.'

CHAPTER 32

Applications

4. **RELIEF FROM SANCTIONS POST-1 APRIL 2013**

[32.26HA] Thevarajah v Riordan
[2015] UKSC 78, [2016] 1 WLR 76, (2015) Times, 23 December

The claimant appellant obtained an unless order against the defendant respondents, and a debarring order in the event of non-compliance. The claimant sought to enforce the order following the defendants' non-compliance, and the defendants made a cross-application for relief from sanctions under CPR r 3.9.

The first instance judge found that the defendants had failed to comply with the unless order, so debarred them from defending the claim and struck out their defence and counter-claim.

The defendants issued a second application for relief from sanctions to be heard on the first day of the relisted trial. The deputy judge granted the defendants relief on the basis of the defendants' submission that they had, by the time of the second application, complied with the unless order.

The claimant's appealed that decision to the Supreme Court.

HELD, ON APPEAL: A second application for relief from sanctions was to be treated as an application to vary or revoke the initial order, pursuant to CPR r 3.1(7). The applicant was, therefore, required to show that there had been a material change of circumstances since the first application for relief was made, in accordance with *Mitchell v News Group Newspapers Ltd* [2013] EWCA Civ 1537, [2014] 2 All ER 430, [2014] 1 WLR 795.

The defendants' subsequent compliance with the unless order could not amount to a material change of circumstances to justify granting relief, absent other facts that could adequately explain away a party's prior default.

[32.26Q] Viridor Waste Management Ltd v Veolia Es Ltd
[2015] EWHC 2321 (Comm)

The defendant applied to strike out the claimant's claim on the basis that the claimant had served its particulars of claim four days late, after earlier attempting to effect service by 2nd class post (which is not a recognised method of service under CPR r 6.20(1)).

The parties had previously agreed to a 28-day extension for service of the particulars and to a stay of the proceedings to explore settlement. The defendant refused to agree to the claimant's application for an extension of time, and instead applied for strike-out.

HELD: In applying the 3-stage test established in *Denton v TH White Ltd* [2014] EWCA Civ 906, [2015] 1 All ER 880, [2014] 1 WLR 3926, and assessing the seriousness and significance of default, it was important to recognise that the particulars were actually received by the defendant only one day late.

The court considered that the defendant's conduct had been unreasonable as it sought to obtain the windfall of strike-out despite it being obvious that consenting to the claimant's application for relief from sanctions was been appropriate. In the

[32.26Q] *Applications*

circumstances, the claimant was awarded its costs on an indemnity basis given that the court found the defendant's application for strike-out had been opportunistic and unreasonable.

[32.26R]　Hockley v North Lincolnshire and Goole NHS Foundation Trust
(19 September 2014, unreported), HHJ Richardson QC

The instant application was made to set aside a default judgment following the defendant's failure to file and serve its acknowledgement of service. The claimant's failure to follow the relevant Pre-Action Protocol meant the court considered that it was in the interests of 'fairness and justice' to set aside the default judgment under the provisions of CPR r 13.3(1)(b).

The claimant appealed the decision.

HELD, ON APPEAL: The relevant considerations in respect of either an application to set aside default judgment under CPR r 13.3, or an application seeking relief from sanctions under CPR r 3.9, were profoundly similar.

Therefore, application of the three stage test established by *Denton v TH White Ltd* [2014] EWCA Civ 906, [2015] 1 All ER 880, [2014] 1 WLR 3926, meant default judgment would be restored on the basis that the failure to file an acknowledge of service is considered serious or significant, and the reason given by the defendant for the breach, namely oversight, was simply not considered a good enough reason for the breach.

5.　INTERIM REMEDIES

(C) INTERIM PAYMENTS

CPR 25.7 – INTERIM PAYMENTS – CONDITIONS TO BE SATISFIED AND MATTERS TO BE TAKEN INTO ACCOUNT

[32.31A]　Eeles v Cobham Hire Services Ltd
[2009] EWCA Civ 204, [2010] 1 WLR 409, [2009] PIQR P273

The Court of Appeal summarised the approach a court should take when considering whether to make an interim payment in a personal injury case, where the trial judge may elect to make a periodical payments order.

HELD, ON APPEAL: A court, applying CPR r 25.7(4), had no power to make an order for any more than a reasonable proportion of the likely amount of the final judgment (estimated on a conservative basis):
(1)　In a case in which a periodical payments order may be made by the trial judge, the correct approach to estimating the final judgment was not to estimate the full capital value of the entire claim, but only the likely capital award. A judge should, therefore, exclude heads of future loss that the trial judge might wish to deal with by a periodical payments order.
(2)　The court's assessment should comprise special damages to date, and general damages, together with interest on both.
(3)　As the practice of awarding accommodation costs (including future running costs) as a capitalised lump sum was well established, it would usually be appropriate to include accommodation costs within the court's assessment of the likely capital award.
(4)　Additional elements of future loss could be included in the assessment, providing the claimant could establish a real need for the interim payment, and only where the judge could confidently predict that the trial judge would wish to

(5) The interim payment should, save in certain circumstances, be a reasonable proportion of the assessment, albeit a reasonable proportion may actually be a high proportion provided that the assessment itself had been a conservative one.
(6) In assessing what was a reasonable proportion, the judge was not required to have regard to what the claimant intended to do with the interim payment.

8. STRIKING OUT STATEMENT OF CASE AS ABUSE OF PROCESS

[32.66B] Lewis v Ward Hadaway (A Firm)
[2015] EWHC 3503 (Ch), [2016] 4 WLR 6

The court was asked to determine whether claimants that had deliberately understated the value of their claims, in order to pay reduced issue fees and to prevent limitation periods from running, were guilty of conduct that amounted to an abuse of process.

HELD: Where it was established that claimant(s), at the time of issue, had every intention of amending their proceedings before service to reflect the true value of their claims, this did amount to an abuse of the court's process, despite the fact that the claimant(s) would subsequently settle the balance of the 'appropriate fee' at the time of amendment.

Despite the court's finding that the claimants' behaviour amounted to an abuse of process, the court determined it would be disproportionate to strike out the claim(s), given the value of the defendant's potential liability, and the fact that the claimant(s) claims were arguable.

However, the fact that, as a result of the abuse, the 'appropriate fee' (per *Page v Hewetts* [2012] EWCA Civ 805) had not been paid at the time of issue meant that a limited number of claims had not actually been brought within their limitation periods, and the defendant was therefore entitled to summary judgment on those claims.

[32.66C] Solland International Ltd, Solland Interiors Ltd, Abner Solland and Grazyna Urszula Solland v Clifford Harris & Co (A Firm)
[2015] EWHC 2018 (Ch), [2015] All ER (D) 33 (Dec)

The defendant applied to strike out a professional negligence claim brought against it by the claimants on the basis that it alleged the claimant's conduct amounted to an abuse of the court's process. The claimant had failed to file its allocation questionnaire within the specified period, or to take any further involvement in the litigation for over two years, only engaging in proceedings once the defendant had made its application for strike out.

HELD, ON APPEAL: Delay alone, no matter how inordinate or inexcusable, could not constitute an abuse of process without also considering the effect of such delay on the possibility of a fair trial, *Purefuture Ltd v Simmons & Simmons* [2001] CP Rep 30.

The substantial passage of time in the immediate case was likely to have had an adverse effect on the recollection of witnesses and the credibility of their oral testimony, which created a substantial risk that a fair trial could no longer be conducted. Accordingly, the claimant's claim was struck out.

Any litigation that was commenced or conducted without an intention to bring it to a proper conclusion amounted to an abuse of process, *Grovit v Doctor* [1997] 2 All ER 417, [1997] 1 WLR 640, [1997] NLJR 633.

PART 33

Part 36 Offers

1. **GENERALLY**

(B) MAKING OFFERS OTHER THAN IN ACCORDANCE WITH CPR PART 36

[33.2A]

'36.2

(2) Nothing in this Section prevents a party making an offer to settle in whatever way that party chooses, but if the offer is not made in accordance with rule 36.5, it will not have the consequences specified in this Section.

Note – Rule 44.2 requires the court to consider an offer to settle that does not have the costs consequences set out in this Section in deciding what order to make about costs.'

(E) FORM AND CONTENT OF A PART 36 OFFER

[33.7]

'36.5

(1) A Part 36 offer must—

(a) be in writing;

(b) make clear that it is made pursuant to Part 36;

(c) specify a period of not less than 21 days within which the defendant will be liable for the claimant's costs in accordance with rule 36.13 or 36.20 if the offer is accepted;

(d) state whether it relates to the whole of the claim or to part of it or to an issue that arises in it and if so to which part or issue; and

(e) state whether it takes into account any counterclaim.

Note – Rule 36.7 makes provision for when a Part 36 offer is made.

(2) Paragraph (1)(c) does not apply if the offer is made less than 21 days before the start of a trial.

(3) In appropriate cases, a Part 36 offer must contain such further information as is required by rule 36.18 (personal injury claims for future pecuniary loss), rule 36.19 (offer to settle a claim for provisional damages), and rule 36.22 (deduction of benefits).

(4) A Part 36 offer which offers to pay or offers to accept a sum of money will be treated as inclusive of all interest until—

[33.8A] *Part 36 Offers*

(a) the date on which the period specified under rule 36.5(1)(c) expires; or

(b) if rule 36.5(2) applies, a date 21 days after the date the offer was made.'

(EA) DEFINITIONS

[33.8A]

'36.3

In this Section—

(a) the party who makes an offer is the "offeror";

(b) the party to whom an offer is made is the "offeree";

(c) a "trial" means any trial in a case whether it is a trial of all issues or a trial of liability, quantum or some other issue in the case;

(d) a trial is "in progress" from the time when it starts until the time when judgment is given or handed down;

(e) a case is "decided" when all issues in the case have been determined, whether at one or more trials;

(f) "trial judge" includes the judge (if any) allocated in advance to conduct a trial; and

(g) "the relevant period" means—

(i) in the case of an offer made not less than 21 days before a trial, the period specified under rule 36.5(1)(c) or such longer period as the parties agree;

(ii) otherwise, the period up to the end of such trial.'

(G) TIME WHEN A PART 36 OFFER IS MADE

[33.10]

'36.7

(1) A Part 36 offer may be made at any time, including before the commencement of proceedings.

(2) A Part 36 offer is made when it is served on the offeree.

Note – Part 6 provides detailed rules about service of documents.'

(H) OFFER AND ACCEPTANCE

[33.13B] DB UK Bank Ltd (t/a DB Mortgages) v Jacobs Solicitors
[2016] EWHC 1614 (Ch)

The defendant made a without prejudice offer (but not a Part 36 compliant offer) dated 28 August 2015.

The claimant made a counter-offer (by way of Part 36) dated 19 May 2016, which was never accepted.

On 22 June 2016, and only five days before trial, the claimant purported to accept the defendant's original without prejudice offer.

The defendant submitted that the claimant's Part 36 counter-offer had effectively rejected its without prejudice offer, such that it was no longer available for acceptance.

HELD, ON APPEAL: Where a Part 36 counter-offer was made in response to an opponent's Part 36 offer, the common law principle of implied rejection would not apply; Part 36 was a self-contained code, per *Gibbon v Manchester City Council* [2010] EWCA Civ 726.

However, the defendant's original offer was not a Part 36 offer but a without prejudice offer only. The impact of any counter-offer must be addressed by reference to common law principles. Therefore, the claimant's Part 36 counter-offer had indeed impliedly rejected the defendant's without prejudice offer, such that it was no longer available for acceptance.

The claim had, therefore, not been settled and would proceed to trial.

Obiter, if the defendant's without prejudice offer had not been impliedly rejected by a counter offer, it would have remained open for acceptance as there was no basis for implying any time limit for acceptance.

(K) CLARIFICATION OF A CPR PART 36 OFFER

[33.18]

'36.8

(1) The offeree may, within 7 days of a Part 36 offer being made, request the offeror to clarify the offer.

(2) If the offeror does not give the clarification requested under paragraph (1) within 7 days of receiving the request, the offeree may, unless the trial has started, apply for an order that the offeror do so.

Note – Part 23 contains provisions about making an application to the court.

(3) If the court makes an order under paragraph (2), it must specify the date when the Part 36 offer is to be treated as having been made.'

(MA) WITHDRAWING OR CHANGING THE TERMS OF A PART 36 OFFER GENERALLY

[33.23A]

'36.9

(1) A Part 36 offer can only be withdrawn, or its terms changed, if the offeree has not previously served notice of acceptance.

(2) The offeror withdraws the offer or changes its terms by serving written notice of the withdrawal or change of terms on the offeree.

Note – Rule 36.17(7) deals with the costs consequences following judgment of an offer which is withdrawn.

(3) Subject to rule 36.10, such notice of withdrawal or change of terms takes effect when it is served on the offeree.

Note – Rule 36.10 makes provision about when permission is required to withdraw or change the terms of an offer before the expiry of the relevant period.

(4) Subject to paragraph (1), after expiry of the relevant period—

[33.23B] *Part 36 Offers*

(a) the offeror may withdraw the offer or change its terms without the permission of the court; or

(b) the offer may be automatically withdrawn in accordance with its terms.

(5) Where the offeror changes the terms of a Part 36 offer to make it more advantageous to the offeree—

(a) such improved offer shall be treated, not as the withdrawal of the original offer; but as the making of a new Part 36 offer on the improved terms; and

(b) subject to rule 36.5(2), the period specified under rule 36.5(1)(c) shall be 21 days or such longer period (if any) identified in the written notice referred to in paragraph (2).'

[33.23B]   Burrett v Mencap Ltd
(14 May 2014, unreported) Ackroyd, DJ

In July 2013, the defendant made a valid Part 36 offer to the claimant, which was neither accepted nor withdrawn.

In January 2014, the defendant served a variation of the July 2013 offer such that the original offer was less advantageous. The varied offer was ultimately accepted by the claimant, but outside the 21 day period from the date the varied offer was served.

The claimant submitted that the Part 36 costs penalties should only apply from the end of the relevant period for the varied offer and not for the original offer.

HELD: In dismissing the claimant's application, it was held that the relevant period set out in the original offer applied, and not relevant period in the varied (and less advantageous) offer.

The court noted that the Part 36 regime allows a party to change the terms of an offer to be less advantageous to the offeree, but did not state that further time is allowed for contemplation of a less advantageous varied offer.

(MB) WITHDRAWING OR CHANGING THE TERMS OF A PART 36 OFFER BEFORE THE EXPIRY OF THE RELEVANT PERIOD

[33.23C]

'36.10

(1) Subject to rule 36.9(1), this rule applies where the offeror serves notice before expiry of the relevant period of withdrawal of the offer or change of its terms to be less advantageous to the offeree.

(2) Where this rule applies—

(a) if the offeree has not served notice of acceptance of the original offer by the expiry of the relevant period, the offeror's notice has effect on the expiry of that period; and

(b) if the offeree serves notice of acceptance of the original offer before the expiry of the relevant period, that acceptance has effect unless the offeror applies to the court for permission to withdraw the offer or to change its terms—

(i) within 7 days of the offeree's notice of acceptance; or

(ii) if earlier, before the first day of trial.

Generally **[33.25C]**

(3) On an application under paragraph (2)(b), the court may give permission for the original offer to be withdrawn or its terms changed if satisfied that there has been a change of circumstances since the making of the original offer and that it is in the interests of justice to give permission.'

(N) ACCEPTANCE OF A CPR PART 36 OFFER

[33.24]

'36.11

(1) A Part 36 offer is accepted by serving written notice of acceptance on the offeror.

(2) Subject to paragraphs (3) and (4) and to rule 36.12, a Part 36 offer may be accepted at any time (whether or not the offeree has subsequently made a different offer), unless it has already been withdrawn.

Note – Rule 21.10 deals with compromise, etc. by or on behalf of a child or protected party.

Note – Rules 36.9 and 36.10 deal with withdrawal of Part 36 offers.

(3) The court's permission is required to accept a Part 36 offer where—

(a) rule 36.15(4) applies;

(b) rule 36.22(3)(b) applies, the relevant period has expired and further deductible amounts have been paid to the claimant since the date of the offer;

(c) an apportionment is required under rule 41.3A; or

(d) a trial is in progress.

Note – Rule 36.15 deals with offers by some but not all of multiple defendants.

Note – Rule 36.22 defines "deductible amounts".

Note – Rule 41.3A requires an apportionment in proceedings under the Fatal Accidents Act 1976 and Law Reform (Miscellaneous Provisions) Act 1934.

(4) Where the court gives permission under paragraph (3), unless all the parties have agreed costs, the court must make an order dealing with costs, and may order that the costs consequences set out in rule 36.13 apply.'

(NA) ACCEPTANCE OF A PART 36 OFFER IN A SPLIT-TRIAL CASE

[33.25C]

'36.12

(1) This rule applies in any case where there has been a trial but the case has not been decided within the meaning of rule 36.3.

(2) Any Part 36 offer which relates only to parts of the claim or issues that have already been decided can no longer be accepted.

(3) Subject to paragraph (2) and unless the parties agree, any other Part 36 offer cannot be accepted earlier than 7 clear days after judgment is given or handed down in such trial.'

[33.26] *Part 36 Offers*

(O) COSTS CONSEQUENCES OF ACCEPTANCE OF A PART 36 OFFER

[33.26]
'36.13

(1) Subject to paragraphs (2) and (4) and to rule 36.20, where a Part 36 offer is accepted within the relevant period the claimant will be entitled to the costs of the proceedings (including their recoverable pre-action costs) up to the date on which notice of acceptance was served on the offeror.

(Rule 36.20 makes provision for the costs consequences of accepting a Part 36 offer in certain personal injury claims where the claim no longer proceeds under the RTA or EL/PL Protocol.)

(2) Where—

(a) a defendant's Part 36 offer relates to part only of the claim; and

(b) at the time of serving notice of acceptance within the relevant period the claimant abandons the balance of the claim,

the claimant will only be entitled to the costs of such part of the claim unless the court orders otherwise.

(3) Except where the recoverable costs are fixed by these Rules, costs under paragraphs (1) and (2) are to be assessed on the standard basis if the amount of costs is not agreed.

(Rule 44.3(2) explains the standard basis for the assessment of costs.)

(Rule 44.9 contains provisions about when a costs order is deemed to have been made and applying for an order under section 194(3) of the Legal Services Act 2007.)

(Part 45 provides for fixed costs in certain classes of case.)

(4) Where—

(a) a Part 36 offer which was made less than 21 days before the start of a trial is accepted; or

(b) a Part 36 offer which relates to the whole of the claim is accepted after expiry of the relevant period; or

(c) subject to paragraph (2), a Part 36 offer which does not relate to the whole of the claim is accepted at any time,

the liability for costs must be determined by the court unless the parties have agreed the costs.

(5) Where paragraph (4)(b) applies but the parties cannot agree the liability for costs, the court must, unless it considers it unjust to do so, order that—

(a) the claimant be awarded costs up to the date on which the relevant period expired; and

(b) the offeree do pay the offeror's costs for the period from the date of expiry of the relevant period to the date of acceptance.

Generally **[33.27]**

(6) In considering whether it would be unjust to make the orders specified in paragraph (5), the court must take into account all the circumstances of the case including the matters listed in rule 36.17(5).

(7) The claimant's costs include any costs incurred in dealing with the defendant's counterclaim if the Part 36 offer states that it takes it into account.'

(P) OTHER EFFECTS OF ACCEPTANCE OF A PART 36 OFFER

[33.27]

'36.14

(1) If a Part 36 offer is accepted, the claim will be stayed.

(2) In the case of acceptance of a Part 36 offer which relates to the whole claim, the stay will be upon the terms of the offer.

(3) If a Part 36 offer which relates to part only of the claim is accepted, the claim will be stayed as to that part upon the terms of the offer.

(4) If the approval of the court is required before a settlement can be binding, any stay which would otherwise arise on the acceptance of a Part 36 offer will take effect only when that approval has been given.

(5) Any stay arising under this rule will not affect the power of the court—

(a) to enforce the terms of a Part 36 offer; or

(b) to deal with any question of costs (including interest on costs) relating to the proceedings.

(6) Unless the parties agree otherwise in writing, where a Part 36 offer that is or includes an offer to pay or accept a single sum of money is accepted, that sum must be paid to the claimant within 14 days of the date of—

(a) acceptance; or

(b) the order when the court makes an order under rule 41.2 (order for an award of provisional damages) or rule 41.8 (order for an award of periodical payments), unless the court orders otherwise.

(7) If such sum is not paid within 14 days of acceptance of the offer, or such other period as has been agreed, the claimant may enter judgment for the unpaid sum.

(8) Where—

(a) a Part 36 offer (or part of a Part 36 offer) which is not an offer to which paragraph (6) applies is accepted; and

(b) a party alleges that the other party has not honoured the terms of the offer, that party may apply to enforce the terms of the offer without the need for a new claim.'

that party may apply to enforce the terms of the offer without the need for a new claim.'

[33.29] *Part 36 Offers*

(R) ACCEPTANCE OF A PART 36 OFFER MADE BY ONE OR MORE, BUT NOT ALL, DEFENDANTS

[33.29]

'36.15

(1) This rule applies where the claimant wishes to accept a Part 36 offer made by one or more, but not all, of a number of defendants.

(2) If the defendants are sued jointly or in the alternative, the claimant may accept the offer if—

(a) the claimant discontinues the claim against those defendants who have not made the offer; and

(b) those defendants give written consent to the acceptance of the offer.

(3) If the claimant alleges that the defendants have a several liability to the claimant, the claimant may—

(a) accept the offer; and

(b) continue with the claims against the other defendants if entitled to do so.

(4) In all other cases the claimant must apply to the court for permission to accept the Part 36 offer.'

(S) CASES IN WHICH THE OFFEROR'S COSTS HAVE BEEN LIMITED TO COURT FEES

[33.29A]

'36.23

(1) This rule applies in any case where the offeror is treated as having filed a costs budget limited to applicable court fees, or is otherwise limited in their recovery of costs to such fees.

(Rule 3.14 provides that a litigant may be treated as having filed a budget limited to court fees for failure to file a budget.)

(2) "Costs" in rules 36.13(5)(b), 36.17(3)(a) and 36.17(4)(b) shall mean—

(a) in respect of those costs subject to any such limitation, 50% of the costs assessed without reference to the limitation; together with

(b) any other recoverable costs.'

2. CPR PART 36 OFFERS NOT TO BE DISCLOSED TO TRIAL JUDGE

(A) RESTRICTION ON DISCLOSURE OF A PART 36 OFFER

[33.30]

'36.16

CPR Part 36 Offers Not To Be Disclosed To Trial Judge [33.31]

(1) A Part 36 offer will be treated as "without prejudice except as to costs".

(2) The fact that a Part 36 offer has been made and the terms of such offer must not be communicated to the trial judge until the case has been decided.

(3) Paragraph (2) does not apply—

(a) where the defence of tender before claim has been raised;

(b) where the proceedings have been stayed under rule 36.14 following acceptance of a Part 36 offer;

(c) where the offeror and the offeree agree in writing that it should not apply; or

(d) where, although the case has not been decided—

(i) any part of, or issue in, the case has been decided; and

(ii) the Part 36 offer relates only to parts or issues that have been decided.

(4) In a case to which paragraph (3)(d)(i) applies, the trial judge—

(a) may be told whether or not there are Part 36 offers other than those referred to in paragraph (3)(d)(ii); but

(b) must not be told the terms of any such other offers unless any of paragraphs (3)(a) to (c) applies.'

CPR 52.12 NON-DISCLOSURE OF PART 36 OFFERS AND PAYMENTS TO AN APPEAL JUDGE

[33.31]

'52.12

(1) The fact that a Part 36 offer or payment into court has been made must not be disclosed to any judge of the appeal court who is to hear or determine –

(a) an application for permission to appeal; or

(b) an appeal,

until all questions (other than costs) have been determined.

(2) Paragraph (1) does not apply if the Part 36 offer or payment into court is relevant to the substance of the appeal.

(3) Paragraph (1) does not prevent disclosure in any application in the appeal proceedings if disclosure of the fact that a Part 36 offer or payment into court has been made is properly relevant to the matter to be decided.

(Rule 36.4 has the effect that a Part 36 offer made in proceedings at first instance will not have consequences in any appeal proceedings. Therefore, a fresh Part 36 offer needs to be made in appeal proceedings. However, rule 52.12 applies to a Part 36 offer whether made in the original proceedings or in the appeal.)'

[33.34] *Part 36 Offers*

3. COSTS CONSEQUENCES OF A CPR PART 36 OFFER

(A) CLAIMANT ADVANCING ALTERNATIVE CASES, ONLY SUCCESSFUL ON ONE

[33.34]

'36.17

(1) Subject to rule 36.21, this rule applies where upon judgment being entered—

(a) a claimant fails to obtain a judgment more advantageous than a defendant's Part 36 offer; or

(b) judgment against the defendant is at least as advantageous to the claimant as the proposals contained in a claimant's Part 36 offer.

(Rule 36.21 makes provision for the costs consequences following judgment in certain personal injury claims where the claim no longer proceeds under the RTA or EL/PL Protocol.)

(2) For the purposes of paragraph (1), in relation to any money claim or money element of a claim, "more advantageous" means better in money terms by any amount, however small, and "at least as advantageous" shall be construed accordingly.

(3) Subject to paragraphs (7) and (8), where paragraph (1)(a) applies, the court must, unless it considers it unjust to do so, order that the defendant is entitled to—

(a) costs (including any recoverable pre-action costs) from the date on which the relevant period expired; and

(b) interest on those costs.

(4) Subject to paragraph (7), where paragraph (1)(b) applies, the court must, unless it considers it unjust to do so, order that the claimant is entitled to—

(a) interest on the whole or part of any sum of money (excluding interest) awarded, at a rate not exceeding 10% above base rate for some or all of the period starting with the date on which the relevant period expired;

(b) costs (including any recoverable pre-action costs) on the indemnity basis from the date on which the relevant period expired;

(c) interest on those costs at a rate not exceeding 10% above base rate; and

(d) provided that the case has been decided and there has not been a previous order under this sub-paragraph, an additional amount, which shall not exceed £75,000, calculated by applying the prescribed percentage set out below to an amount which is—

(i) the sum awarded to the claimant by the court; or

(ii) where there is no monetary award, the sum awarded to the claimant by the court in respect of costs—

Amount awarded by the court	Prescribed percentage
Up to £500,000	10% of the amount awarded
Above £500,000	10% of the first £500,000 and (subject to the limit of £75,000) 5% of any amount above that figure.

(5) In considering whether it would be unjust to make the orders referred to in paragraphs (3) and (4), the court must take into account all the circumstances of the case including—

(a) the terms of any Part 36 offer;

(b) the stage in the proceedings when any Part 36 offer was made, including in particular how long before the trial started the offer was made;

(c) the information available to the parties at the time when the Part 36 offer was made;

(d) the conduct of the parties with regard to the giving of or refusal to give information for the purposes of enabling the offer to be made or evaluated; and

(e) whether the offer was a genuine attempt to settle the proceedings.

(6) Where the court awards interest under this rule and also awards interest on the same sum and for the same period under any other power, the total rate of interest must not exceed 10% above base rate.

(7) Paragraphs (3) and (4) do not apply to a Part 36 offer—

(a) which has been withdrawn;

(b) which has been changed so that its terms are less advantageous to the offeree where the offeree has beaten the less advantageous offer;

(c) made less than 21 days before trial, unless the court has abridged the relevant period.

(8) Paragraph (3) does not apply to a soft tissue injury claim to which rule 36.21 applies.

Note — Rule 44.2 requires the court to consider an offer to settle that does not have the costs consequences set out in this Section in deciding what order to make about costs.'

(i) COSTS CONSEQUENCES EXTEND TO FAILURE TO PARTICIPATE IN ADR

[33.41H] Thai Airways Internal Public Co Ltd v KI Holdings Co Ltd (formerly Koito Industries Ltd) and Asia Fleet Services (Singapore) PTE Ltd
[2015] EWHC 1476 (Comm), [2015] 3 Costs LR 545

The claimant made a Part 36 offer, and ultimately obtained judgment for nearly three times the amount it had offered to accept.
 The claimant sought its costs assessed on the indemnity basis from the date of expiry.
 The defendant argued it would be unjust to make such an order because it alleged the claimant failed to disclose evidence relied upon in a timely manner.

[33.41H] *Part 36 Offers*

HELD: It would be unjust to subject the defendant to the financial risks of not accepting the claimant's Part 36 offer until such time as the defendant was in a position to take an informed view on quantum.

Once the defendant had received the claimant's expert evidence, the court found that the defendant would have had ample information to enable it to take a realistic view about the value of the claim.

Accordingly, the claimant was entitled to its costs assessed on the indemnity basis, not from the date of expiry of its Part 36 offer, but from 21 days after the date of the claimant's expert report, together with its costs assessed on the standard basis for the period after expiry of its Part 36 offer.

[33.41I]   **Worthington v 03918424 Ltd**
(16 June 2015, unreported), Harrison, DJ

The claimant was injured in an incident in 2010 for which the defendant admitted liability by June 2011, although it maintained concerns regarding causation. As a result of the defendant's concerns, it obtained surveillance, which was disclosed to the experts who concluded that they could no longer support the claimant.

The claim was valued by the claimant in the order of half a million pounds, yet a Part 36 offer of £40,000, which was made in May 2014, was ultimately accepted out of time. The defendant applied for an appropriate costs order.

HELD: The court found that the claimant exaggerated his claim in the extreme and that, in the absence of such exaggeration, the matter would have likely been resolved by 30 June 2012 or thereabouts.

The claimant was entitled to its costs on the standard basis up to and including 30 June 2012. However, the defendant was entitled to its costs from that date, assessed on an indemnity basis, together with the entirety of its costs of, and incidental to, the gathering of the surveillance evidence (even those incurred prior to the expected date of conclusion in June 2012). The defendant was also entitled to its costs of the application, assessed on the indemnity basis.

[33.41J]   **Sugar Hut Group Ltd v AJ Insurance Service (a partnership)**
[2016] EWCA Civ 46, [2016] All ER (D) 51 (Feb)

A claimant that chose not to accept a defendant's global Part 36 offer, which included a specified sum in respect of business interruption losses totalling £600,000 (gross), and that was awarded £570,000 (gross) in respect of that head of loss at trial was deprived of its costs from the expiry of the relevant period and ordered to pay the defendant's costs relating to the assessment of damages from that date.

The judge found that it had been unreasonable for the claimant to have pursued a business interruption claim for £860,000 after the expiry of the relevant period, despite recognising that the claimant had beaten the defendant's global offer.

The claimant appealed.

HELD, ON APPEAL: The defendant's global offer had been beaten, and the figure of £600,000 in respect of the business interruption claim had not actually been a distinct and free-standing offer that the claimant could have accepted without compromising other heads of loss.

Whilst significant parts of the claimant's claim had failed, that did not mean that the claimant had been unreasonable in pursuing each part. The claimant's failure to succeed on every part of its claim had already been reflected by the first instance judge's reduction (30%) in the claimant's costs.

The judge at first instance had erred by effectively treating the defendant's global offer as having been successful when that was not the case. There was, therefore, no basis upon which to deprive the claimant of its costs after expiry of the relevant period, much less require them to pay the defendant's costs.

Costs Consequences of a CPR Part 36 Offer [33.46A]

(ii) OFFER TO SETTLE A CLAIM FOR PROVISIONAL DAMAGES

[33.46A]

'36.18

(1) This rule applies to a claim for damages for personal injury which is or includes a claim for future pecuniary loss.

(2) An offer to settle such a claim will not have the consequences set out in this Section unless it is made by way of a Part 36 offer under this rule.

(3) A Part 36 offer to which this rule applies may contain an offer to pay, or an offer to accept—

(a) the whole or part of the damages for future pecuniary loss in the form of—

(i) a lump sum;

(ii) periodical payments; or

(iii) both a lump sum and periodical payments;

(b) the whole or part of any other damages in the form of a lump sum.

(4) A Part 36 offer to which this rule applies—

(a) must state the amount of any offer to pay or to accept the whole or part of any damages in the form of a lump sum;

(b) may state—

(i) what part of the lump sum, if any, relates to damages for future pecuniary loss; and

(ii) what part relates to other damages to be paid or accepted in the form of a lump sum;

(c) must state what part of the offer relates to damages for future pecuniary loss to be paid or accepted in the form of periodical payments and must specify—

(i) the amount and duration of the periodical payments;

(ii) the amount of any payments for substantial capital purchases and when they are to be made; and

(iii) that each amount is to vary by reference to the retail prices index (or to some other named index, or that it is not to vary by reference to any index); and

(d) must state either that any damages which take the form of periodical payments will be funded in a way which ensures that the continuity of payments is reasonably secure in accordance with section 2(4) of the Damages Act 1996⁴ or how such damages are to be paid and how the continuity of their payment is to be secured.

(5) Rule 36.6 applies to the extent that a Part 36 offer by a defendant under this rule includes an offer to pay all or part of any damages in the form of a lump sum.

(6) Where the offeror makes a Part 36 offer to which this rule applies and which offers to pay or to accept damages in the form of both a lump sum and periodical payments, the offeree may only give notice of acceptance of the offer as a whole.

[33.46A] *Part 36 Offers*

(7) If the offeree accepts a Part 36 offer which includes payment of any part of the damages in the form of periodical payments, the claimant must, within 7 days of the date of acceptance, apply to the court for an order for an award of damages in the form of periodical payments under rule 41.8. (Practice Direction 41B contains information about periodical payments under the Damages Act 1996.)

[33.46B]

'36.19

(1) An offeror may make a Part 36 offer in respect of a claim which includes a claim for provisional damages.

(2) Where the offeror does so, the Part 36 offer must specify whether or not the offeror is proposing that the settlement shall include an award of provisional damages.

(3) Where the offeror is offering to agree to the making of an award of provisional damages, the Part 36 offer must also state—

(a) that the sum offered is in satisfaction of the claim for damages on the assumption that the injured person will not develop the disease or suffer the type of deterioration specified in the offer;

(b) that the offer is subject to the condition that the claimant must make any claim for further damages within a limited period; and

(c) what that period is.

(4) Rule 36.6 applies to the extent that a Part 36 offer by a defendant includes an offer to agree to the making of an award of provisional damages.

(5) If the offeree accepts the Part 36 offer, the claimant must, within 7 days of the date of acceptance, apply to the court for an award of provisional damages under rule 41.2.'

5.   DEDUCTION OF BENEFITS

CPR 36.15 – DEDUCTION OF BENEFITS

[33.49]

'36.22

(1) In this rule and rule 36.11—

(a) "the 1997 Act" means the Social Security (Recovery of Benefits) Act 19975;

(b) "the 2008 Regulations" means the Social Security (Recovery of Benefits)(Lump Sum Payments) Regulations 2008;

(c) "recoverable amount" means—

(i) "recoverable benefits" as defined in section 1(4)(c) of the 1997 Act; and

(ii) "recoverable lump sum payments" as defined in regulation 1 of the 2008 Regulations;

(d) "deductible amount" means—

Deduction of benefits **[33.49]**

(i) any benefits by the amount of which damages are to be reduced in accordance with section 8 of, and Schedule 2 to the 1997 Act ("deductible benefits"); and

(ii) any lump sum payment by the amount of which damages are to be reduced in accordance with regulation 12 of the 2008 Regulations ("deductible lump sum payments"); and

(e) "certificate"—

(i) in relation to recoverable benefits, is construed in accordance with the provisions of the 1997 Act; and

(ii) in relation to recoverable lump sum payments, has the meaning given in section 29 of the 1997 Act, as applied by regulation 2 of, and modified by Schedule 1 to, the 2008 Regulations.

(2) This rule applies where a payment to a claimant following acceptance of a Part 36 offer would be a compensation payment as defined in section 1(4)(b) or 1A(5)(b)8 of the 1997 Act.

(3) A defendant who makes a Part 36 offer must, where relevant, state either—

(a) that the offer is made without regard to any liability for recoverable amounts; or

(b) that it is intended to include any deductible amounts.

(4) Where paragraph (3)(b) applies, paragraphs (5) to (9) will apply to the Part 36 offer.

(5) Before making the Part 36 offer, the offeror must apply for a certificate.

(6) Subject to paragraph (7), the Part 36 offer must state—

(a) the gross amount of compensation;

(b) the name and amount of any deductible amounts by which the gross amount is reduced; and

(c) the net amount of compensation.

(7) If at the time the offeror makes the Part 36 offer, the offeror has applied for, but has not received, a certificate, the offeror must clarify the offer by stating the matters referred to in paragraph (6)(b) and (c) not more than 7 days after receipt of the certificate.

(8) For the purposes of rule 36.17(1)(a), a claimant fails to recover more than any sum offered (including a lump sum offered under rule 36.6) if the claimant fails upon judgment being entered to recover a sum, once deductible amounts identified in the judgment have been deducted, greater than the net amount stated under paragraph (6)(c).

(Section 15(2) of the 1997 Act provides that the court must specify the compensation payment attributable to each head of damage. Schedule 1 to the 2008 Regulations modifies section 15 of the 1997 Act in relation to lump sum payments and provides that the court must specify the compensation payment attributable to each or any dependant who has received a lump sum payment.)

(9) Where—

(a) deductible amounts have accrued since the Part 36 offer was made; and

(b) the court gives permission to accept the Part 36 offer,

the court may direct that the amount of the offer payable to the offeree shall be reduced by a sum equivalent to the deductible amounts paid to the claimant since the date of the offer.

(Rule 36.11(3)(b) states that permission is required to accept an offer where the relevant period has expired and further deductible amounts have been paid to the claimant.)'

(A) GUIDANCE ON HOW TO DEDUCT BENEFITS

[33.50A] Crooks v Hendricks Lovell Ltd
[2016] EWCA Civ 8, 166 NLJ 7684

A claimant appealed against a decision that it had failed to beat a defendant's part 36 offer, which was made for '£18,500 net of CRU (a certificate of recoverable benefits issued by the Compensation Recovery Unit (CRU)) and inclusive of interim payments in the sum of £18,500'.

At the time of the defendant's offer, the amount payable to the CRU was £16,262, and at trial the claimant was ultimately awarded £29,550 (ie less than the gross sum of £34,762). However, prior to trial but after the date of the defendant's part 36 offer, the claimant appealed against the CRU certificate, and a revised certificate showing deductible benefits of £6,760 was only made available after trial.

The defendant's case was that, notwithstanding the subsequent reduction in the sum payable to the CRU, the claimant had failed to beat the defendant's offer at the time when judgment was actually delivered.

HELD, ON APPEAL: The regime in CPR r 36.14 (now r 36.17) applied to circumstances as they were once judgment had been given, but not only at the moment of delivery.

The court would not be obliged to make a decision on costs in ignorance of the outcome of the CRU review, given that the liability to the CRU had not yet crystallised.

The defendant's offer had not sought to anticipate the result of the CRU process, after any review or appeal, nor had it identified a hypothetical gross sum. The claimant had in fact beaten the defendant's Part 36 offer.

7. RTA PROTOCOL AND EL/PL OFFERS TO SETTLE

(A) SCOPE

[33.55] Note For detail of the application of the RTA Protocol (to personal injury claims valued at between £1,000 and £25,000 arising from road traffic accidents on or after 31 July 2013), please see elsewhere in this volume.

'36.24

(1) Where this Section applies, Section I does not apply.

(2) This Section applies to an offer to settle where the parties have followed the RTA Protocol or the EL/PL Protocol and started proceedings under Part 8 in accordance with Practice Direction 8B ("the Stage 3 Procedure").

(3) A reference to the Court Proceedings Pack Form is a reference to the form used in the relevant Protocol.

RTA Protocol And EL/PL offers to settle **[33.59]**

(4) Nothing in this Section prevents a party making an offer to settle in whatever way that party chooses, but if the offer is not made in accordance with this Section, it will not have any costs consequences.'

(B) FORM AND CONTENT OF A PROTOCOL OFFER

[33.56]

'36.27

A Protocol offer—

(a) is treated as exclusive of all interest; and

(b) has the consequences set out in this Section only in relation to the fixed costs of the Stage 3 Procedure as provided for in rule 45.18, and not in relation to the costs of any appeal from the final decision of those proceedings.'

(C) TIME WHEN A PROTOCOL OFFER IS MADE

[33.57]

36.26

(1) The Protocol offer is deemed to be made on the first business day after the Court Proceedings Pack (Part A and Part B) Form is sent to the defendant.

(2) In this Section "business day" has the same meaning as in rule 6.2.

(D) GENERAL PROVISIONS

[33.58]

'36.27

A Protocol offer—

(a) is treated as exclusive of all interest; and

(b) has the consequences set out in this Section only in relation to the fixed costs of the Stage 3 Procedure as provided for in rule 45.18, and not in relation to the costs of any appeal from the final decision of those proceedings.'

(E) RESTRICTIONS ON THE DISCLOSURE OF A PROTOCOL OFFER

[33.59]

'36.28

(1) The amount of the Protocol offer must not be communicated to the court until the claim is determined.

(2) Any other offer to settle must not be communicated to the court at all.'

[33.60] *Part 36 Offers*

(F) COSTS CONSEQUENCES FOLLOWING JUDGMENT

[33.60]

'36.29

(1) This rule applies where, on any determination by the court, the claimant obtains judgment against the defendant for an amount of damages that is—

(a) less than or equal to the amount of the defendant's Protocol offer;

(b) more than the defendant's Protocol offer but less than the claimant's Protocol offer; or

(c) equal to or more than the claimant's Protocol offer.

(2) Where paragraph (1)(a) applies, the court must order the claimant to pay—

(a) the fixed costs in rule 45.26; and

(b) interest on those fixed costs from the first business day after the deemed date of the Protocol offer under rule 36.26.

(3) Where paragraph (1)(b) applies, the court must order the defendant to pay the fixed costs in rule 45.20.

(4) Where paragraph (1)(c) applies, the court must order the defendant to pay—

(a) interest on the whole of the damages awarded at a rate not exceeding 10% above base rate for some or all of the period starting with the date specified in rule 36.26;

(b) the fixed costs in rule 45.20;

(c) interest on those fixed costs at a rate not exceeding 10% above base rate; and

(d) an additional amount calculated in accordance with rule 36.17(4)(d).'

[33.60A]   Broadhurst v Tan, Taylor and Smith
[2016] EWCA Civ 94, [2016] 1 WLR 1928, 166 NLJ 7689

Claimants that had issued claims, which were subject to the fixed costs regime for low value personal injury cases, had both made Part 36 offers that were rejected by the defendants. Ultimately, each claimant obtained judgment for a sum that was more advantageous than the terms of their offer and argued that there were entitled to their costs assessed on an indemnity basis, rather than being limited to fixed costs in accordance with CPR Part 45, Part IIIA.

HELD, ON APPEAL: Where a claimant had made a successful Part 36 offer in a low value personal injury claim, they should not be limited to fixed costs only, but instead be awarded fixed costs to the last staging point provided by CPR r 45.29C and Table 6B, and then costs to be assessed on the indemnity basis from the date when the offer became effective.

(G) DEDUCTION OF BENEFITS

[33.61]

'36.30

For the purposes of rule 36.29(1)(a) the amount of the judgment is less than the Protocol offer where the judgment is less than that offer once deductible amounts identified in the judgment are deducted.

Note — 'Deductible amount' is defined in rule 36.22(1)(d).'

CHAPTER 34

Trial

1. PRELIMINARY MATTERS

(C) CONSEQUENCES OF FAILURE TO ATTEND TRIAL

APPLICANT MUST SHOW A 'GOOD REASON' FOR FAILING TO ATTEND

[34.4A] Stuart John Gentry v Miller and UK Insurance

[2016] EWCA Civ 141, (2016) Times, 21 April

The claimant sought damages following a road traffic accident for which the first defendant's insurer admitted liability. Ultimately, the claimant entered default judgment on 8 August 2013 and the court subsequently assessed damages at a disposal hearing on 17 October 2013 where neither the first defendant nor their insurer was in attendance.

On 25 November 2013, solicitors acting for the first defendant applied to set aside the default judgment and, on 10 February 2014, the solicitors acting for the first defendant sought the court's permission to cease acting for the first defendant and to join the insurer as second defendant, alleging that the claim was fraudulent. On 26 February 2014, the solicitors made an application on behalf of the second defendant to set aside both the default judgment and the order assessing damages.

The district judge set aside both orders and concluded that claims pertaining to allegations of fraud should be exempt from the usual considerations governing relief from sanctions, including the tests in *Mitchell v News Group Newspapers Ltd* [2013] EWCA Civ 1537, [2014] 2 All ER 430, [2014] 1 WLR 795 and *Denton v TH White Ltd* [2014] EWCA Civ 906, [2015] 1 All ER 880, [2014] 1 WLR 3926.

HELD, ON APPEAL: In determining the application for relief in accordance with CPR r 39.3, a court was required to consider the requirements of r 39.3(5) before turning to the tests in '*Mitchell*' and '*Denton*'.

In the immediate case, the insurer had not been 'a party who failed to attend the trial' under CPR r 39.3(5) at the time damages had been assessed. In any event, the court had been required by r 39.3(5)(a) and by the tests in '*Mitchell*' and '*Denton*' to consider whether the applicant had acted promptly once it had learned of the order(s). It had not, nor had it protected its interests by instructing solicitors to accept service of proceedings following the admission of liability.

There had to be finality to the litigation and the rules of court must be obeyed. A default judgment could not be set aside as a matter of course simply owing to an arguable allegation of fraud.

Instead, the applicant insurer would be required to vindicate its rights by bringing a new action based on fraud, *Royal Bank of Scotland plc v Highland Financial Partners LP* [2013] EWCA Civ 328, [2013] All ER (D) 65 (Apr) applied.

CHAPTER 35

Appeals

1. **PRELIMINARY MATTERS**

(B) ROUTES OF APPEAL

[35.9] 3.3

The court or judge to which an appeal is to be made (subject to obtaining any necessary permission) is set out in the tables below–

Table 1 deals with appeals in proceedings other than family and insolvency proceedings;

Table 1 – Proceedings other than family or insolvency proceedings

Court	Deciding judge	Nature of claim	Interim / final	Destination
County	District judge	Pt 7 Claim	Interim	Circuit judge in the county court
		Pt 7 Claim (not MT)	Final	
		Pt 7 Claim (MT)	Final	Court of Appeal
		Pt 8 Claim	Interim / final	Circuit judge in the county court
		Other	Interim / final	
		Specialist	Interim	
			Final	Court of Appeal
	Circuit judge including a recorder or a district judge who is exercising the jurisdiction of a Circuit judge	Pt 7 Claim	Interim	single judge of the High Court
		Pt 7 Claim (not MT)	Final	
		Pt 7 Claim (MT)	Final	Court of Appeal

133

[35.9] *Appeals*

Court	Deciding judge	Nature of claim	Interim / final	Destination
High	Master	Pt 8 Claim	Interim / final	single judge of the High Court
		Other	Interim / final	single judge of the High Court
		Specialist	Interim	single judge of the High Court
			Final	Court of Appeal
	Master	Pt 7 Claim	Interim	single judge of the High Court
		Pt 7 Claim (not MT)	Final	single judge of the High Court
		Pt 7 Claim (MT)	Final	Court of Appeal
		Pt 8 Claim	Interim / final	single judge of the High Court
		Other	Interim / final	single judge of the High Court
		Specialist	Interim	single judge of the High Court
			Final	Court of Appeal
	single judge of the High Court	Any	Interim / final	Court of Appeal

   3.7 A decision is to be treated as a final decision for destination of appeal purposes where it –
(a)   is made at the conclusion of part of a hearing or trial which has been split into parts; and
(b)   would, if it had been made at the conclusion of that hearing or trial, have been a final decision.
   3.8
(1)   The following are examples of final decisions –
- a judgment on liability at the end of a split trial;
- a judgment at the conclusion of an assessment of damages following a judgment on liability.

(2)   The following are examples of decisions that are not final –
- a case management decision (within the meaning of paragraph 4.6);
- a grant or refusal of interim relief;
- summary judgment;
- striking out a claim or statement of case;
- a summary or detailed assessment of costs;
- an order for the enforcement of a final decision.

(C) PERMISSION

CPR 52.3 – Permission

[35.10]

'(1) An appellant or respondent requires permission to appeal –

(a) where the appeal is from a decision of a judge in the County Court or the High Court, except where the appeal is against –

(i) a committal order;

(ii) a refusal to grant habeas corpus; or

(iii) a secure accommodation order made under section 25 of the Children Act 1989; or

(b) as provided by Practice Direction 52.

(Other enactments may provide that permission is required for particular appeals)

(2) An application for permission to appeal may be made –

(a) to the lower court at the hearing at which the decision to be appealed was made; or

(b) to the appeal court in an appeal notice.

(Rule 52.4 sets out the time limits for filing an appellant's notice at the appeal court. Rule 52.5 sets out the time limits for filing a respondent's notice at the appeal court. Any application for permission to appeal to the appeal court must be made in the appeal notice (see rules 52.4(1) and 52.5(3))

(Rule 52.13(1) provides that permission is required from the Court of Appeal for all appeals to that court from a decision of the County Court or the High Court which was itself made on appeal)

(3) Where the lower court refuses an application for permission to appeal—

(a) a further application for permission may be made to the appeal court; and

(b) the order refusing permission will specify—

(i) the court to which any further application for permission should be made; and

(ii) the level of the judge who should hear the application.

(4) Subject to paragraph (4A) and except where a rule or practice direction provides otherwise, where the appeal court, without a hearing, refuses permission to appeal, the person seeking permission may request the decision to be reconsidered at a hearing.

(4A)

(a) Where a judge of the Court of Appeal or of the High Court, a Designated Civil Judge or a Specialist Circuit Judge refuses permission to appeal without a hearing and considers that the application is totally without merit, the judge may make an order that the person seeking permission may not request the decision to be reconsidered at a hearing.

(b) For the purposes of subparagraph (a) "Specialist Circuit Judge" means any Circuit Judge in the County Court nominated to hear cases in the Mercantile, Chancery or Technology and Construction Court lists.

[35.10] Appeals

(4B) Rule 3.3(5) will not apply to an order that the person seeking permission may not request the decision to be reconsidered at a hearing made under paragraph (4A).

(5) A request under paragraph (4) must be filed within 7 days after service of the notice that permission has been refused.

(6) Permission to appeal may be given only where –

(a) the court considers that the appeal would have a real prospect of success; or

(b) there is some other compelling reason why the appeal should be heard.

(7) An order giving permission may –

(a) limit the issues to be heard; and

(b) be made subject to conditions.

(Rule 3.1(3) also provides that the court may make an order subject to conditions)

(Rule 25.15 provides for the court to order security for costs of an appeal)

2 The Appellant

Practice Direction to CPR 52C –Extension of time for filing appeallant's notice.'

2. THE APPELLANT

(A) THE APPELLANT'S NOTICE

FILING AND SERVICE OF THE APPELLANT'S NOTICE CPR 52.4 — APPELLANT'S NOTICE

[35.20B]   R (on the application of Hysaj) v Secretary of State for the Home Department, Fathollahipour v Aliabadienisi, May v Robinson

[2014] EWCA Civ 1633, [2015] 1 WLR 2472, (2015) Times, 22 January

The three appellants applied for extensions of time to file their appellant's notice(s). The Court of Appeal conjoined the hearings in order to provide general guidance on the approach to be adopted for such applications to extend time.

HELD, ON APPEAL: Although CPR r 52.6 gave no guidance as to the principles on which applications for extension of time should be considered, such applications were equivalent to applications for relief from sanctions and should be governed by the principles in CPR r 3.9.

The 3 stage approach set out in *Mitchell v News Group Newspapers Ltd* [2013] EWCA Civ 1537, [2014] 2 All ER 430, [2014] 1 WLR 795 and *Denton v TH White Ltd* [2014] EWCA Civ 906, [2015] 1 All ER 880, [2014] 1 WLR 3926, must, therefore, be applied.

The merits of the substantive appeal would have little significance when considering whether to extend time.

CHAPTER 36

Accidents Abroad

2. APPLICABLE LAW

(D) THE BRUSSELS I REGULATION

[36.5A] Hoteles Pinero & Keefe (by his litigation friend Eyton) v Mapfre Mutualidad Compania De Seguros Y Reaseguros SA

[2015] EWCA Civ 598, [2016] 1 WLR 905, [2016] Lloyd's Rep IR 94

Mr Keefe was seriously injured by a piece of hotel equipment while on holiday in Tenerife in October 2006. He initially sued the hotel's management company in Spain but, after the decision in Odenbreidt was published, he sought to sue the hotel's insurers, Mapfre, directly in England. He argued that articles 9 and 11 of the Brussels I regulation provided grounds for this approach to jurisdiction. [The numbering of the articles is that of the original regulation rather than the re-cast version, but nothing turns on this.]

If the jurisdiction argument succeeded it would logically follow, in a case before Rome II applied, that the quantum of damages would be regarded as procedural and therefore governed by the law of the court, ie English law. In any event, the applicable substantive law - which would govern the issue of liability - was agreed to be Spanish.

The claim was valued (assuming liability attached) at around £5 million on the English basis whereas its value if assessed under Spanish principles would be much lower, of the order of €800,000. An important relevant factor was that the hotel's insurance policy was subject to a limit of indemnity of around €600,000 and for this reason the claimant sought to join the hotel to the direct action which he had started in England against its insurer Mapfre. The hotel applied for an order that the English court did not have jurisdiction to hear the claim against it.

HELD: In May 2013 the hotel's application was dismissed by the Master and in October 2013 a High Court judge upheld that decision. In July 2015 the Court of Appeal in turn confirmed that the English courts had jurisdiction because of articles 11 & 9 of the regulation.

The Court of Appeal was:

'unable to accept that the exercise by the English court of jurisdiction over the hotel amounts in this context to an impermissible ouster of the jurisdiction of the Spanish courts. It is no more than a consequence of the combination of two principles: that the injured person as the weaker party in a direct claim against the insurer is entitled to sue in the courts of his own place of domicile (Articles 11(2) and 9(b)); and that, if the court has jurisdiction over the insurer in relation to a direct claim, it also has jurisdiction over the insured, if the law under which the direct claim arises permits the insured to be joined in the same action.'

In addition, the court was alive to the effect that this decision on jurisdiction would have on the valuation of the claim (if liability attached), pointing out that:

'it is hard on the hotel to find that because its insurer has been sued in this country it faces a liability for damages considerably greater than would have been the case if it had been sued in Spain, but that is primarily a consequence of the differences between English and Spanish law in relation to the assessment of damages . . . '

[36.5A] *Accidents Abroad*

Subsequently, in November 2015, the Supreme Court granted permission to appeal.

(E) TRANSITIONAL ARRANGEMENTS

[36.22A] Vann v Ocidental-Companhia de Seguros SA
[2015] EWCA Civ 572, [2015] All ER (D) 36 (Jun)

The insurer, Occidental, appealed the finding that the pedestrians were not contributorily negligent. The application of Portuguese law pursuant to article 4(1) of Rome II was not contested. The point at issue was an aspect of the judge's decision on the factual evidence.

HELD: The Court of Appeal observed that it was not disputed that relevant Portuguese principles were essentially the same as the English law on contributory negligence.

The judge had drawn an inference from the facts that the injured pedestrians had kept a proper look out. That was not a permissible inference because the judge had found, consistent with the expert evidence, that the Portuguese driver had his headlights on. The crossing pedestrians ought therefore to have noticed him approaching but, by continuing to cross the road, it must follow that they did not take reasonable care for their safety. However, the driver was nevertheless principally at fault for driving too fast. A reduction of 20% should be made for the contributory negligence of the pedestrians.

[36.24] Winrow v Hemphill & Ageas Insurance
[2014] EWHC 2164 (QB), 164 NLJ 7629

The claimant was the wife of a British army officer stationed in Germany at the time of the accident in November 2009. She worked at an army school. The defendant driver, who was at fault in the accident, was the wife of another British officer and was also living in Germany at the time. Her car was insured with Ageas, based in England. The claimant brought proceedings in England in 2011 after having returned to the UK. The key issue was the correct applicable law under article 4 of Rome II. The claimant argued that it should be English law, under either article 4(2) or article 4(3).

HELD: Given that the accident happened in Germany and the damage occurred there, German law would apply under article 4(1) unless either of the exceptions was made out. Article 4(2) required for the claimant and *'the person claimed to be liable'* to have a common habitual residence at the time when the damage occurs. Following one aspect of *Jacobs v Motor Insurers' Bureau*, the judge found that *'the person claimed to be liable'* in article 4(2) meant the defendant driver and not the insurer. It was therefore irrelevant that the insurer was registered in England. On the facts, the claimant was not *'at the time when the damage occurs'*, habitually resident in the UK but in Germany. Her husband and family had been established there for several years. She was employed in Germany and her children were being educated there. A stated intention eventually to return to the UK was not sufficient and the exception in article 4(2) was not made out.

The claimant's alternative argument was that the tort was *'manifestly more closely connected'* with England under article 4(3). The judge found this to be a high threshold but, unlike article 4(2), the test in 4(3) has no temporal limitation to *'the time when the damages occurs'*. Connecting factors to England were that the parties were resident in England when proceedings were issued here, both were English nationals, and the claimant's injuries required ongoing care and treatment in England. However, the accident had occurred in Germany, the parties were at the time habitually resident there (the claimant for some eight years previously) and the claimant continued to live there for a year and a half after the accident. The judge found that the high threshold required of article 4(3) was not met in this case, because *'taking into account all the circumstances, the relevant factors do not indicate a manifestly closer connection of the tort with England than with Germany.'* German law therefore applied according to article 4(1).

[36.25] Bianco (Widow and Administratrix of the estate of the late Vladimiro Capano on behalf of herself and dependant children) v Bennett

[2015] EWHC 626 (QB), [2015] All ER (D) 178 (Mar)

The claimant's husband was killed in a road traffic accident in Surrey in February 2011. At the time, he was living in Italy but had been commuting to the UK for a short while on weekly basis as part of an engineering project. Proceedings were issued in England seeking damages under English law, ie the Fatal Accidents Act 1976 (FAA) and under the Law Reform (Miscellaneous Provisions) Act 1934 (LRMPA). The parties agreed a 2:1 apportionment of liability against the defendant. The damages sought by the claimant under both Acts were around £500,000.

However, in addition, recovery was also sought of sums of around £340,000 and £65,000. These were described as subrogated claims which related, respectively, to amounts paid or to be paid to the family by the Italian Workers Compensation Authority and by the deceased's employers. It was argued that these were recoverable under Article 85 of Regulation (EC) No 883/2004 on the Co-ordination of Social Security Systems, which is set out below:

'1. If a person receives benefits under the legislation of one Member State in respect of an injury resulting from events occurring in another Member State, any rights of the institution responsible for providing benefits against a third party liable to provide compensation for the injury shall be governed by the following rules:

(a) *where the institution responsible for providing benefits is, under the legislation it applies, subrogated to the rights which the beneficiary has against the third party, such subrogation shall be recognised by each Member State;*

(b) *where the institution responsible for providing benefits has a direct right against the third party, each Member State shall recognise such rights.'*

HELD: On the material before him as pleaded, the judge found that the supporting Italian law which might provide for subrogation or direct claims (at (a) or (b) above) was not proven. The subrogated claims could not be brought within the applicable English law, that being the FAA and the LRMPA. On the one hand they were not causes of action possessed by the deceased before his death, so the LRMPA could not vest them in his estate. On the other, the FAA provided only for recovery of damages for bereavement, for loss of dependency and funeral expenses. No other heads of damage were recoverable and hence the subrogated claims were outside it.

The judge was also asked to decide the position assuming the Italian law had been proven and it had been shown that subrogation was possible under its provisions. He essentially reached the same decision this obiter point. The law applicable to the dispute was English Law because the damage occurred in England. As the subrogated claims were not recoverable in English law, it followed that - regardless of the rights of subrogation that might exist in Italian law - they were not recoverable by the claimant on behalf of the Italian payers.

[36.26] Syred v Powszecnny Zaklad Ubezpieczen (PZU), Bednorz & HDI Gerling

[2016] EWHC 254 (QB), [2016] All ER (D) 157 (Feb)

The claimant, an English resident, was a rear seat passenger injured in an accident in Poland in February 2010. The drivers were Polish and the cars were insured by Polish and German insurers PZU and HDI. There was no dispute that article 4(1) of Rome II designated Polish law as the applicable law and that it governed questions of contributory negligence and quantum because of article 15.

The claimant admitted not wearing a seatbelt and thus the question of what deduction to make arose. The experts on Polish law agreed that failure to wear a seatbelt in the rear seat was negligent and raised the question whether this negligence caused the injuries or made them worse than they would otherwise have been.

HELD: The burden of proving foreign law falls on the party seeking to rely on it which, here, was the defendant insurer(s). They would be required to show that the failure to wear the seat belt caused the injuries or made them worse. The judge found that although the claimant was thrown from the vehicle and sustained head injuries, he would have done so in any event because he would have been forced violently against the car's frame had he been wearing a seat belt. The defendants had failed to establish that the head injury would have been less severe.

The parties had agreed that the claim for pecuniary losses should be assessed in accordance with English law, subject to giving credit for state benefits received. Although the applicable Polish law requires that credit be given for all benefits, the claimant sought to argue that the equivalent English legislation (on compensation recovery) should apply. If it did apply, the claimant would have to give credit only for benefits received in the five years after the accident. His argument was that this rule was an overriding mandatory provision in accordance with article 16 of Rome II: 'Nothing in this Regulation shall restrict the application of the provisions of the law of the forum in a situation where they are mandatory irrespective of the law otherwise applicable to the non-contractual obligation.'

The judge dismissed this argument on the basis that the English legislation on compensation recovery could hardly be said to be so critical to the protection of the political social or economic order of the UK as to override a rule of Polish law which was properly designated by the Rome II regulation.

[36.27]   Moreno v Motor Insurers' Bureau

[2015] EWHC 1142 (QB), [2016] UKSC 52, [2015] All ER 213 (Apr)

The claimant was injured in Greece in 2011 by an uninsured driver. No other car was involved in the accident. She pursued the MIB under the 2003 Regulations (Motor Vehicles (Compulsory Insurance) (Information Centre and Compensation Body Regulations 2003 (SI 2003/37)). But for the statutory rights under these regulations, Rome II would have applied and would have designated Greek law as the applicable law and it would, under article 15, have applied to the assessment of damages.

HELD: The judge was however bound by the earlier Court of Appeal' decisions of *Jacobs v Motor Insurers' Bureau* and *Bloy* and *Ireson v Motor Insurers' Bureau* regarding the 2003 Regulations. He therefore found that the claimant's damages should be assessed according to English law. 'Leapfrog' permission to appeal was granted to the Supreme Court.

On 3 August 2016 the Supreme Court unanimously allowed the MIB's appeal and held that the damages should be assessed according to Greek law. In this respect, it expressly overruled the earlier Court of Appeal decisions in *Jacobs* and *Bloy*. The various European Motor Insurance Directives had put in place a scheme for compensating victims of road traffic accidents that should be interpreted in English law so as to deliver consistent compensation regardless of whether a driver, an insurer or a home or host state's guarantee fund was pursued. The 2003 Regulations should therefore be understood in that context. Lord Mance gave the judgment of the court and concluded that:

> '. . . the Directives . . . do not leave it to individual member states to provide for compensation in accordance with any law that such states may choose. On the contrary, they proceed on the basis that a victim's entitlement to compensation will be measured on a consistent basis, by reference to the law of the state of the accident, whichever of the routes to recovery provided by the Directives he or she invokes.'

Although it is not clear if anything turns on it, it should nevertheless be noted that his preferred formulation here - *'the law of the state of the accident'* - differs slightly from the test applied in article 4.1 of the Rome II regulation, below (bold emphasis added):

> 'Unless otherwise provided for in this Regulation, the law applicable to a non-contractual obligation arising out of a tort/delict shall be **the law of the country in which the damage occurs** irrespective of the country in which the event giving rise to the damage occurred and irrespective of the country or countries in which the indirect consequences of that event occur.'

[36.28] Marshall v Motor Insurers' Bureau, Pickard & Generali, Pickard v Motor Insurers' Bureau

[2015] EWHC 3421 (QB), [2016] PIQB Q65

The claimants were injured in France in 2012. The accident was caused by an uninsured driver colliding with them, with an English registered Ford Fiesta (owned by Mr Pickard and insured with RSA and in which they had been travelling) and with a French breakdown vehicle. Mr Marshall was killed in the accident and his widow pursued the MIB (acting as proxy for the Fonds de Garantie (FdG), its French counterpart), Mr Pickard and Generali, the insurer of the recovery vehicle. Mr Pickard pursued the MIB.

HELD: French law applied under the general rule of article 4(1) of Rome II. On the facts, it was possible that French law could be partly displaced by article 4(2) in favour of English law, but only in respect of the claim by the passenger's widow against the driver of the Fiesta, as both had a common habitual residence in England at the time of the damage. Turning to article 4(3), the judge found that this provision, on these facts, operated to designate French law. The centre of gravity of the tort was in France and the claim was *'manifestly more closely connected'* with that country.

Mr Marshall had been trapped by the Fiesta's trailer and the recovery truck. As a matter of French law, the judge found that the involvement (*'l'implication'*) of these two insured vehicles in his fatal accident meant that the FdG was not liable to his widow in French law.

Under the 2003 Regulations (The Motor Vehicles (Compulsory Insurance) (Information Centre and Compensation Body Regulations 2003 (SI 2003/37), the MIB would only be liable to ' . . . *compensate the injured party in accordance with the provisions of Article 1 of the second motor insurance directive as if it were the body authorised* . . . ' (reg 13(2)). The FdG was 'the body authorised' in France and, because it was not liable in French law, the MIB would not be liable to Mrs Marshall.

Mr Pickard had been thrown clear by the impact with the uninsured car. No other vehicle was involved in his accident and therefore the FdG, and hence the MIB, would be liable in respect of that claim. The judge found that *'on the law as it stands as at the date of this judgment the assessment of damages on the part of the MIB will be governed by English law, and the assessment of damages on the part of RSA and Generali will be governed by French law.'*

It is understood that the Court of Appeal has granted permission to appeal.

[36.29] Howe v Motor Insurers' Bureau

[2016] EWHC 640 (QB), 166 NLJ 7694

The claimant was injured by an uninsured vehicle in France in 2007. The accident pre-dated the Rome II regulation but the applicable law was not disputed.

HELD: The claim failed because it was statute barred under French law. It was also time barred under the 2003 Regulations.

[36.29] *Accidents Abroad*

Notwithstanding, the judge, who was taken to *Marshall v Motor Insurers' Bureau* (above), examined the question if the MIB would be liable only if the Fonds de Garantie is liable. He found that he was bound the decisions of the Court of Appeal in *Jacobs v Motor Insurers' Bureau* and *Bloy* and *Ireson v Motor Insurers' Bureau* [2013] EWCA Civ 1543, [2014] Lloyds Rep 75, [2014] PIQR P171 to find that the MIB is not liable (under the 2003 Regulations) only if the Fonds de Garantie is liable.

This is therefore a different conclusion than that reached in *Marshall* some four months earlier. The judge observed that *'It is of course for the Supreme Court to decide whether the Courts of Appeal in Jacobs and Bloy were correct when they hear the Moreno appeal in the summer of 2016. Until then, I find it is impermissible and unnecessary for me to consider in any more detail MIB's arguments as to the construction of Regulation 13(2)(b).'*

As with the *Marshall* case immediately above, it is understood that this decision is also being appealed.

CHAPTER 37

General Principles of Quantum

1. FORSEEABILITY

(D) SECOND INDENT

[37.17A]   XP v Compensa Towarzystwo SA
[2016] EWHC 1728 (QB)

The claimant claimed damages for personal injuries and consequential losses following two road traffic accidents. The first occurred in Poland, and the damages consequent on it fell to be determined according to Polish law. The second accident occurred in the UK. Both defendants admitted liability but disputed the damages claimed, and disputed their relative contribution to the claimant's loss and damage. Accident 1 had caused the claimant to miscarry a pregnancy at 16 weeks which caused her physical and psychiatric injury. Accident 2 caused an exacerbation of the claimants' PTSD, plus orthopaedic injuries. It was established that the combined effects of both accidents lead the claimant to be unemployed for a period of two years. The court was asked to consider the causative potency in respect of accident 1 and accident 2. The defendant invited the court to consider the authority of *Christine Reaney v University Hospital of North Staffordshire and Mid Staffordshire NHS Foundation Trust* [2015] EWCA Civ 1119, [2015] All ER (D) 16 (Nov). The court should ask the 'but for' question: but for accident 2, what would have the difference have been? The judge did not consider that this was a *Reaney* type case. It was not possible to separate neatly the effects of accident 1 and accident 2. The case better fitted with the approach taken in *Rahman v Arearose Ltd* [2001] QB 351, [2000] 3 WLR 1184. In respect of the claim for past loss of earnings, the judge was unable to distinguish between the effects of accident 1 and 2. The defendants therefore shared the losses on a 75/25, ie 75% of the loss is attributable to the first accident and 25% to the second.

4. ECONOMIC LOSS

(C) SPECIAL RELATIONSHIP

[37.38A]   Burgess v Lejonvarn
[2016] EWHC 40 (TCC), 164 Con LR 165

In proceedings brought against an architect by her employers, who were seeking damages in contract and tort, the court was required to determine, as preliminary issues, whether she had concluded a contract with them or owed them a duty of care. The architect had been a friend of her employers (the claimant). The architect had

[37.38A] *General Principles of Quantum*

recommended the services of a contractor, for no fee, to complete the earthworks and hard landscaping in connection with a garden reservation. It had been the parties' intention for the architect to then complete the second stage of 'soft landscaping' thereafter. The project did not reach the second stage, however, as the employers deemed the work of the contractor to have been defective.

The claim in contract failed, however it was held that there was a claim in tort. The cases of *Hedley Byrne & Co Ltd v Heller & Partners Ltd* [1964] AC 465, [1963] 2 All ER 575, [1963] 3 WLR 101, HL and *Henderson v Merrett Syndicates Ltd (No 1)* [1995] 2 AC 145, [1994] 3 All ER 506, [1994] 3 WLR 761, were applied.

It was held that the architect had provided a series of professional services for the employers in respect of the project. Although her provision of those services was gratuitous in the sense that she only intended to seek specific payment for the second phase once the earthworks element had been completed; the fact that the services were gratuitously provided did not mean that they were informal or social in context. The evidence was that the architect had provided a series of professional services to the employers. It followed that the architect had owed a duty of care to the employers to exercise reasonable skill and care in the provision by her of professional services acting as an architect and project manager on the project.

(D) ABSENCE OF ACTIONABLE INJURY

[37.38B]   Greenway v Johnson Matthey plc
[2016] EWCA Civ 408, [2016] All ER (D) 207 (Apr)

Five chemical process operators appealed against a decision that their claims against the respondent employer arising out of their exposure to platinum salts in the workplace were claims for pure economic loss and not personal injury.

Chlorinated or halogenated platinum salts were produced during the refining process undertaken at the employer's chemical factory. Owing to the risk of sensitisation through exposure to the salts, the employer required employees to undergo regular skin prick testing. The appellants were found to have become sensitised and were removed from work involving contact with platinum. They claimed substantial damages for loss of earnings. Platinum sensitisation was symptomless and did not adversely affect day-to-day life. However, it created a susceptibility to developing a platinum allergy if exposure continued. The employer accepted that it had failed in its statutory duties regarding workplace cleaning. The appellants claimed in tort and contract. The judge held at first instance that they had not suffered any physical injury as was necessary to give them a cause of action in tort. He found that the losses they claimed to have suffered were outside the scope of the relevant contractual duty owed to them and that they could only recover nominal damages for breach of contract.

The initial decision was upheld and the appeal was dismissed. The appellants had not suffered an actionable injury. The employer had breached its duty to take all necessary and reasonable steps to ensure its employees' safety at work, but that duty, whether in contract or tort, was focused on protecting employees from physical injury, not from economic harm. A standard term or duty of care requiring an employer to protect an employee from economic loss could not be implied into contracts of employment.

7. ILLEGALITY

[37.66C] McCracken (a protected party suing by his mother and litigation friend Deborah Norris)

[2015] EWCA Civ 380, [2016] Lloyd's Rep IR 171, [2015] PIQR P305

Two 16 year old boys had been riding a stolen motorbike dangerously on a cycle path adjacent to a road junction. The claimant was riding as a pillion passenger. The first defendant was the driver of the trials bike. A collision occurred between the trials bike and the defendant's minibus. At first instance, the minibus driver was found to have been contributory negligent in causing the claimant's injuries, but the claimant's damages were reduced by 45% (including the agreed 15% for failure to wear a helmet) to reflect his own responsibility for his injuries.

The decision at first instance was appealed by the minibus driver. It was held that the judge had not erred in finding the minibus driver negligent for failing to properly check at the junction before colliding with the stolen motorbike; and nor had the judge erred in rejecting the minibus driver's defence of *ex turpi causa*. The accident had two causes, the dangerous driving of the bike and the negligent driving of the minibus. The claimant's injury had been the consequence of both. The fact that the criminal conduct had been one of the two causes was not a sufficient basis for the *ex turpi causa* defence to succeed.

On appeal, the damages payable to the seriously injured pillion passenger were further reduced to reflect his contributory negligence. The passenger's contributory negligence was re-assessed at 65%, 20% more than that attributed to him at first instance.

[37.66D] Smith (by his mother and litigation friend Mrs Banner) v Stratton

[2015] EWCA Civ 1413, [2015] All ER (D) 259 (Dec)

The claimant was one of four young men in a car which struck a parked vehicle, whilst the driver was attempting to outrun the police. The MIB's case was the four men were in a joint enterprise of drug dealing. There was no direct evidence on that issue but only circumstantial evidence. The judge accepted the circumstantial evidence that the claimant was involved in drug dealing from the car.

The test for 'ex turpi' set out in *Joyce v O'Brien* [2013] EWCA Civ 546, QB was applied, ie was the injury caused by a manifestation of a foreseeable increased risk from joint enterprise.

The judge was prepared to link the risk of the loss of control in travelling at an unsafe speed to the criminal activity, namely drug dealing and attempting to evade the police. The claim was dismissed.

[37.66E] Beaumont & O'Neill v Ferrer

[2016] EWCA Civ 768

The claimant's appealed against the first instance decision, which found that the defendant had done nothing wrong in driving off when the door of his taxi, through which the claimants' subsequently tried to exit the taxi, was left open.

By way of background, six men ordered a taxi, which they had all previously agreed not to pay for, instead intending to escape at an opportune moment at or near their destination.

Three of the men, seated in the middle row of the defendant's taxi, escaped near their intended destination whilst the vehicle was stationary. They left the sliding door open for the claimants, who were seated in the back row, to also escape.

The defendant moved off from a stationary position, partly as a result of panic and partly to impede the claimants' escape.

[37.66E] *General Principles of Quantum*

The two claimants, who had been seated in the back row of the vehicle, were undeterred by the fact the vehicle was once again moving and intended to escape through the open door.

In the course of escaping from the moving vehicle, both claimants sustained personal injuries.

HELD: The appeal was unsuccessful. The principle of *ex turpi causa* precluded the claimants from recovering damages, despite a finding of negligence on the part of the defendant taxi driver. However his negligence was not considered causative of the claimants' injuries. He had moved off from a stationary position, during the course of the passengers' escape when he knew they were neither wearing seat belts and the door from which they would escape had been opened. The court found that the defendant had done nothing to put either claimant in the position where they were poised to exit the vehicle, once the vehicle began moving each claimant had the opportunity to retake their seats and put their seat belts back on and had they done so, would not have sustained their injuries.

CHAPTER 38

Quantification of Damages

3. DAMAGES FOR PAIN, SUFFERING AND LOSS OF AMENITY

(D) PSYCHIATRIC ILLNESS

[38.41A]   Easton v B & Q plc

[2015] EWHC 880 (QB), [2015] All ER (D) 40 (Apr)

The defendant successfully defeated allegations of breach of duty. It was argued the claimant's psychiatric illness and consequential loss caused by work-related stress was not foreseeable at any stage.

HELD: The court held that the claimant's psychiatric illness, on a proper application of the principles of *Hatton v Sutherland* [2002] EWCA Civ 76, [2002] 2 All ER 1, [2002] ICR 613 was bound to fail at the first hurdle – foreseeability. The claimant had ten years management experience of large retailers and had not given history of psychiatric or psychological problems. The defendant had no indication that the claimant would suffer psychiatric illness. Furthermore, there was nothing about store managers in general which would give rise to a foreseeable risk.

[38.43A]   Lisa Diane Wild and Ian Daniel Wild v Southend University Hospital NHS Foundation Trust

[2014] EWHC 4053 (QB), [2014] All ER (D) 46 (Dec)

The second claimant was present with his wife at hospital when it was discovered that their unborn son had died in the womb and he also present when the baby was delivered stillborn. He brought a case against the defendant NHS Trust on the basis that he had sustained psychiatric injuries due to the shock of being present when the baby's death in the womb was discovered and this had been compounded by the subsequent wait and witnessing of the delivery of his stillborn son. His claim was presented on the basis of his being a secondary victim.

HELD: Whilst the defendant admitted clinical negligence and settled the first claimant's claim as she was the primary victim, the judge dismissed the second claimant's claim as it held that he did not satisfy the control mechanisms for secondary victims derived from *Alcock v Chief Constable of South Yorkshire* [1992] 1 AC 310, [1991] 4 All ER 907, [1991] 3 WLR 1057 and applied *Taylor v Novo (UK) Ltd* [2014] EWCA Civ 194, [2014] QB 150. Although he witnessed the consequences of the defendant's negligence this did not satisfy as witnessing horrific events leading to a death or serious injury.

[38.43B]   Liverpool Woman's Hospital NHS Foundation Trust v Ronayne

[2015] EWCA Civ 588, 145 BMLR 110, [2015] PIQR P337

In July 2008, the claimant's wife was admitted to a hospital administered by the defendant NHS trust, where she underwent a hysterectomy. A few days after discharge the claimant's wife became unwell and her condition deteriorated over 24

[38.43B] *Quantification of Damages*

hours. The condition of the claimant's wife was a consequence of the negligence of the trust in the performance of the hysterectomy. The claimant alleged at trial that he had suffered psychiatric injury in the form of post-traumatic stress disorder (PTSD), consequent upon the shock of seeing his wife's sudden deterioration. The judge rejected his claim of PTSD, but nonetheless found that he had suffered from a frank psychiatric illness. His claim for damages as a secondary victim of the trust's admitted negligence succeeded and he was awarded damages of £9,165.88. The trust appealed.

HELD: The principal issue was whether the events concerned were of a nature capable of founding a secondary victim case, namely were they in the necessary sense 'horrifying'. The appeal would be allowed.

The claimant fell far short of those cases which had been recognised by the law as founding secondary victim liability. It had not been a case where there had been a sudden appreciation of an event. There had been a series of events over time.

[38.43C]   Shorter v Surrey and Sussex Healthcare NHS Trust
[2015] EWHC 614 (QB), 144 BMLR 136

The claimant sought damages for psychiatric injury from the defendant NHS trust which had been responsible for the care of her sister LS, who had died in May 2009 as a result of the admitted breach of the defendant's duty of care. The claimant had been made aware of her sister's collapse, and subsequently went to support her sister. She was present with her sister following her hospital admission until she pronounced dead. The defendant had already settled various claims for damages in respect of the death of LS, and on behalf of her estate. The claimant based her case on the fact that she had a close relationship with LS, and alleged that, as a 'secondary victim' she was aware of her sister's collapse and of what happened afterwards. She submitted that she had suffered a number of different episodes which together amounted to a seamless single traumatic event, beginning with news that her sister's condition had deteriorated significantly and that she had suffered a sub-arachnoid haemorrhage which had been undiagnosed and untreated, and ending with her death. The claimant alleged that she had sustained psychiatric injury taking the form of a major depressive episode.

HELD: The claim would be dismissed. It was settled law that, in very limited circumstances, a secondary victim of a breach of duty was entitled to recover damages for psychiatric injury occurring as a result of the death or serious physical injury of a near relative, caused by the negligence of a third party. It was difficult for a secondary victim to meet the criteria necessary for a successful claim by satisfying the 'control mechanisms' which had to be surmounted in order to recover damages.

6.   LOSS OF EARNING CAPACITY

(A) ADULT

[38.94A]   Billett v Ministry of Defence
[2015] EWCA Civ 773, [2016] PIQR Q1

The claimant, who had been in the army, had suffered with a non-freezing cold injury to his feet sustained while engaged on exercises, with unsuitable footwear, during his employment with the defendant. He was awarded damages for pain, suffering loss of amenity and for future loss of earnings calculated by reference to the Ogden tables. The defendant successfully challenged an award of £99,000 for loss of earning capacity arrived at using an adjusted multiplier/reduction factors approach. This case is the first time the Court of Appeal has considered the reduction factors set out in Tables A-D of the Ogden tables, which apply contingencies other than mortality to multipliers for earnings related losses. However, as the claimant was on the outer fringe of the broad spectrum of the disability, his loss of future earnings should not have been calculated by reference to the Ogden tables and should have been calculated on the basis of a *Smith v Manchester City Council (or Manchester Corpn)* (1974) 17 KIR 1, 118 Sol Jo 597 approach.

[38.94B] Murphy v Ministry of Defence

[2016] EWHC 3 (QB)

The claimant had been a serving soldier in the army since 2006. In 2010, he was serving in Afghanistan. Whilst in the process of unloading a goods vehicle, a roll of fabric struck him on the back of the neck. The claimant went on to develop chronic widespread pain (fibromyalgia). He was subsequently discharged from the army in September 2013. By the date of trial, the claimant had been working as an Estate Workforce Manager for the NHS, earning £45,000 per annum gross.

In determining whether the claimant was considered to be disabled, as set out in the Equality Act 2010, the judge had regarded the test for disability as set out under the Act. Whilst the judge did find the claimant to be disabled, the level of that disability was considered to be modest in nature. Having regard to the claimant's particular circumstances and the factual matrix of this case, it was not a case considered well suited to the use of the Ogden tables. The judge found the case of *Billett v Ministry of Defence* [2015] EWCA Civ 773 to be the most useful guide. The claimant had been in work since leaving the army. His employment was secure. He was handicapped on the labour market, but that handicap was limited. He would, however, be more limited in his choice of employment. The judge found this case to be more suited to a *Smith v Manchester* calculation. The claimant was awarded the sum of £50,000, which represented in the region of two years loss of earnings.

HELD: When calculating past loss of earnings, *Billett v Ministry of Defence* [2015] All ER (D) 256 (Jul) was applied. It had to be remembered that the army way of life was what the claimant had wanted. He would have fulfilled that ambition, but for the accident. He would have done his duty and he would have received the income and the payments/bonuses referred to. Comparing the hypothetical uninjured claimant with the injured claimant, the hypothetical uninjured claimant would willingly have endured the less attractive aspects of army life and he would have been paid accordingly. There was no logic to discount any of those payments. In terms of future loss even though the claimant was disabled, a sufficient adjustment to the disabled multiplier was too contrived an exercise. An appropriate award would be in the region of two years' loss of earnings and an award amounting under this head of £50,000.

That award was on top of the multiplier/multiplicand based award for loss of earnings based on what the claimant would have earned in the army compared to what he will earn during the period to when he would have left the army in 2030, which needed to be calculated.

8. LOSS OF PENSION

WORKPLACE PENSIONS

[38.105A] In October 2012, the Government introduced requirements for employers to enrol eligible employees into a workplace pension scheme. Contributions would be made by employers, employees or both, dependent upon

[38.105A] *Quantification of Damages*

the earnings and age of the employee. The Government supported the scheme indirectly through pension tax relief, as income tax was not levied on contributions by employees.

Information about the scheme and the employer's duties are available on the Pensions Regulator's website.

'Auto-enrolment' is a term that is commonly used for this scheme. However, it describes only one class of employee effected by the changes. Only employees meeting certain criteria are automatically enrolled (see below). The aim of automatic enrolment was to encourage savings for retirement.

Types of employees:
(1) If an employee is between 22 and the state pension age (SPA) and:
  (a) earning more than £10,000, the employee must be automatically enrolled into the workplace pension scheme unless the employee chooses to opt out; and
  (b) if in that age bracket but earning between £10,000 and the threshold wage of £5,824, the employee can <u>ask</u> to be enrolled and the employer must make contributions.
(2) If an employee is aged 16-22 and SPA – 74 and above the threshold earnings of £5,824, but not earning more than £10,000, they can ask to be part of a workplace pension which must then be provided and the employer must make contributions.
(3) If an employee is below the threshold earnings of £5,824 they can ask to be part of a workplace pension scheme but the employer does not have to make any contributions.

The maximum earning against which contributions are calculated is £42,385.

9. CARE AND NURSING

(A) GRATUITOUS CARE

[38.112A] Massey v Tameside & Glossop Acute Services NHS Trust
[2007] EWHC 317 (QBE), [2007] All ER (D) 301 (Feb)

The claimant suffered from dyskinetic cerebral palsy with dystonia as a result of negligent care by the defendant during his birth. The claimant's mother cared for the claimant for which she received carers allowance. The issue arose as to whether sums received by way of carer's allowance should be deducted from the claim for past care.

The court ruled that to the extent that the carer had received benefits in respect of her voluntary care, the claimant did not need a sum of money to give proper recompense for that care. Accordingly, sums received by the carer by way of carer's allowance, should be deducted from past care to ensure there would be no double recovery.

[38.112B]   R (on the application of ZYX) v Walsall Metropolitan Borough Council
[2014] EWHC 1918 (Admin), [2015] 1 All ER 165, [2014] PTSR 1356

The claimant had who was severely disabled had substantial assets. She sought judicial review of the decision by the defendant authority to charge her for the full cost of social care services it provided to her. The claimant's substantial capital assets were from damages paid to her in settlement of a substantial personal injury claim. A deputy had been appointed and the court ordered that the deputy could withdraw no more than £50,000 per annum from the claimant's damages, for her use and benefit.

HELD: The whole of the claimant's capital fell within paragraph 44(1)(b) of Sch 10 to the Income Support (General) Regulations 1987, SI 1987/1967. The defendant authority's stance in charging for the cost of social care was unlawful insofar as it took into account the capital derived from the claimant's personal injury claim.

(C) PROFESSIONAL/PAID CARE

[38.118A]   Reaney v University Hospital of North Staffordshire NHS Trust and Mid Staffordshire NHS Foundation Trust

[2015] EWCA Civ 1119, [2015] All ER (D) 16 (Nov)

The claimant was a 61 year old T7 paraplegic due to a spontaneous spinal inflammatory condition. Whilst in hospital she developed pressure sores as a result of the defendant's admitted negligence. At first instance, the claimant recovered all of the costs of her care needs, even though she was a T7 paraplegic pre-negligence. At first instance, Foskett J held that the defendant had to take the claimant as it found her. If the defendant's negligence worsened the claimant's condition, the defendant had to compensate for the worsened position. The Court of Appeal did not accept that approach. It accepted the defendant's argument that the correct approach was to compare the pre and post-accident needs; liability only extended to additional needs caused by the negligence. The Court of Appeal distinguished between quantitative and qualitative differences in care needs. If the defendant's negligence caused care and other needs which were substantially the same as pre-accident needs, but different only in the quantity needed, the defendant was liable only for additional needs. However, if the needs were qualitatively different, ie different in type and expertise then those needs were caused entirely by the negligence.

[38.118B]   Lamarieo Manna (a child and protected party by his father and litigation friend, Samuel Manna) v Central Manchester University Hospitals NHS Foundation Trust

[2015] EWHC 2279 (QB), [2015] All ER (D) 39 (Aug)

The claimant sustained severe brain damage at birth. He was 18 at time of trial. There was no dispute that the claimant would require an extremely high level of privately paid care for the remainder of his life. The day care regime in place, at the date of trial, was the provision of one carer to meet the claimant's needs. The claimant's care expert contended for two home-based day carers being available at all times. The defendant challenged the proposed care package on the basis that the pre-trial arrangement of one day carer would be adequate in the future. The claimant's day care package was accepted by the trial judge. The defendant expert had overlooked the fact that the ability to manage with the existing one carer arrangement was largely due to the claimant's mother offering the role of second carer. The authorities have established that a tortfeasor cannot avoid payment for commercial care in reliance of the fact that a family member has in the past demonstrated their ability to care for a claimant. That family member is not obliged as carer or case manager and is entitled to be freed from the need for constant supervision (see *Iqbal v Whipps Cross University Hospital Trust* [2007] EWCA Civ 1190, [2008] PIQR P161; *Massey v Tameside & Glossop Acute Services NHS Trust* [2007] EWHC 317 (QBE), [2007] All ER (D) 301 (Feb); and *Crofts v Merton* [2009]).

[38.118C] *Quantification of Damages*

[38.118C] Harman v East Kent Hospitals NHS Foundation Trust

[2015] EWHC 1662 (QB), [2015] PIQR Q92

The claimant suffered from severe autism and significant cognitive impairment. The defendant hospital admitted liability. At the date of trial, the local authority was providing residential accommodation and education for 44 weeks per year. The local authority would probably continue to fund this arrangement until the claimant, who was 13 at trial, would attain the age of 25.

The defendant challenged the claim for funding for the claimant's placement as a local authority were providing funding. Mr Justice Turner reviewed the cases of *Sowden v Lodge* [2004] EWCA Civ 1370, [2005] 1 All ER 581, [2005] 1 WLR 2129, *Crofton v National Health Service Litigation Authority* [2007] EWCA Civ 71, [2007] 1 WLR 923, [2007] LGR 507 and *Peters v East Midlands Strategic Health Authority* [2009] EWCA Civ 145, [2010] QB 48, [2009] 3 WLR 737. He concluded that the effect of *Peters* was that the claimant was entitled to pursue the defendant rather than having to rely on statutory obligations. Further, even if the local authority would continue to pay, the claimant was free to elect not to receive those payments; simply because funding was being paid and would continue, it did not assist the defendant's argument. In response to the defendant's offer of an indemnity should future funding falter it was said: 'The right of recovery against the tortfeasor in this category of case cannot be diluted by the offer of an indemnity'.

The judge was satisfied that the claimant's parents were genuine in their wish to fund privately the claimant's accommodation. Therefore the defendant's attempts to avoid the impact of '*Peters*' was unsuccessful.

10. OTHER FUTURE LOSSES

(B) ACCOMMODATION COSTS

[38.131A] Lamarieo Manna (a child and protected party by his father and litigation friend, Samuel Manna) v Central Manchester University Hospitals NHS Foundation Trust

[2015] EWHC 2279 (QB), [2015] All ER (D) 39 (Aug)

The claimant sustained severe brain damage at birth. He was 18 at date of trial. The claimant's parents had divorced some years prior to the trial.

The claimant's natural father (and litigation friend) had not seen the claimant for a number of years but wished to become involved again in his care.

The claimant recovered the cost of two properties on a *Roberts v Johnstone* basis to allow time with each parent, with carers accommodated in each home. The defendant did not dispute the availability of a second *Roberts v Johnstone* claim in principle, but disputed that it was justified and supported on the facts.

HELD: The judge viewed it as inconceivable that where divorced parents living apart but sharing the care of a negligently injured child, that the child could not claim for necessary adaptations and purchases of a new home for each parent. If the claimant was going to regularly spend time with his father and restore the relationship they had for the first 16 years of his life, then recovery of the second *Roberts v Johnstone* award should not be barred in principle.

It was emphasised that the decision was reached on particular evidence before the court and was not to be regarded as establishing any wider precedent in respect of such recovery.

[38.131B] Robshaw (a child) v United Lincolnshire Hospitals NHS Trust

[2015] EWHC 923 (QB) TLQ/13/0433, [2015] All ER (D) 167 (May)

The claimant, who was aged 12 at the date of trial, suffered significant brain damage following negligence mishandling at his birth. Liability for negligence was admitted. One of the issues which the court was required to consider at the assessment of Assessment of Damages Hearing was the claim for the cost of installing a pool at the claimant's home. A consensus was reached between the accommodation experts that a swimming pool would provide the claimant with enjoyment and both physical and psychological benefits. Whilst the availability of a public pool, 40 minutes away, was considered to be reasonable by the judge, the 29C temperature was agreed to be too cold for the claimant who needed a pool temperature of 32C. The judge determined that the evidence demonstrated that the only way in which the need for the claimant to go swimming regularly was by home provision: - 'just providing pleasure would not ordinarily be sufficient and real and tangible benefits would need to be demonstrated'.

Note: See also *HS v Lancashire Teaching Hospitals NHS Trust* [2015] All ER (D) 167 (May). William J awarded damages on a lifelong basis to the claimant in attending the pool with private hydrotherapy facilities rather than the expensive installation of a pool at home and he did not consider the provision of a home hydrotherapy pool would be a reasonable head of damage.

(C) DIY AND HOUSEKEEPING

[38.132A] Mr Jason Seers v Creighton & Sons Ltd

[2015] EWHC 959 (QB)

The claimant was a man who had always worked and had joined the defendant firm as a fabricator welder. During the course of his employment in March 2010 the claimant suffered a lower back injury. The defendant sought to redeploy the claimant in a supervisory role due to difficulties in undertaking his employment. The claimant's symptoms became worse as a result of which he underwent operative treatment in September 2012 and again in June 2013 as a result of which he never returned to work for the defendant. The claimant took up part time work as a driver and his earnings were a fraction of what he earned with the defendant.

It was submitted to the court that the claimant's claim for DIY costs should attract the standard rate for inability to undertake DIY and that standard rate being £750.00 per annum.

HELD: The trial judge, Mr Justice William Davies, did not believe a standard rate should apply on the basis that people's disabilities are variable. The claimant could not undertake heavy work but it was not suggested that he was incapable of doing any work around his home. The trial judge doing the best he could assessed the annual rate in this case at £350.00 subject to the appropriate multiplier. In relation to cost of gardening the claimant was able to submit evidence to the court that they paid a gardener during the summer months between £20.00-£25.00 per week. The evidence was not challenged and granted by the trial judge, again subject to the appropriate multiplier.

Whilst the claimant sought to recover the cost of decorating on a multiplier/multiplicand basis the court had no direct evidence in relation to the cost of decorating. Whilst the trial judge could infer that there will be some costs of future decorating that would otherwise have been saved by the claimant doing the work himself, as to the exact cost of that on an annual basis it was impossible for the trial judge to assess. In those circumstances a lump sum of £3,000.00 was awarded.

[38.132B] *Quantification of Damages*

[38.132B]   **Mosson v Spousal (London) Ltd**
[2015] EWHC 53 (QB), [2016] 4 WLR 28

The claimant died after a prolonged illness and mesothelioma. The claim was brought by his widow on behalf of the estate and as a dependant.

A number of heads of claim had been agreed between the parties but the court had to decide an award in relation to inter alia, loss of services and loss of intangible benefits.

The claimant had claimed loss of services including gardening and general home maintenance based on the assumption that the claimant would have worked ten hours per week in the provision of the aforementioned services for the rest of his life. A claim for £5,000.00 per annum was pleaded. There was no evidence as to the commercial cost of replacing these services, furthermore little allowance appears to have been made for the fact that as the claimant got older he would have been less and less able, regardless of his illness, to carry out DIY and maintenance.

HELD: The deceased did provide a valuable service to his family and it was right to allow some allowance in respect of this. The trial judge allowed a figure of £1,500.00 per annum.

17. DEDUCTION FROM DAMAGES

(D) PENSION

[38.185A]   **Lamarieo Manna (a child and protected party by his father and litigation friend, Samuel Manna) v Central Manchester University Hospitals NHS Foundation Trust**
[2015] EWHC 2279 (QB), [2015] All ER (D) 39 (Aug)

he claimant sustained severe brain damage at birth. He was 18 at date of trial.

The claimant claimed, in addition to his future loss of earnings, the loss of additional contributions the employer would have made, which in this case was to be based on compulsory employer contributions from age 22. The claimant successfully recovered the sum of £15,967 based on an assumed compulsory employer provision amounting to £700 per annum.

18. SOCIAL SECURITY BENEFITS

(H) CHALLENGING THE RECOVERABILITY OF BENEFITS)

(i)   REVIEW OF CERTIFICATE

[38.203A] A request for mandatory reconsideration can be made if the compensation claim is settled and the compensator has paid the CRU all the monies due as listed on the certificate.

The introduction of the Welfare Reform Act 2012 introduced changes from 28 October 2013 to the Appeals process so that more disputes against DWP decisions can be resolved without the need for referral to Her Majesty's Court and Tribunal Service. The key changes are mandatory reconsideration and direct lodgement.

The CRU must be given the opportunity to formally reconsider its decision before an appeal can be made. This process is known as mandatory reconsid-

eration. The compensator can ask the CRU for a mandatory reconsideration of a certificate of benefits. The CRU will then look at all the evidence and decide if the certificate should either be:
(1) Changed and a partial refund issued.
(2) Revoked and a full refund issued.
(3) Confirmed as correct.

Written notice will be sent out to the compensator and this is known as a mandatory reconsideration notice.

Appeals
(1) If the compensator still believes that the certificate is wrong after having received a mandatory reconsideration notice an Appeal can be made. An appeal must be made in writing and sent directly to HMCTS. A copy of the mandatory reconsideration notice must be sent with the Appeal as the appeal will not go ahead without it. The mandatory reconsideration notice will also tell you where to send your appeal form. You must make an Appeal within one month after the date of the mandatory reconsideration notice has been sent.

An appeal against a certificate of recoverable benefits may be made on the grounds of:
- that any amount, rate or period specified in the certificate is incorrect;
- the certificate shows benefits and/or a lump sum payments which were not paid as a result of the accident, injury or disease;
- benefits and/or lump sum payments listed which have not and are not likely to be paid to the injured person have been brought into account; and
- the compensation payment was not as a consequence of the accident, injury or disease.

(2) An appeal under this section may be made by made by:
- the person who applied for the certificate of recoverable benefits;
- in a case where the amount of compensation payment has been calculated under Section 6; or
- the injured person or other person to whom the payment is made.

(3) No appeal may be made under this section until:-
- the claim giving rise to the compensation payment has been finally disposed of; and
- the liability under Section 6 has been discharged.

You can use the tribunal's Notice of Appeal form which can be found at (http://hmctsformfinder.justice.gov.uk/HMCTS/GetForm.do?court_forms_id=4395) in order to submit your Appeal.

19. RECOVERY OF NHS CHARGES

(B) CHARGES

[38.211] The following NHS treatment and ambulance journey charges are recoverable by the DWP:

[38.211] *Quantification of Damages*

Accident Date (after)	Out-patient charge	In-patient per day	Ambulance journey (each & every)	Cap in any one claim	Classes affected
01.04.2004	£473	£582		£34,800	Motor
01.04.2005	£483	£593		£35,500	Motor
01.04.2006	£505	£620		£37,100	Motor
29.01.2007	£505	£620	£159	£37,100	Motor and casualty
01.04.2008	£547	£672	£165	£40,179	Motor and casualty
01.04.2009	£566	£695	£171	£41,545	Motor and casualty
01.04.2010	£585	£719	£177	£42,999	Motor and casualty
01.04.2011	£600	£737	£181	£44,056	Motor and casualty
01.04.2012	£615	£755	£185	£45,153	Motor and casualty
01.04.2013	£627	£770	£189	£46,046	Motor and casualty
01.04.2014	£637	£783	£192	£46,831	Motor and casualty
01.04.2015	£647	£770	£796	£47,569	Motor and casualty
01.04.2016	£665	£817	£817	£48,849	Motor and casualty

(I) APPEALS

[38.218A] The Welfare Reform Act 2012 introduced changes to the Appeals process so that more disputes against DWP decisions could be resolved without the need for referral to Her Majesty's Courts and Tribunal Service (HMCTS).

The key changes are mandatory reconsideration and direct lodgement. Certificates of NHS charges are not subject to mandatory reconsideration, but are subject to direct lodgement to HMCTS from 7 November 2013.

If you believe the information on the certificate of NHS charges is wrong, you can still ask the CRU to look at the case again under the review process before making an Appeal. You can use the tribunal's Notice of Appeal form which can be found at (http://hmctsformfinder.justice.gov.uk/HMCTS/GetForm.do?court_forms_id=4395) in order to submit your Appeal.

If you think the certificate of NHS charges is wrong following a review, you can make an Appeal. Your Appeal must be made in writing giving reasons why you think the certificate of NHS charges is wrong. An Appeal form is available on the HMCTS website.

Any appeal must be sent directly to HMCTS. The address where to send your Appeal can be found on the HMCTS website. You must also include a copy of the certificate of NHS charges with your Appeal otherwise it will be sent back.

An Appeal must be made within three calendar months after the latest of:
(1) The date on the certificate of NHS charges.
(2) The date on which the compensation payment was made to the injured party.
(3) If the certificate has been reviewed the date the certificate was confirmed or a fresh certificate was issued.

HMCTS will contact you if the appeal is late and ask why it was not made on time. Good reason must be given as to why the appeal was made late.

An appeal must be made on one or more of the following grounds:
(4) An amount specified in the certificate of NHS charges is incorrect.
(5) An amount specified takes into account treatment which is not NHS treatment received by the injured person or in respect of their injury at an NHS charges.
(6) The ambulance which transported or treated the injured person is not an NHS ambulance service.
(7) The payment on the basis of which the certificate of NHS charges was issued is not compensation payment.

For appeal purposes Orders for provisional damages in personal injury cases made under or by virtue of s 32A(2)(a) of the Senior Court Act 1981, s 12(2)(a) of the Administration of Justice Act 1982 or s 51(2)(a) of the County Court Act 1984 are to be treated as having been finally disposed of.

In accordance with Health and Social Care (Community Health and Standards) Act 2003 an Appeal may be made to a Commissioner against any decision of an Appeal Tribunal, under s 158, on the grounds that the decision was erroneous on a point of law.

20. INTEREST

(G) RATE OF INTEREST

[38.246A] Oyesanya v Mid-Yorkshire Hospital NHS Trust

[2015] EWCA Civ 1049, [2015] 5 Costs LR 911

The Court of Appeal has noted that r 12.6 of the CPR provides an entitlement to interest up to the judgment rate on a default judgment. However the Court of Appeal found that the convenience of using the Judgments Act 1838 rate of 8% was so much in excess of the rate generally awarded as to make it inappropriate.

HELD: The Appeal Court held that the default position in a commercial case is to award 1% above base rate unless that would be unfair in either direction.

CHAPTER 39

Damages in Fatal Cases

2. WHO HAS THE RIGHT OF ACTION?

(A) LIABILITY TO THE DECEASED

[39.12A]   Kadir v Mistry
[2014] EWCA Civ 1177

The claimant's wife died of gastric cancer. It was admitted that the defendants were negligent in delaying the diagnosis. However, absent the negligence, the cancer would inevitably have caused the claimant's wife's death, albeit at a later stage. The claimant claimed for pain suffering and loss of amenity as well as damages for mental anguish caused by the claimant's wife's awareness that her life expectancy had been reduced, pursuant to s 1(1)(b) of the Administration of Justice Act 1982.

HELD: The claimant could not recover for pain, suffering and loss of amenity. Absent the negligence, the claimant's wife would have been in the same position in respect of pain, suffering and loss of amenity and invasive treatment, albeit later. The claimant could recover damages for anguish for reduced life expectancy as his wife feared, on good grounds, that her life expectancy had been reduced by the late diagnosis. Mental anguish was proven over the three month period prior to her death. A relevant factor was her having four young children.

3. DAMAGES RECOVERABLE

(B) DEPENDENCY

(ii)   MULTIPLIER AND MULTIPLICAND

[39.41B]   Knauer (Widower and Administrator of the estate of Sally Ann Knauer, Deceased) v Ministry of Justice
[2016] UKSC 9

The case of *Knauer v Ministry of Justice* [2016] UKSC 9 successfully challenged the long established approach of fixing multipliers from the date of death in fatal accident cases. In *Knauer* the claimant argued the multiplier should be set at the date of trial, rather than at date of death. The trial judge felt bound by the approach in *Cookson v Knowles* [1979] AC 556 to calculate the multiplier from date of death, but he would have done so if it had been possible for him to take that approach. A leapfrog certificate was granted to appeal to the Supreme Court. The judgment from the Supreme Court confirmed that the multiplier is to be assessed at date of trial, thereby overruling *Cookson v Knowles* and *Graham v Dodds* [1982] 1 WLR 880.

The Supreme Court took the opportunity to review the correct date as at which to assess the correct multiplier when calculating damages for future loss in claims under the Fatal Accidents Act 1976. The claimant dies of mesothelioma.

[39.41B] *Damages in Fatal Cases*

HELD: The correct date is the date of trial or settlement and not, as was previously the case, the date of death. *Cookson v Knowles* and *Graham v Dodds* not followed. The Supreme Court's reasoning was that assessing the multiplier from the date of death and using the Ogden discounted multipliers leads to a discount for accelerated receipt of past loss. The earlier decisions were from a different era where the use of actuarial tables was not routine. Further, it was now possible to deal with the uncertainties over what would have happened to the deceased between death and the trial date.

(C). FUNERAL AND OTHER EXPENSES

[39.68A]   Mosson v Spousel (London) Ltd

[2016] EWHC 53 (QB)

The claimant died of mesothelioma, primary liability was not disputed. The court had to consider whether certain heads of loss were recoverable in law, namely the cost of funeral expenses, probate and the loss of 'intangible benefits' - an award to reflect the loss of the value and convenience of having someone who was willing to provide services out of love and affection.

HELD: Whilst funeral expenses could be claimed, the defendant was not liable to pay the cost of the wake, a memorial bench and the costs of clothing for the funeral - *Gammell v Wilson* [1982] AC 27 followed.

The costs of probate could not be recovered as there was no reference to this cost in the Law Reform (Miscellaneous Provisions) Act 1934.

The loss of intangible benefits would not attract damages. There were advantages as well as disadvantages to using contractors to replace the services and the inconvenience would be a non-financial loss, which was already covered by the bereavement award.

CHAPTER 40

Credit Hire

1. ENFORCEABILITY

(E) THE CANCELLATION OF CONTRACTS MADE IN THE CONSUMER'S HOME OR PLACE OF WORK ETC. REGULATIONS 2008 (SI 2008/1816) – FOR CONTRACTS MADE BEFORE 13 JUNE 2014

[40.14A] **Sobrany v UAB Transtira**
[2016] EWCA Civ 28, [2016] Lloyd's Rep IR 266

The claimant and defendant were involved in a road traffic accident, the defendant accepting fault for the collision. The claimant hired a replacement car from a credit hire company and additionally took out a free policy of insurance to cover the cost of the hire charges which provided coverage limited to £100,000. The hire company acted as the insurer's agents. The claimant, after hiring for a short time, switched hire vehicles and signed a second hire agreement. The total credit hire charges for both vehicles were £142,751. The claimant claimed under the policy of insurance for the full hire charges. The claimant issued proceedings against the defendant to recover this sum as a subrogated claim being brought on behalf of the insurers. The defendant argued that there was only one policy of insurance which related to the hire of the first vehicle. The hire charges relating to the second vehicle were not subrogated and the agreement fell foul of the Cancellation of Contracts made in the Consumer's Home or Place of Work etc. Regulations 2008 and was unenforceable. Alternatively they argued that recoverable hire was limited to £100,000, being the extent of the policy coverage. During the trial the claimant gave evidence that two policies of insurance existed. At first instance the district judge found that the two policies were substantially similar and that recovery was limited to the first period only. The matter was appealed on the grounds:
(1) Whether the district judge ought to have considered the evidence that two policies existed.
(2) Whether the district judge had come to the right conclusion.

In addition, the respondent sought to introduce new evidence at appeal that cancellation notices existed thereby ensuring compliance with the Cancellation of Contracts Regulations and that only one policy of insurance had existed.

HELD, ON APPEAL, TO THE COURT OF APPEAL: The court refused to allow the new evidence to be admitted. The cancellation notices could have been produced long before trial and should have formed part of disclosure. However, with respect to the claimant's evidence at trial that two policies of insurance existed it was within the discretion of the judge to allow this to be used and arguments based on this point to be put forward. In respect of the judge's finding the appeal court found it was incorrect to limit the claimant to recovering the first period of hire only. On the district judge's findings the claimant had a first policy to cover the shorter period of hire and the second policy for the much larger balance. Furthermore the insurer had paid the whole of the hire charges. Judgment was awarded for just over £100,000 charges as the respondent had made a concession as to the recoverable period of hire.

[40.14B] *Credit Hire*

[40.14B]   Ali v Spirit Motor Transport Ltd
(12 May 2014, unreported) LTL

The claimant, a taxi driver, pursued a claim for credit hire charges for £33,211.75 incurred following a road traffic accident on 30 November 2011. The claimant hired for a total of 113 days and ultimately concluded hiring when the credit hire company indicated that they were not prepared to provide ongoing hire. The claimant therefore temporarily repaired his vehicle using money borrowed from friends. The defendants' challenges included arguments that as the claimant's damaged vehicle was a profit making chattel and he had hired a replacement at a cost of £294 per day, he was only entitled to the lesser of the cost of hire or the profit the chattel would have earned if it had not been damaged. The claimant signed a rental agreement rendering him responsible for credit hire charges. The agreement did not include a cancellation notice. It was therefore argued that the rental agreement was unenforceable as it did not comply with the requirements of the Cancellation of Contracts made in the Consumer's Home or Place of Work etc. Regulations 2008.

HELD: The court found that the rental agreement was not subject to the Regulations. The claimant had hired a vehicle for use as a taxi and in addition for domestic/social purposes (with the claimant's own business accounts conceding that his vehicle was used 25% of the time for domestic reasons). The court relied upon the judgment in *Aggouche v TNT UK Ltd* which confirmed that acquisition for dual purposes (as a consumer and for business use) was not a consumer acquisition subject to the Regulations unless the trade use was negligible. As the trade use was 75% it could not be considered negligible.

2.   NEED

(C) LEASE CARS

[40.19A]   Ali v Spirit Motor Transport Ltd
(12 May 2014,unreported),LTL

For facts of this case see para **[40.14B]**.

HELD: The court accepted the defendant's argument in relation to the sum recoverable being the loss of profit when this was less than the daily hire rate. The claimant's counsel had raised no arguments in response to this submission. The court did consider that in addition to the loss of profit of £52.20 per day (calculated based on the claimant's accounts) the claimant could recover a further sum as the vehicle was hired for social/domestic use. Both counsel agreed a figure of £15 per day for the loss of use. The court therefore allowed a daily rate of £67.20.

4.   RATE

(A) RECOVERABLE RATE

[40.35A]   Stevens v Equity Syndicate Management Ltd
[2015] EWCA Civ 93, [2015] 4 All ER 458, [2015] RTR 257

The claimant was involved in a non-fault collision whilst driving his Audi A4. Whilst he was without his damaged vehicle he obtained a replacement on credit terms from

Accident Exchange. He hired for 28 days at a total cost of £5,764.80. At first instance the Recorder was required to determine the recoverable daily rate. Basic hire rate (BHR) evidence was before him in the form of a single report. The Recorder focused on rates where the excess on the vehicle was nil as this was the same as the hire car. The evidence included a cluster of mainstream hire companies whose rate included a nil excess all charging a daily rate of between £60 and £66 plus VAT. He therefore took the average of those rates and found the BHR to be £63.16 plus VAT. The claimant appealed the decision and prior to the appeal it was agreed by the parties that the Recorder was incorrect to take an average rate. On appeal Burnett J confirmed that to identify the irrecoverable benefits included in credit hire you should look at the difference between what was charged on credit hire and what the claimant would have paid if he had gone in to the local hire market. He said that claimants should be cross examined on what they would have done had they had to pay themselves (subjective approach). In this case he suggested that the claimant would have paid as little as possible. Burnett J therefore suggested that the Recorder should have used one of the lower rates of hire. As there was no detriment to the claimant in the finding, the appeal was dismissed. The claimant appealed once more to the Court of Appeal. The claimant argued that the exercise of finding a BHR and identifying the charge included for additional benefits was an objective exercise and what a claimant would have paid is irrelevant. The appellant contended that it is for the defendant to prove the BHR and where there was evidence which showed companies charging more than the credit hire company then the credit hire charge was recoverable as it could not be said it included a charge for the additional benefits.

HELD ON APPEAL, TO THE COURT OF APPEAL: The nature of the court's exercise in considering BHR evidence is to strip out the irrecoverable costs of the additional services provided. The difficulty is created as the credit hire companies do not value these benefits. Attempts to value them at a later stage will involve some imprecision. The best to be hoped for is a reasonable approximation. A reasonable estimate is the charge of the use of a car from an ordinary hire company. This does not mean considering what the claimant would have been prepared to pay. The analysis is an objective one as confirmed in *Pattni v First Leicester Buses Ltd* [2010] All ER (D) 201 (Nov) (see para **[40.45]**).The task is to determine what the charge would be for a reasonable person in the claimant's position hiring a car of the kind hired.

Note It should be noted that on 22/23 February 2017 the Court of Appeal will consider whether to grant permission to appeal in the matter of *McBride v UKI* in respect of the third ground of appeal that *Stevens v Equity Syndicate Management Ltd* is incompatible with previous case law.

(B) ASSESSMENT OF RATE EVIDENCE

[40.39A] Stevens v Equity Management Services Ltd

[2015] EWCA Civ 93, [2015] 4 All ER 458, [2015] RTR 257

For facts of the case see para **[40.35B]**.

HELD, ON APPEAL, TO THE COURT OF APPEAL: Where the rates contained within the BHR evidence vary, it is reasonable to suppose that the lowest reasonable rate quoted by a mainstream supplier for the hire of such a vehicle to a person such as the claimant is a reasonable approximation of the BHR. When faced with many rates the judge should identify a rate for the hire in the claimant's geographical area, of a car of the type hired by the claimant. If this results in one rate, that is the BHR. Where there are several rates then the lowest reasonable rate quoted by a mainstream supplier or a local reputable supplier will be the basic hire rate. The suggestion that the highest figure in the group of rates would be considered would be manifestly unjust particularly considering that the credit hire companies are in the best position to

[40.39A] *Credit Hire*

confirm the cost of the additional services but are not required to do so due to the size of the task. Burnett J erred in his methodology but not in the answer he came up with. If he had followed the correct approach the rate awarded would have been a little less. The appeal was therefore dismissed.

[40.39B]   **Lawson v Mullen**

(22 June 2015, unreported), LTL

The claim arises out of a non-fault road traffic accident which occurred on 15 July 2014. The claimant pursued a claim for hire charges of £7,384.05 being the amount charged by On Hire under a credit agreement. The claimant did not seek to rely upon impecuniosity. Basic hire rate evidence confirmed the cost of a similar vehicle for the assessed period to be £2,500.12. In addition the district judge allowed the cost of excess reduction at £11.99 per day, which reduced the excess to £500, and the costs of an additional driver at £10 per day. The total assessed figure was £3,115.84. The district judge had noted that the credit hire vehicle was provided with a nil excess. He confirmed however that it was a matter for the court to decide if a £500 excess was out of the ordinary in relation to the particular type of hire or for the particular type of vehicle. He found that he was satisfied that it was not unduly just in the circumstances. The matter was appealed on the basis that the judge was wrong to conclude that the BHR quote was for a like for like vehicle as it did not provide for a zero excess. Therefore the judge ought not to have substituted the BHR for the credit hire rate.

HELD, ON APPEAL: In many cases it may well be reasonable for a claimant to obtain hire with a nil excess but the over-arching test is whether the charges incurred by the claimant are reasonable having regard to the basic hire rates available elsewhere. The overriding test is one of reasonableness having regard to the basic hire rates available in the market. It is a question of fact and degree. In other words if the credit hire rate is only marginally or at least not very substantially higher than the BHR available and the former includes nil excess whereas the latter does not, then a court might conclude that it would be reasonable for the hirer to incur the somewhat higher rate. The district judge was entirely right in concluding that it was unreasonable to incur hire charges of nearly £7400 where a basic hire rate for the same period for an equivalent car, albeit with a £500 excess, was approximately £3115. The claimant as a matter of legal principle does not have an inalienable right to hire a vehicle with a full waiver excess. In many situations it may be reasonable for a claimant to obtain a replacement vehicle with a nil excess but where, as here, there is a gross disparity between what the credit hire company charged and the basic hire rate, with the only additional advantage being the waiver of a £500 excess, it may well be unreasonable for the claimant to incur that additional cost.

[40.39C]   **Taj v Isran**

(22 October 2015, unreported), LTL

The claimant pursued a claim for credit hire charges. At first instance the district judge was required to identify the recoverable basic hire rate (BHR). BHR evidence was adduced in the form of a witness statement from a rate analyst who had conducted a survey of car hire companies in the claimant's geographical area for vehicles which were similar to the car hired by the claimant. The rates were approximately 25% of the sum charged by the credit hire company. This was the only evidence on BHR before the court. At the assessment of damages hearing the district judge rejected the BHR evidence on the grounds that it was obtained some 17 months after hire and was therefore not contemporaneous evidence of the basic hire rate at the time that the claimant entered into the credit hire agreement. The defendant appealed.

HELD, ON APPEAL: The defendant's appeal was successful. The district judge had erred and was wrong in principal to have rejected the BHR evidence on account of its lack of contemporaneity. Even where the evidence was not ideal judges should use the evidence before them to assess the BHR as confirmed in *Bent v Highways and Utilities Construction and Allianz* [2011] EWCA Civ 1539 (see para **[40.37]**). Having allowed the appeal HHJ Stacey then went on to substitute her assessment of the rate.

Note On 21 January 2016 the Court of Appeal granted permission to appeal in the matters of *McBride v UKI and Clayton v UKI*. Both are credit hire matters and the issues will relate to the recoverable rate. *McBride* will consider how the courts should deal with BHR evidence which is adduced and the quotes relate to cars with an insurance excess where the hire car was provided with a nil excess, and the proper meaning of the terms 'reasonable mainstream supplier rate' and 'reasonable supplier rate'. *Clayton* will relate to how the issue of excess waivers should be dealt with and what adjustments can be made to BHR awards if the defendant's BHR evidence is not exactly comparable.

9. OTHER

[40.46]   Phillips v Willis

[2016] EWCA Civ 401, [2016] All ER (D) 149 (Apr)

For facts of case see para **[20.57A]**.

HELD, ON APPEAL, TO THE COURT OF APPEAL: A personal injury claim, in which general damages had been agreed leaving only the recoverable rate for the credit hire charges to be determined by the court, was erroneously exited from the MOJ portal. The first instance court had sufficient evidence before it to determine the appropriate rate of hire following the stage 2 procedure, and should have done so at a stage 3 hearing rather than to exit the claim from the portal and require further evidence from the claimant to determine the appropriate rate of hire. MOJ portal claims where the only matter in dispute is rate, and where sufficient evidence has been provided at stage 2, are suitable to be resolved within the MOJ process.

CHAPTER 41

Costs

2. CONDITIONAL FEE AGREEMENTS (CFAS)

(A) FORMALITY OF REQUIREMENTS

[41.33A] 8 Representative Claimants v MGN Ltd

[2016] EWHC 855 (Ch), [2016] All ER (D) 127 (Apr)

The claimants alleged that they were the victims of invasion of privacy by the defendant. Eight cases were taken to trial and the claimants were awarded judgment. Each claimant had entered into a CFA and taken out ATE insurance cover. The claimants' bills of costs were served and the defendant argued in the points of dispute that the additional liabilities were not recoverable as a matter of law because the legislation was incompatible with the convention on human rights.

HELD: The CFA regime, which allowed the recovery of success fee and ATE insurance premiums in defamation and privacy cases, was not incompatible with Article 10 of the European Convention on Human Rights.

[41.33B] Coventry v Lawrence

[2015] UKSC 50, [2016] 2 All ER 97, 165 NLJ 7663

On appeal the defendant argued that payment of the additional sums for the success fee and ATE insurance premium was contrary to Article 6 of the European Convention on Human Rights or Article 1 of the First Protocol.

HELD: By a majority of 5:2, their Lordships held that a claimant's right to recover any success fee and ATE premium from an unsuccessful defendant under the Access to Justice Act 1999 did not infringe either Article 6 or Article 1 of the First Protocol to the Convention, or both of those provisions.

(B) ENTERING INTO CFAS

[41.34A] Milton Keynes NHS Foundation Trust v Hyde

[2016] EWHC 72 (QB), 166 NLJ 7688

The claim was settled by consent order. The claimant had initially been issued with a CLS funding certificate which limited the funding to £43,000. Her solicitors later reviewed the cost of the work and realised it was reaching the prescribed limit. The Legal Services Commission (LSC) refused to increase the funding. The claimant's solicitors therefore advised their client to enter into a CFA. The solicitors did not ask the LSC to discharge the funding certificate.

HELD ON APPEAL: Appeal dismissed. The CFA was enforceable. Public funding was utilised up to the date of expiry of the certificate and a CFA thereafter. There was no attempt to seek additional payment from the claimant. There was no evidence of deception on the part of the claimant's solicitors.

[41.34B] *Costs*

[41.34B] Ramos v Oxford University NHS Trust

(2 February 2016, unreported) Senior Costs Office

The claimant had the benefit of a CLS funding certificate. However, this funding would not cover expert fees over a rate of £180 per hour. The solicitors therefore recommended their client enter into a CFA backed by an ATE insurance premium. The claimant's funding certificate was discharged.

HELD: The claimant had been unable to make an informed choice about a change from public funding to a CFA and ATE insurance arrangement. As a result the success fee and ATE insurance premium were not recoverable.

(C) ASSIGNMENT OF CFAS

[41.35A] Jones v Spire Healthcare Ltd

Case No: A13YJ811

Prior to April 2013 the claimant entered into a CFA with her solicitors, who later became insolvent. The portfolio of personal injury work was transferred to another firm of solicitors by way of a general deed of assignment but as the claimant was happy with the transfer she also signed a separate deed of assignment in January 2014.

The court at first instance held that the benefit of the CFA was validly assigned but the burden was not. This meant that the claimant's new firm under the purported assignment could recover costs incurred by the dissolved firm but had no entitlement to any subsequent costs incurred by itself.

The second assignment, signed by the claimant, was found to be a novation based on the terms of the original CFA. As it did not provide for the success fee to be limited to 25% of damages it failed to comply with s 58(4B) of the Courts and Legal Services Act 1990 and was therefore unenforceable.

The claimant appealed in relation to the disallowance of the post-assignment costs, and the defendant appealed in relation to the allowance of the pre-assignment costs.

HELD, ON APPEAL: The claimant's appeal was allowed and the defendant's cross appeal dismissed. It was held that both the burden and the benefit of the CFAs were assigned by the first firm of solicitors to the second firm and there was a valid retainer allowing recovery of both pre-and-post assignment costs.

In respect of the defendant's appeal the judge rejected the argument that the benefit of the original CFA could not be transferred to the second firm of solicitors as the previous firm were in liquidation. He considered the proposition that a solicitor could not assign such agreements without continuing to exist as a legal entity as one which would have a chilling effect on the business arrangements of legal service providers. If that were the case there would be no value in CFA assignments in progress if the benefit of the work undertaken could not be recovered.

[41.35B] Budana v Leeds Teaching Hospitals NHS Trust

(14 September 2015, unreported) Kingston-upon-Hull County Court

The claimant entered into a CFA with a firm of solicitors who subsequently notified her that they were no longer dealing with personal injury litigation and arranged for another firm to take over conduct of the claim. The first solicitors then sought to assign her claim and CFA to the second firm of solicitors. The claimant signed letters of instruction for the second firm of solicitors and a deed of transfer. The second CFA stated that it was only to be effective in the event that the deed of assignment did not allow the solicitors to recover their costs.

The defendant questioned whether the purported assignment of the original CFA was effective as a matter of law. The issues were:
(a) whether, at the date of the transfer, there was a CFA to assign;
(b) whether a CFA, being a contract for personal skills, could be assigned; and
(c) if it could, whether there was novation.

HELD: The first solicitors had terminated the retainer before assignment by way of the letter. The court was bound by the ratio in *Jenkins v Young Brothers Transport Ltd* [2006] EWHC 151 (QB) which meant that the benefit and burden could be assigned as an exception to the rule. The first solicitor's costs were not recoverable.

[41.35C]   Aileen Webb v Bromley London Borough Council

(18 February 2016, unreported) Senior Costs Costs Office

The claimant entered into a CFA with a firm of solicitors which had to close in January 2014 after the death of what was effectively the sole principal of the firm. His former partner discussed the situation with the claimant, setting out a number of options which included the claim being passed to the firm he was now working at. The claimant agreed and an assignment took place. The question was whether on the particular facts of the case whether the CFA had been terminated and a new one entered into with the new firm.

HELD: On the facts there was no assignment. The CFA had been terminated and a new CFA entered into. On that basis the new CFA was found to be unenforceable. It had failed to comply with s 58(4B) of the Courts and Legal Services Act 1990 which specified the success fee is subject to a maximum of 25% of general damages and damages for pecuniary loss other than future pecuniary loss. However, the CFA in place provided for a success fee of 100% as it was based on that in place pre-April 2013.

(D) BACKDATING OF CFAS

[41.38A]   O'Brien (John Joseph) (a protected party suing by his father and litigation friend Authur O'Brien) v Michael Shorrock and Motor Insurers Bureau

[2015] EWHC 1630 (QB), [2015] 4 Costs LO 439

Two issues arose as a result of a detailed assessment of the claimant's costs:
(a) whether the 100% success fee claimed, and reduced by the Master to 75%, should have been reduced further to either 5% or, alternatively, 67%; and
(b) whether the claimant should have recovered a retrospective success fee under the back-dated CFA.

HELD: The defendant's argument that the risk of the claimant losing was so low that no more than a 5% success fee should be recoverable was not sustainable. The matter had proceeded to a trial on the identity of the defendant driver. If the claimant had not won on this issue he would have lost under the CFA, which as a matter of construction did not cover a payment award from the MIB under the untraced driver's scheme.

However, the Master should have reduced the success fee to 67% despite the matter proceeding to trial on a preliminary issue as the risk assessment had provided the prospects of success of winning under the CFA at 60%.

The Notice of Funding had failed to comply with CPR r 44.3B(1) as it had specified the date when the CFA had come into force (6 November 2008) not the actual date when it was made (21 October 2009). The MIB should have been informed that the CFA was backdated. However as the litigation had not been affected relief was

[41.38A] *Costs*

granted. A reduced success fee of 20% was awarded up 20 October 2009, the day prior to signature of the CFA, to take into account the failure to comply with the rules.

[41.38B]   Roshan Ghising v Secretary of State for the Home Department

[2015] EWHC 3706 (QB), [2015] All ER (D) 213 (Dec)

At detailed assessment the cost judge concluded that the claimant could not recover success fees for either solicitor or counsel for work undertaken prior to the date of their CFAs. Whilst retrospective success fees could be allowed, this was a matter of discretion in each and every case.

The claimant appealed, arguing that it was reasonable to recover a retrospective success fee. Applications had been made for CLS funding in July 2012 but as no decision had been made by December 2012 CFAs were entered into.

HELD ON APPEAL: Appeal allowed. There was no evidence that the defendant would have dealt with the matter any differently had the CFAs been entered into at the outset and no prejudice had been suffered by it. The risk presented was not materially different in July 2012 than in December 2012, when the respondent was notified that the CFAs had been entered into. The wording of the CFA was not ambiguous and was capable of covering a retrospective position.

(F) TERMINATION OF CFAS

[41.41A]   Diann Blankley (by her litigation friend Andrew MG Cusworth) v Central Manchester & Manchester Children's University Hospitals NHS Trust

[2015] EWCA Civ 18, [2015] 1 WLR 4307, 165 NLJ 7639

This case raised the question of whether:
(a)   a CFA is automatically terminated where the claimant who entered into it loses mental capacity; and
(b)   if so, whether the litigation friend had in some way 'adopted' the CFA.

The judge at first instance concluded that there was no retainer in place after the appointment of the litigation friend and struck out the costs covering that period. The claimant successfully appealed. The defendant was granted permission to appeal to the Court of Appeal.

HELD ON APPEAL: Appeal dismissed. Their Lordships agreed with Philips J who concluded that supervening mental incapacity of a principal did not frustrate or terminate the retainer. It might cause a delay in performance of the obligation to provide instructions but that would be a matter for the enforcement of the contract terms. The CFA provided that the retainer would terminate on the death of the claimant, which indicated the parties to the contract did not regard incapacity as being a ground for terminating it. If the CFA had terminated then the litigation friend would not have been able to adopt it and would have needed to enter into a new CFA.

(G) THE CANCELLATION OF CONTRACTS MADE IN A CONSUMER'S HOME OR PLACE OF WORK ETC. REGULATIONS 2008

[41.43A]   Cox v Woodlands Manor Care Home Ltd
[2015] EWCA Civ 415, [2015] 3 Costs LO 327

The claimant brought a claim resulting from an employers' liability incident. The claimant suffered serious injuries, such that a personal attendance at her home was necessary to provide initial instructions to her solicitor.

At the first detailed assessment the defendant contended that as the Consumer's Home or Place of Work etc. Regulations 2008 (the Regulations) had not been fully complied with the CFA was unenforceable. The claimant and her solicitor submitted witness evidence stating that their intention was for the CFA only to come into effect once the relevant funding enquiries had been completed, that the CFA had therefore not been entered into at the claimant's home and the Regulations did not apply. Annexed to the claimant's solicitor's witness statement was a letter sent to the claimant stating that the funding enquiries were complete and that she would 'continue' to act under the terms of the CFA. Her solicitor conceded the use of the word 'continue' was unfortunate and out of context.

District Judge Britten accepted the claimant's evidence and held that the CFA did not come into effect until the claimant's solicitor had completed funding enquiries relating to potential legal expenses insurance. The district judge's decision was overturned on appeal. The claimant in turn appealed to the Court of Appeal and was initially denied permission. However, after an oral hearing this was granted.

HELD ON APPEAL: Appeal dismissed. The CFA was held to have been entered into on the date that it was signed in the claimant's home. As a notice of cancellation had not been provided to the client the regulations had been breached. Therefore the contract between the claimant and her solicitor was deemed unenforceable. The bill of costs was assessed at £nil and the defendant awarded their detailed assessment costs throughout the process, including those relating to the two appeals.

(H) WRONG NAMED PARTY

[41.44A]   Linda Engeham v London & Quandrant Housing Trust Ltd, Academy of Plumbing Ltd (In voluntary liq), sub nom Linda Engeham v London & Quandrant Housing Trust Ltd and Academy of Plumbing Ltd (In Voluntary Liq)
[2015] EWCA Civ 1530

The appeal raised an important question about the proper construction of the Law Society model CFA 2000 edition.

The claimant was injured after a bathroom ceiling fell on her. She sued her landlord (first defendant) and the plumbing company (second defendant). The claim against both defendants was settled under a *Tomlin* Order upon payment of £10,000 by the second defendant. The claimant had entered into a CFA that was stated to cover her claim 'against the defendants London Quadrant Housing Group' but did not mention the second defendant. As such the principal costs officer in the Senior Courts Costs Office held a 'win' had not been achieved against the party named in the CFA and the costs claimed were therefore not recoverable under that agreement. This decision was upheld on appeal to the Master. However, this decision was overturned by the High Court on appeal. The second defendant therefore appealed to the Court of Appeal.

[41.44A] *Costs*

HELD ON APPEAL: Appeal dismissed. The 'win' clause in the CFA was not limited by reference to the identity of a person who actually pays the damages and the claimant could recover her costs against the first defendant.

7. FIXED RECOVERABLE COSTS

(A) FIXED RECOVERABLE BASE COSTS AND DISBURSEMENTS IN ROAD TRAFFIC ACCIDENTS OCCURRING ON OR AFTER 6 OCTOBER 2003

[41.94A]   Shahow Qader v Esure Services Ltd

[2015] All ER (D) 295 (Oct)

The claimants were involved in a road traffic accident in October 2013 and pleaded they expected to recover between £5,000 and £15,000 in damages. The defence pleaded fraud and the case was allocated to the multi-track. At first instance the district judge ruled that fixed costs under the CPR r 45.29A would apply to the case and refused the claimants permission to appeal.

HELD ON APPEAL: Appeal dismissed. CPR r 45.29A was clear and there was no need for the court to interpret the rule. Although fraud had been pleaded the claim was still a low value personal injury road traffic accident and the implementation of fixed recoverable costs did not offend the overriding objective. Further, the CPR r 45.29J provided a material safeguard against injustice. It is open to the court to award costs exceeding the fixed sums at the conclusion of the case if it considers there are exceptional circumstances to do so.

[41.94B]   Jonathan Mills v Farmfoods Distribution Ltd; Matthew Salter v Muller UK & Ireland Group LLP

(27 November 2015, unreported) Leeds CC

The conjoined appeals dealt with the question of whether the fixed costs regime in Part IIIA of CPR r 45 applies where a claim has been commenced under the Employers Liability and Public Liability Protocol but has exited that process as a result of applications being made by the claimants for pre-action disclosure. At first instance the court assessed the costs of the applications on the standard basis. The defendants appealed, arguing the fixed costs regime should apply.

HELD ON APPEAL: Appeal allowed. It was clear from the wording of CPR r 45.29A that the section relating to fixed costs applied where a claim is started under the pre-action Protocol but no longer continues under it. That applied in the period between the exit from the Protocol and the issue of proceedings and therefore included the applications for pre-action disclosure.

[41.94C]   Mendes v Hochtief (UK) Construction Ltd

[2016] EWHC 976 (QB), [2016] All ER (D) 18 (May)

The claimant was involved in a road traffic accident in August 2014 and brought a claim under the RTA Protocol Scheme. Proceedings were issued and the matter proceeded to trial in December 2015 but compromised before the hearing actually commenced. Costs were governed by the fixed recoverable costs matrix set out in CPR r 45.29C, table 6B. The recorder refused to award the fixed trial advocacy fee as the trial had not yet commenced. The claimant appealed.

HELD ON APPEAL: Appeal allowed. It was clear from the way the rules had been written that the costs did not fall within section B of the table which covered costs incurred on or after listing but prior to the date of trial. The costs therefore fell to be assessed in section C which included the fixed trial advocacy fee.

[41.94D] Sean Phillips v Carol Willis

[2016] EWCA Civ 401, [2016] All ER (D) 149 (Apr)

The Court of Appeal considered the question of how the court should deal with low value road traffic accident claims where the personal injury element has been resolved and only a modest dispute about car hire charges remains.

The claim started in the RTA Protocol that pre-dated the one introduced on 31 July 2013. It proceeded to stage 3 due to a dispute over car hire charges. The difference between the parties' offers was just £462. Proceedings were correctly issued under CPR r 8. At the hearing the district judge informed the parties that as the only issue between them was the amount of the hire charges the action would proceed under CPR r 7 on the small claims track and listed a further hearing for directions. The decision was appealed to a circuit judge and upheld as he considered the appellate court could not interfere with the district judge's case management decision in exercise of his powers under paragraph 7.2 of Practice Direction 8B. The claimants sought a further appeal.

HELD ON APPEAL: Appeal allowed. The case did not fall within the ambit of paragraph 7.2 of Practice Direction 8B and the district judge had no power under that paragraph to make the order he did. Lord Justice Jackson considered that once a case was within the RTA protocol it did not automatically exit when the personal injury case settled. The process was there to narrow issues between the parties and it was to be expected that the sums in dispute at stage 3 would be much smaller than at the beginning of the process.

12. INTEREST ON COSTS UNDER CPR PT 44

[41.127A] Excalibur Ventures LLC v Texas Keystone Inc

[2015] EWHC 566 (Comm), 165 NLJ 7645

The defendants had successfully defended a claim brought by the claimants which was funded by nine other companies introduced at various stages. They were ordered to pay the defendants costs on the indemnity basis. The issue arose as to whether the court should award 8% interest to apply from a date earlier than the costs order and whether an interim payment was appropriate.

HELD: The funders' liability for interest at the judgment rate would accrue only from the date on which they had been found liable for costs, not the earlier date when judgment against the claimant was entered. The court considered the rate of 8% very significantly above current commercial rates.

It was reasonable to order an interim payment of 80% be made given that costs had been awarded on an indemnity basis.

[41.148A] *Costs*

15. MEDIATION

[41.148A] Annie Morris v Sandra Sanda Htay

(2 February 2015, unreported) Kingston upon Hull CC

The claimant's bill of costs totalled £161,184. Shortly after service of detailed assessment proceedings the claimant made an offer to accept £45,000. The defendant did not respond to this offer and made no offer when serving points of dispute. The claimant later reduced the offer to £36,590.97. The bill was assessed by the court at £28,850.98. The defendant invited the court to depart from the usual order for costs in favour of the claimant, relying on the significant reduction applied to the bill. The claimant argued that the defendant had refused to engage in mediation or to make any offer above £nil.

HELD: The court made no order as to costs of the detailed assessment proceedings as both parties had failed to comply with the overriding objective. The reduction to the claimant's bill of costs of 82% was exceptional. However, the need to proceed to an assessment had been largely caused by the defendant's failure to make any offer or to actively consider alternative dispute resolution.

[41.148B] Reid v Buckinghamshire Healthcare NHS Trust

[2015] EWHC B21 (Costs)

The claimant was awarded more than its own costs Part 36 offer at detailed assessment. During the detailed assessment proceedings the claimant had offered the defendant an opportunity to mediate, which was declined.

HELD: The defendant was ordered to pay an additional 10% in costs due to the failure to beat the claimant's Part 36 offer. Indemnity costs were awarded to the claimant from the date that the defendant received the offer to mediate.

[41.148C] Bristow v The Princess Alexander Hospital NHS Trust

(4 November 2015, unreported), Senior Costs Office

The claimant lodged a bill of costs totalling £239,000 which was reduced to £135,486.90 at detailed assessment. As this figure was higher than the defendant's offers the claimant sought to recover detailed assessment costs. In addition the defendant refused to mediate as they considered:
(1) The parties were far apart.
(2) The assessed figure was much close to their offers than those made by the claimant.

HELD: The master penalised the claimant for including items within the bill of costs that should not have been claimed. The claimant was therefore only entitled to 80% of the detailed assessments costs. However, the court also ruled the defendant should have engaged in mediation and had to pay those costs on the indemnity basis to reflect this.

22. PROPORTIONALITY

[41.216A] Finglands Coachways Ltd v O'Hare (a protected party by his sister and litigation friend Ms Portia Crees)

[2014] EWHC 1513 (QB), [2014] 4 Costs LO 668

The claimant suffered serious and extensive brain injuries following a road traffic accident. Quantum was valued in the region of £3-4 million. Liability was denied and the claimant discontinued his claim 11 days before trial following a joint meeting between the experts. The defendant was therefore entitled to its costs. The defendant's bill totalling £60,101.80 was assessed at £37,803.89 by District Judge Iyer. At the detailed assessment the judge referred to the necessity test. The defendant objected to this reference as the claimant had not raised proportionality in his points of dispute (a prerequisite to considering necessity). The defendant appealed.

HELD, ON APPEAL: The defendant submitted that the judge had erred in principle by assessing the costs by reference to the stricter test of necessity, as opposed to reasonableness. However, Mr Justice Cranston could find nothing which confines the proportionality template to costs as a whole and excluded its application to individual items. In assessing costs under the old version of the CPR a court could consider on an item by item basis whether a particular item of costs was proportionate and necessary even if costs were proportionate on a global basis. Existing authorities did not preclude this finding and the appeal was dismissed.

[41.216B]   Savoye & Savoye Ltd v Spicers Ltd

[2015] EWHC 33 (TCC), [2015] 1 Costs LR 99

The claimants sought to enforce an adjudicator's decision in its favour against the defendant. The claim was worth £889,300. The issue was whether the underlying contract between the parties was a construction contract involving construction operations. There was judgment in favour of the claimants by way of enforcement of the decision. The claimant's bill of costs totalled £201,790.66 and fell to be assessed under the new proportionality test pursuant to CPR r 44.3.

HELD: The case revolved around a relatively narrow issue of fact and there were limited issues of principle to be resolved. Further, the arguments raised in proceedings had already been rehearsed in the adjudication. Akenhead J concluded that costs were disproportionate and assessed the claimants' bill at £96,465, a reduction of £105,325.66. In arriving at this substantially lower figure, the judge took into consideration a number of factors including the relationship between the amount of costs claimed, the amount in issue, the amount of time spent by solicitors and counsel in relation to the total length of hearing and the importance of the case to either party.

[41.216C]   Hobbs v Guy's and St Thomas' NHS Foundation Trust

[2015] EWHC B20 (Costs)

The claim related to injuries and losses suffered by the claimant's late husband following a delay in receiving medical treatment. Evidence was obtained from a number of experts and the claim finally settled for £3,500 plus costs. The claimant's bill of costs totalling £32,329.12 was reduced to £9,879.34 at provisional assessment by Master O'Hare. The claimant requested an oral hearing which included a judgment on proportionality in the context of low value claims.

HELD: Two tests of proportionality applied (referred to as the old *Lownds* test and the new *Jackson* test). The Master stated that proportionality was not the lowest amount which the claimant could reasonably have been expected to spend in order to have this case conducted and presented proficiently but involved consideration of the amount of sums in issue and that proportionality trumps necessity. The axe of proportionality was swung upon particular items of work rather than at reasonable costs incurred as a whole. Although it was reasonable for the claimant to incur these costs it would be unfair to expect the defendant to pay for them. Notwithstanding some minor adjustments to the costs claimed, the claimant fared no better at the oral hearing.

[41.217A] *Costs*

23. QUALIFIED ONE WAY COSTS SHIFTING (QOCS)

[41.217A]   Landau v Big Bus Co Ltd and Pawel Zeital

[2013] EWHC 3281 (QB), [2013] All ER (D) 64 (Oct)

The claimant brought a claim against the defendants for personal injuries and consequential losses following a road traffic accident. The claim was dismissed at first instance and on appeal. The claimant had entered into two CFAs; one pre-1 April 2013 (first instance) and the other post-1 April 2013 (appeal). The claimant contended that the claim at first instance and on appeal were different proceedings and therefore QOCS applied to the appeal. The defendants contended that the entire case, including the appeal, was one set of proceedings which therefore deprived the claimant of QOCS protection. The defendants further argued that the wording of the CPR clearly distinguished between 'matter' and 'proceedings' and that the matter might give rise to more than one set of proceedings.

HELD: The costs judge preferred the defendants' arguments. He found that it was Parliament's intention that a pre-1 April 2013 CFA entered into in respect of the matter would disapply QOCS in any proceedings arising out of that matter. The costs judge was aided by the Court of Appeal authority of *Wagenaar v Weekend Travel Ltd (t/a Ski Weekend)* [2014] EWCA Civ 1105, [2016] 1 All ER 643, [2015] 1 WLR 1968, in which the appeal court defined 'proceedings' as effectively meaning a 'claim' and therefore QOCS protection did not apply.

[41.217B]   Hassan v Cooper and Accident Claims Consultants Ltd

[2015] EWHC 540 (QB), [2015] RTR 288

The claimant was involved in a road traffic accident. Despite there being a genuine collision, the claimant had dishonestly exaggerated her claim for damages. Credit hire and recovery and storage charges totalled £47,853.12 but it was found that the invoice for repair costs was a forgery. The defendant was granted permission to plead fraud and bring a Part 20 clam for exemplary damages.

HELD: The court awarded exemplary damages to the defendant/Part 20 claimant and the claimant/Part 20 defendant's original claim was struck out. The claimant/Part 20 defendant's fundamental dishonesty brought it within the exceptions under CPR r 44.16 (1) which removed the QOCS shield and he was liable to pay the defendant's costs.

[41.217C]   Howe v Motor Insurers' Bureau

[2016] EWHC 884 (QB)

The claimant's personal injury claim failed due to limitation and he was ordered to pay 85% of the defendant's costs. The central point for the judge to consider was the wording of CPR r 44.13(1) 'This Section applies to proceedings which include a claim for damages – (a) for personal injuries'.

The MIB argued that the claim brought against it by the claimant was not a claim for damages for personal injury but rather a civil debt recoverable by legislation and therefore the MIB's liability did not come within the QOCS provisions. The defendant relied upon the Court of Appeal decision in *Wagenaar* in considering the purpose of QOCS.

HELD: The matter was one of construction. The claimant's claim against the MIB was not one for damages for personal injuries. The claimant did not therefore have protection under the QOCS regime and orders for costs made against him could be enforced in the usual way.

[41.217D] Parker v Butler
[2016] EWHC 1251 (QB)

The claimant's fast track road traffic accident claim was dismissed at first instance. His appeal was also dismissed, although for different reasons to those arrived at by the first instance judge. It was common ground that the QOCS regime applied to the case as the accident had occurred on 10 April 2013. The claims notification form was submitted on 12 July 2013 before the fixed recoverable costs regime was introduced. The successful defendant's costs were therefore assessed by HHJ Edis at £2,795.21 including VAT. The question was whether the claimant's QOCS protection extended to the appeal.

HELD: The claimant's appeal formed part of the same proceedings. There was no difference between the parties, the relief sought or the nature of the claim at trial and on appeal. Therefore QOCS protection under CPR r 44.13 applied and the defendant could only enforce the order with the permission of the court.

24. RELIEF FROM SANCTIONS

[41.221A] Long v Value Properties Ltd and Ocean Trade Ltd
[2014] EWHC 2981 (Ch), [2015] 3 All ER 419, [2014] 5 Costs LR 915

The claimant's solicitors failed to serve a statement of reasons when commencing detailed assessment proceedings and were therefore in breach of costs practice direction paragraph 32.5(1)(c). CPR r 44.3B imposed an automatic sanction that any 'additional liability' is not recoverable.

The claimant's solicitors subsequently provided the necessary information and the Master noted that the period of prejudice (if any) lasted no more than three weeks. The error was rectified promptly and the application for relief from sanction made promptly. At first instance it was found that despite the breach being trivial and little prejudice had been caused the Master felt bound by *Mitchell v News Group Newspapers Ltd* [2013] EWCA Civ 1537, [2014] 2 All ER 430, [2014] 1 WLR 795 to refuse relief and disallowed the success fee. The claimant appealed.

HELD ON APPEAL: HHJ Barling considered the later decision of *Denton v TH White Ltd* [2014] EWCA Civ 906, [2015] 1 All ER 880, [2014] 1 WLR 3926 and concluded that in the context of its surrounding circumstances the breach of the practice direction was neither serious nor significant. The claimant had commenced detailed assessment proceedings well within the three month limit imposed by the CPR, once the breach was brought to attention of the claimant it was remedied swiftly and the application for relief was brought very quickly. The defendants had preferred to take advantage of the claimant's oversight by choosing not to inform the claimant of the default earlier, and after points of dispute were served declined to cooperate and avoid the need for an application for relief. Appeal granted.

[41.221B] Caliendo and another company v Mishcon de Reya (a firm)
[2015] EWCA Civ 1029, [2015] All ER (D) 99 (Oct)

The claimants were 3½ months late in serving notice of the existence of a CFA and ATE insurance premium. The claimants made an application for relief from sanctions which was opposed by the defendants. The court considered the three stage approach set out by the Court of Appeal in *Denton v T H White Ltd* [2014] EWCA Civ 906, [2015] 1 All ER 880, [2014] 1 WLR 3926 and concluded that the defendants could not show that they had been prejudiced and would have acted any differently had no breach occurred. The claimants' application was allowed. The defendants appealed.

[41.221B] *Costs*

HELD: Appeal dismissed. The judge's decision whether or not to grant relief was an exercise of his discretion. His decision did not constitute an error in principle nor was it plainly wrong. The appellant court could see no justification for interfering with the discretion.

[41.221C] Stuart John Gentry v Miller
[2016] EWCA Civ 141, (2016) Times, 21 April

The claimant was involved in a road traffic accident. Proceedings were issued and judgment was given for the clamant. The matter was listed for a disposal hearing and the claimant was awarded damages and costs. The second defendant applied to set aside the judgments and raised concern about possible fraudulent activity on the part of the claimant and the first defendant. The judgments were set aside and the claimant's appeal was dismissed. Permission to bring a second appeal was granted.

HELD: Appeal allowed. The *Denton* test was applied. The court at first instance should not have granted relief from sanctions. The delay of two months by the defaulting party in applying for relief was inexcusable, notwithstanding the allegations of fraud. Although such allegations may in some cases excuse an insurer from taking steps to protect itself, here the insurer missed every opportunity to do so and it had to face the consequence of its own actions. The insurer would have to pursue what remedies it could by way of a new fraud action.

28. THIRD PARTY FUNDING OF LITIGATION

(B) LIABILITY INSURERS

[41.250A] Legg v Sterte Garage Ltd and Aviva UK Ltd
[2016] EWCA Civ 97, [2016] All ER (D) 215 (Feb)

There were two possible causes of oil contamination of the claimants properties:
(a)   a 1997 single incident resulting in a spillage of some 300 litres of diesel from an above ground tank; and
(b)   gradual leakage up to 20,000 llitres of diesel oil from underground storage tanks or associated pipe work.
   The first defendant's insurance policy would cover the first cause but not the second.
   The claimants commenced proceedings on the basis of the 1997 incident. As a result the first defendant's insurers took over conduct of and funded the defence as they were obliged to do under the insurance policy. Further expert evidence was obtained which revealed the second potential cause and the claimants amended the pleadings to reflect this. As a result the insurer abandoned the defence of the claim as the policy would not cover the potential second cause. The claimants obtained judgment against the first defendant, which went into liquidation. The first instance judge granted the claimants' application for a non-party costs order against the insurer, who were added as a second defendant and ordered to pay the claimant's costs. The decision was appealed.

HELD ON APPEAL: Appeal dismissed. The claimant had never abandoned the pleading relating to the 1997 incident. The second defendant's support of the initial defence of the main action had caused the claimant to incur additional costs and the second defendant was unable to demonstrate that the first instance judge's exercise of discretion was flawed.

(E) DIRECTORS

[41.260A]   Deutsche Bank AG v Sebastian Holdings Incorporated
[2016] EWCA Civ 23, [2016] 4 WLR 17, (2016) Times, 25 February

A bank obtained a money judgment against a company for US$243,023,089 in proceedings relating to the operation of accounts maintained by the company with the bank for trading in foreign currencies, shares and financial products. The company was further ordered to pay the bank 85% of its costs of the proceedings, said to amount to about £60 million, on the indemnity basis. The company's counterclaim was dismissed.

The company failed to pay the judgment and costs. The bank obtained a non-party costs order under s 51 of the Supreme Court Act 1981 against its sole director and shareholder, requiring him to pay the bank £36,204,891 on account of its costs. It was found the shareholder had controlled and funded the litigation, had stood to benefit personally from it, and had such a close connection with the company that it would not be unjust to bind him to the court's findings. The shareholder appealed.

HELD ON APPEAL: Appeal dismissed.